The Space of

DEATH

Michel Ragon

The Space of

DEATH

A Study of Funerary Architecture,

Decoration, and Urbanism

TRANSLATED BY

Alan Sheridan

UNIVERSITY PRESS OF VIRGINIA

Charlottesville

Translation copyright 1983
by the Rector and Visitors of the University of Virginia
First published 1983

Originally published in 1981 as
*L'espace de la mort: Essai sur l'architecture, la
décoration et l'urbanisme funéraires* by Michel Ragon

© Editions Albin Michel 1981

Library of Congress Cataloging in Publication Data
Ragon, Michel.
The world of the dead.
Translation of: L'espace de la mort.
Bibliography: p.
Includes index.
1. Tombs—History.   2. Mausoleums—History.
3. Funeral rites and ceremonies—History.   4. Cemeteries
—History.   5. Tombs—France—History.   6. Mausoleums—
France—History.   7. Funeral rites and ceremonies—
France—History.   8. Cemeteries—France—History.
I. Title.
GT3320.F3313   1983   393'.1   83–5958
ISBN 0–8139–0995–3

Printed in the United States of America

to Robert Sabatier

BECAUSE IN 1967 HE HAD

THE THEN CURIOUS IDEA

OF WRITING A *Dictionary of Death*,

AND BECAUSE FOR THIRTY YEARS

HE HAS BEEN MY FRIEND

CONTENTS

III / THANATOS *and the Goddess of Reason, or Rational Death*

Introduction

The Soul Wandering

without a House

The dead had no houses of their own. . . . They might go every Saturday and visit the house where their widow or widower still lived with their children. They might temporarily occupy their old bedroom.

Emmanuel Le Roy Ladurie, *Montaillou*

The human body is an architecture which, like the architecture of a house or of any other building, comprises a structure (the ossature), tensile elements (the muscles, the nerves), filling (flesh), facing (the skin), and a whole system of internal machinery (pumps, pipes, filters), which is connected to the outside by orifices and through which liquids and gases circulate.

The structure of the human body is astonishingly light (while being flexible and mobile), since it weighs only one-tenth of the whole. That is to say, the mass of a body weighing 150 pounds is supported by a skeleton weighing only 15 pounds.

Oddly enough, ever since mankind began to think, men have felt nothing but disgust for the "filling" of the bodies of their dead, and a fascination for the structure. A horror of the decomposing corpse is a

[3

constant in all civilizations and gave rise to the ritual of mourning performed by the survivors, which lasted as long as the decomposition of the body. But, contrary to what most historians of death have believed, not all peoples have venerated their dead, and some, for quite long periods in history, have quite simply abandoned their corpses.[1] When confronted by a dead body, the Yakuts of upper Asia felt such terror that they fled. The Yafars of New Guinea left their dead to rot where they lay; the Sudanese Djurs abandoned them to termites; the Nilotic Masai threw them to the hyenas, and the natives of the Solomon Islands to sharks. The primitive Veddas offered their dead to carnivores, and the Parsees, in order not to pollute the ground, exposed them to vultures.

Alexandra David-Neel describes how, after a week of rituals, the body of a dead Dopka is carried to the mountains where, after being cut up into pieces, "it was abandoned as a supreme offering to the vultures."[2]

Nevertheless, without burial, without a cult of the bones, we would know nothing of the existence of Peking or Neanderthal man. The heads of Homo sapiens (10,000 B.C.) discovered by anthropologists had in fact been decapitated and preserved. Neanderthal man dug graves in which he scattered the broken bones mixed with offerings of chipped flint implements. Cro-Magnon man sprinkled red ocher over the bones. Orientated along the north-south axis, these skeletons were adorned with a headdress, bracelets, and shells. Sometimes prehistoric man gathered the skeletons of his dead together in collective tombs, like the "children's grotto" near Menton. Natural hollows, dry-stone huts, upright stones, and flagstones forming small dolmens are the first known burial places. Why were such burials carried out, and why were such primitive tombs constructed? It could not have been for reasons of health, since the living space was immense. Why this methodical arrangement of the bones, and this particular respect given to the skull, which, as we shall see, was to be the object of a cult in itself: was it a naive denial of biological fact? Did they wish to preserve the body in order to extend its life? Or did they, on the contrary, wish to prevent it ressuscitating and returning? Certain Neanderthal skeletons, found heavily bound, might suggest the last hypothesis.

From earliest times men have been concerned to preserve two things: the structure of the body (the skeleton) and its motive force (the soul). If

---

[1] "Man is the animal who buries his dead" (L. V. Thomas, *Anthropologie de la mort* [Paris: Payot, 1975]). "No human group is uninterested in its corpses" (Françoise Charpentier, *La Mort* [Paris: Classiques Hachette, 1973]). "No primitive group abandons its dead" (Edgar Morin, *L'Homme et la mort dans l'histoire* [Paris: Corréa, 1951]).

[2] Alexandra David-Neel, *Mystiques et magiciens du Tibet* (Paris: Plon, 1929).

the soul, having escaped from the body, had a life of its own, which could be kept going by religious observance, what could be done, on the other hand, with that now empty, cumbersome body, which, once the soul has departed, soon begins to decompose and stink?

To get rid of the dead body in the most effective way possible seems to have been the concern of all primitive civilizations. One of the most effective, and at the same time most economical, was obviously to eat it. In the animal world the only act in relation to death is the eating of the body by carnivores. Although animals certainly have sexual rituals, they do not appear to have funerary rites. Cannibalism soon became, for men, one rite among others. In Australia, Oceania, Africa, and South America, endocannibalism was the rite by which the body was eaten only by the relations of the deceased. In Indonesia, Melanesia, and Polynesia, the products of the decomposition of the corpse were mixed with the food of the tribe. The Guianese Indians made a liquor from the ashes of the dead and drank it. The Acuacats reduced the skeletons of their ancestors to powder and swallowed it. Burning the body and mixing the ashes with food and drink was a fairly common, more refined form of cannibalism. In this technique of the digested dead, the space of death is quite simply that of another body. Continuity of the life of the clan is thus absolute.

Another way of annihilating the corpse is still practiced: incineration. In fact, in the history of mankind, inhumation has played only a secondary role, millions of human beings having been burned to ashes ever since the troglodytes of Gezer, who, it seems, were the first to practice cremation, five or six thousand years ago, before the arrival of the Semites.

What is to be done with the corpse? William Crooke has classified funerary rites into thirteen categories: (1) cannibalism, (2) dolmens and other stone monuments, (3) exposure to wild animals and birds of prey, (4) burial under piles of stone, (5) in a cave, (6) in a house, (7) immersion in water, (8) in a tree, (9) on a platform, (10) in an urn, (11) in a contracted position, (12) in a niche, (13) concealed burial, eliminating any external mark.[3]

Many peoples, in fact, have buried their dead in trees. In the first century A.D., the Tungus and Kirghiz rolled their dead in reeds or tied them to ropes and hung them from branches.[4]

[3] William Crooke, *Death and Disposal of the Dead*, Encyclopaedia of Hastings.

[4] Jean-Paul Roux, *La Mort chez les peuples altaïques, anciens et mediévaux d'après les documents écrits* (Paris: Maisonneuve, 1963).

THE SPACE OF DEATH

In New Guinea the dead man, wrapped in a sheath of palm leaves, was placed on a platform, in his own garden. His close relations lit a fire under the body and smoked it as one would meat. In Europe, in the Middle Ages, this strange custom of hanging the dead from the branches of trees, in the hope of drying them out, sometimes reappeared, much to the horror of the religious authorities.

Like cremation and cannibalism, drying avoids the physical horror of decomposition. So, too, does embalming, which the ancient Egyptians brought to a high degree of perfection and which, for European kings and princes, continued from the end of the Middle Ages to the early nineteenth century, and still survives in the United States for ordinary citizens.

According to Genesis, it took forty days to embalm the body of Jacob. This was embalming on the cheap, imitated of course from the Egyptian technique which, according to Herodotus, required eighty days of work. The Egyptian practitioners eliminated all putrescible parts of the body without impairing the rest, asepticized the substances by magnetism, and stopped any fermentation by complete sterilization. After pulling out the brain through the nostrils, the embalmer opened up the belly of the corpse, and pulled out the viscera, which were then placed in canopic jars. He then took out the heart, which was replaced by a stone beetle. The corpse was then soaked in brine for a month. It was then taken out and dried for about sixty days, the empty body having been previously stuffed with silt, sand, resin, sawdust, bits of cloth, aromatics, and onions, making sure, in the case of women, that the breasts were given their full shape. The mummy was then rolled up in linen wrappings soaked in bituminous substances and placed in a wooden coffin shaped around the form of the human body, which was then put in a stone sarcophagus. But, unlike modern embalmers, who preserve the body in its usual appearance, the Egyptian mummies were complete only when dressed and masked. If this adornment is removed what one sees are skeletons covered with black, dried skin, rather horrible in appearance. The Egyptian embalmings were in fact only tanned bodies.[5]

Other peoples protected their corpses from corruption by filling the emptied bodies with cedar chippings. Alexander the Great was embalmed in wax and honey. The body of Jesus, wrapped in linen, was, in the Jewish manner, scented with aromatics. Following the same prin-

---

[5] Mummification was also practiced in the Inca civilization. Mummified bodies were as numerous in ancient Peru as in ancient Egypt. But the bodies, instead of being laid out, were bent in a crouching position, with the knees brought up to the chin.

ciple, the corpses of kings in the Middle Ages were stuffed with salt and aromatic plants. Saint Louis, who died at Tunis, was cut up into pieces, boiled in wine and water until the flesh came away from the bone, and his skeleton brought to Saint-Denis in a silver reliquary. Nelson's body was brought from Trafalgar to London in a barrel of brandy.

What is to be done with the corpse? This question has always obsessed the survivors. Embalming looks like a victory over the putrefaction of the body. But are Egyptian mummies eternal bodies or similacra? Contrary to what is often believed, the mummified corpse of the Egyptian was not a naive way of cheating eternity of the body, but a representation intended to attract, by means of this physical body, the psychic double. The mummy was merely a pivot intended to trap the "astral body," which Christianity turned into the "glorious body" of the Elect. The Egyptian tombs, so obviously houses of the dead, were merely a receiver, a medium, intended to receive psychic radiation from the beyond. The mummy was simply a symbolic object summoning the psychic reality it represented. That is why, in order to attract the posthumous radiation of the dead man, the object-medium had to be impregnated with all his memories. This is why the dead man's utensils and furniture were buried with him in the tomb. The Egyptian grave, then, was a sort of apparatus for communicating with the beyond. The proliferation of graves and mummies on Egyptian soil made that country, for thousands of years, an extraordinary and unique storehouse of immutable corpses and houses of the dead. This was carried to such a point that the cities of the dead became more important than the residences of the living. But if the Egyptians allowed their imprisoning graves to proliferate, it was also to make sure that their dead were reincarnated only in Egypt, thus ensuring that the empire would always have the same number of souls, though in different bodies.[6] If one considers the extraordinary duration of the Egyptian civilization, the Egyptians seemed to have succeeded in their aim for at least 2,500 years.

These Egyptian mummies still fascinate us. From the sixteenth century the Islamicized Egyptians traded in false mummies, recent corpses prepared with asphalt and pitch, since European physicians recommended mummy's flesh to cure bruises. Thus Francis I always carried on his person a small packet of pulverized mummy, mixed with rhubarb, ready to be taken in case of a fall. In the seventeenth century no scholar's library, no collection of curiosities, no pharmacy was complete without

---

[6]René Kopp, *Variétés sur la Vérité*, vol. 1, *La Science et la mort dans l'Egypte ancienne* (Paris, 1932).

[7

its Egyptian mummy, either complete or in fragments. Fouquet's country house, at Saint-Mandé, was decorated with two mummies in their decorated coffins, which had been sold to him as those of the pharaohs Cheops and Cephren.[7]

But there are even more extraordinary mummies than the Egyptian ones: I am referring to natural mummies, that is to say, bodies that have remained incorruptible without any preparation. Such a phenomenon was seen by the church, of course, as the evident sign of a miracle and of the sanctity of the person in question. This was made all the easier in that Theresa of Avila was the best-known example of the incorruptibility of the flesh. Theresa of Avila died on October 4, 1582, at Alba, and her body was placed, without any special preparation, in a wooden coffin, which was then buried in a very deep ditch beneath the nuns' choir screen. Stone, chalk, and damp soil covered the coffin. For nine months a very strong smell of lilies, jasmine, and violets rose from the tomb and perfumed both the chapel and the convent. The religious authorities were intrigued, and had the body exhumed a year later. The coffin was found broken, and filled with soil and water. The dead woman's clothes had disintegrated, but the body had remained intact. It was put into a new coffin and buried again. In 1585 it was decided to take Theresa's body to Avila. The tomb was opened again, and the body found to be as intact as before. In 1604 and again in 1616, that is to say, thirty years after the initial burial, the body had still not altered. The sanctity of Theresa of Avila having thus been proved, the heart was taken out and placed in a crystal vase; thereafter a rib, then the right foot, and several pieces of flesh were given away as relics.

But the Catholic Church had carefully concealed the fact that, just a century before the death of Theresa of Avila, on April 14, 1485, under the pontificate of Innocent VIII, workers quarrying marble on the Appian Way uncovered a white marble sarcophagus in which lay the outstretched body of a girl, who stared out at them with wide open eyes. There could be no question that it was the body of a young Roman girl who had died some 1,500 years before. The next day the marveling crowd carried the uncorrupted corpse in triumph to the Capitol. Innocent VIII, concerned at this enthusiasm for a "pagan," had the body removed in secret, and it has never been seen again.

We now know that no miracle is involved and that natural mummification is possible in dry air, by sterilization caused by the sun or by freezing. Since the body of Theresa of Avila was covered with moss, it

[7] Legrand d'Aussy, *Des sépultures nationale* (Paris, 1798).

8]

has also been suggested that nature might have used "antibiotic processes to preserve certain dead bodies from the attacks of destructive microorganisms."[8]

Natural mummies, called morchi, were regarded as miraculous by the Russian people, so to convince them of the absurdity of this belief the Soviet government allowed the mummies to crumble no less miraculously into dust under the eyes of the crowd in 1919. As Hubert Larcher reminds us, this did not prevent "that same revolutionary government from having Lenin's body mummified and presenting the remains, the stitches concealed under wax, and carefully supervised by Drs. Vorobieyev and Zbarski to the wonderment of half a million people a year."[9]

The dismemberment of the body, which was practiced in the case of Saint Theresa is a curious custom that seems to be bound up with the triumphal years of the Catholic Church, since it does not appear before the eleventh century. However, the church tried at first to dissuade its faithful from mutilating corpses in this way. In 1299 Pope Boniface VIII even went so far as to ban it altogether.

But to no avail: the most powerful monarchs were "carved up" after their deaths and different parts of their body buried in different places. This was no doubt a way of imitating the holy martyrs, whose relics were scattered throughout Christendom. The first king to be cut up in this way seems to have been William the Conqueror, who died in 1087; his body was buried in the Abbaye aux Dames, at Caen, his heart in Rouen Cathedral, and his entrails at Châlus. In 1199 Richard Lion-Heart bequeathed his body to the abbey of Fontevrault, his heart to Rouen, and his entrails to the abbey of Charroux. In 1226 Louis VIII, king of France, died at Montpensier; his entrails and heart remained in Auvergne, while the rest of his body was taken to Saint-Denis. In 1285 Philip III, nicknamed the Bold, died at Perpignan on his return from a "crusade" in Aragon, and his body, like that of his father, Saint Louis, was boiled in water and wine. The bones and heart were then sent to Saint-Denis, while the flesh and entrails remained at Narbonne. Du Guesclin, who died in 1380, had four tombs: one for his flesh at Montferrand, one for his heart at Dinan, one for his entrails at Le Puy, and, an exceptional privilege for someone who was not a prince of the blood royal, a tomb for his bones at Saint-Denis.

---

[8] Hubert Larcher, *Le Sang peut-il vaincre la mort?* (Paris: Gallimard, 1957). In soil that is not too clayey the decomposition of flesh may take five years. But a soil rich in neutral salts helps to dry the body. This is why natural mummies have been found in the subterranean galleries of the Dominicans and Franciscans in Toulouse.
[9] Ibid.

On January 1, 1793, a member of the Convention, Louis Legendre, who had, it is true, been a butcher before the revolution, proposed to the Jacobin club that the body of Louis XIV be cut up into eighty-three pieces, one piece being sent to each of the eighty-three French departments to fumigate the eighty-three trees of liberty.

It should be noted that it is always the bones that are transported to the solemn burial place. Over and over again we find this fascination for the structure of the body, which I referred to at the beginning of this book. It has been the concern of a number of civilizations to get rid of those parts of the body that decompose rapidly and to preserve only the skeleton. Thus the burial was sometimes carried out in two stages. The first, a temporary burial, lasted until the flesh came off the skeleton, while the second, definitive one, preserved only the skull and bones. The Indians of North America, the Oceanians, and the early peoples of northern Europe exposed their corpses to the air and to birds of prey on top of scaffolding or trees. The bones were then collected, cleaned, and buried beneath tumuli. According to popular medieval belief, the dead flesh was cursed. A rapid dissolution of the body was desirable. Hence the success of the cemetery of the Saints-Innocents, in Paris, where the ground, it was said, rapidly devoured the body. In the fifteenth century certain people even requested in their will that a little soil from the cemetery of the Saints-Innocents be placed in their coffin. Only the bones, the noble part to be preserved, were collected in ossuaries.

"In Brittany," writes Prosper Mérimée, "the relations of a dead person have the body exhumed after some years. The bones are collected and put into a small building next to the church, called the reliquary. Sometimes the dead person's head is kept and put in a box. . . These ossuaries arouse neither disgust nor respect in the peasants. I have seen several of them sheltering from the rain, others eating there. Some waited for me to walk by before making love there with their mistresses."[10]

The grimacing skeleton that invaded the iconography of the late Middle Ages seems to have been unknown to Greco-Roman antiquity. On the other hand, the cult of the skull goes back to Peking man (440,000 to 220,000 B.C.). Veneration for skulls is to be found in all primitive religions as well as in all the great religions of antiquity. Cortez's Spaniards, counting the skull-trophies in Mexican temples, found 136,000. The Toltecs cut off the skulls and used them as bowls. The Gauls cut off the

---

[10] Prosper Mérimée, *Notes d'un voyage dans l'ouest de la France* (Paris, 1836). Mérimée appears to be horrified by the ossuaries, and says that there are few churches in Brittany where one does not find skulls in their boxes.

heads of their dead enemies and brought them back to their villages, suspended from the necks of their horses, then nailed them as trophies in front of their houses. In New Caledonia widows kept the skulls of their husbands in baskets. In Brittany each family had its own skull boxes, small wooden coffers, shaped like an ark and surmounted by a cross. These coffers, which had openings allowing one to see the contents, were painted in gray, white, or black and bore an inscription: "Here lies the head of. . ."[11]

The head of Saint John the Baptist, martyrs carrying their heads in their hands, the guillotined at the time of the Terror, skulls on funeral drapes and on pirates' black flags, the skulls of the hussars and of the SS—what a strange fascination!

But, in addition to the skull, there is another part of the body that seems more noble than the others. This is the heart. Charlemagne had the bodies of Roland, Oliver, and Turpin opened and their hearts taken out. Is there not a parallel between the ceremony of the deposition of the hearts of princes in the Val-de-Grâce, which began with the death of Anne of Austria in 1666, and the devotion to the Sacred Heart, which was propagated at the same time by Father Grignon de Montfort and the Jesuits? This cult cropped up again in 1793, when the Sacred Heart in red material was pinned on the chests of the insurgent Vendéens.

But in that same year, 1793, on Sunday, July 28, Marat's heart was presented to the Parisian crowd on a bier in the Luxembourg Gardens. And what are we to make of Charles Maurras's last wish that after his death his heart be put in his mother's needlework box?[12]

In the architecture of the body, then, there grew up a cult of the structure (the skeleton), of the cranium (which contains the brain-computer), and of the principal pump (the heart).[13] But on these fetishistic cults there was soon superimposed another cult, that of the spirit,

[11] Jacques Marcireau, *Rites étranges dans le monde* (Paris: Laffont, 1974). In New Guinea decorated skulls painted with motifs representing the social status of the deceased were placed in the Men's House. After leaving the head of the corpse to rot until the flesh fell away, it was cleaned, then covered with an overmodeling of clay to give it back its former face. The eyes were treated with the help of shells, and human hair was used.

[12] Philippe Ariès, *L'Homme devant la mort* (Paris: Seuil, 1977).

[13] The cult of the skeleton has turned to mockery in Mexico and Spain. In Castille, Aragon, and Navarre, on November 1 and 2, people eat "*huesos de Santos*" (saints' bones), almond paste representing bones stuffed with yellow cream simulating the marrow. In modern Spain one can buy plastic keyrings representing a skeleton which, on opening its jaws, reveals a naked woman. Disarticulated skeletons, moving in every direction, are suspended from the front and back of cars. One also finds in Spain keyrings made of gilt metal with a plastic skeleton with glass eyes, and parafin candles shaped like skulls.

or soul, which escapes from the body at death. The body is the soul's first house. Once the body has decomposed, the soul wanders, without a house.

Throughout the Middle Ages, right up to the late seventeenth century, the annihilation of the body did not seem to present a problem. If there was a fear of death, it concerned the salvation of the soul, the immortal soul thanks to which the Christian benefited from a myth of equality. Faced with the inequality of earthly conditions, the survival of the soul revealed a sort of "democracy of the beyond."[14]

This was a quite new phenomenon in the history of men, for although Plato had said that the immortality of the soul was a risk to be incurred, although the ancient Greeks believed that their deceased continued to live in a "house of the blessed," Euripides was nevertheless surprised that a slave might think of death, since he had no existence; no civil existence, therefore no soul.

In the Christian world, king and serf had an egalitarian soul. But to the immortality of the soul, the *idée-force* of Greek philosophy inherited from Egyptian esotericism, Christianity added another curious, and to say the least incredible, belief: the resurrection of the body.

Although recent statistics show that 40 percent of the French population now believe that there is nothing after death,[15] belief in the survival of the human spirit after death has been universal nonetheless, and it is quite possible to believe with James Frazer that "in the present state of our knowledge the immortality of the soul cannot be proved, but it is equally impossible to prove the contrary."[16]

On the other hand, belief in the resurrection of the flesh is the folly of an early Christianity still imbued with its Judaic origins. Since bodies were to be ressucitated as such, the early Christians had little concern for corpses. They merely forbade the burning of them, on the grounds that it might make the resurrection of the flesh more difficult. Already, in their discussions, the rabbis before the coming of Christ expressed concern as to how martyrs, whose limbs had been dispersed by executioners, might gather their bodies together. They also asked themselves whether the dead rose naked or dressed in the clothes in which they had been buried. Would the bodies be cured of their illnesses and infirmities? Would the risen have a digestive system, nails, hair? Would the skin and flesh appear first, or the nerves and bones? The Sadducees, who did not

[14] Jean Baudrillard, *L'Echange symbolique et la mort* (Paris: Gallimard, 1976).
[15] Statistics for 1973, according to Georges Heuse, *Guide de la Mort* (Paris: Masson, 1975).
[16] Sir James Frazer, *The Fear of the Dead* (London: Macmillan, 1933).

believe in the resurrection of the body, had tried to embarrass Jesus by asking him how women married in turn to seven brothers might, after the resurrection, be the wife of a single man? Because certain rabbis taught that those buried in Palestine would be the first, and perhaps even the only ones, to rise, there resulted a rush to get buried in the Valley of Josaphat. Fortunately, through the magnanimity of the God of Israel, it was later arranged that the Just who had died in exile would be brought by subterranean passages to the frontiers of Palestine and resuscitated.[17]

For the Jews and for the Christians, then, the tomb was only a temporary resting place. The body slept there until the resurrection. But very soon the Christian dead, like others, grew tired of waiting for the resurrection of the flesh and began to walk about. Le Roy Ladurie notes that, in the accounts given at the Inquisition of the peasants of Montaillou, the *vertical* movement of souls is contrasted with "the *horizontal* wanderings of ghosts."[18] This world of ghosts, closely bound up with our own, is the world of souls without houses. That is why those ghosts reappear so often in their former places of residence. Old Breton stories tell how they want to come back and warm themselves by the hearth, asking help in getting their time in purgatory reduced, making reparation for some misdeed, paying off a debt, giving warnings. Camille Flammarion published a whole file on ghosts, supported by letters.[19] He tells us how these dead came back as a result of mutual oaths, promises, commitments. They are dead who wish to pay their debts, carry out tasks which they have left undone, or revenge themselves on the living. "We all live, without knowing it," Camille Flammarion adds, "in the midst of an unknown psychic environment. The atmosphere contains not only chemical elements, oxygen, nitrogen, carbonic acid, steam, etc., but also psychic elements. Everything is full of souls."[20]

The Greeks, who called their dead "the more numerous," were fond of sleeping in tombs in order to dream of the dead and to question them.

This notion that "mankind is made up of more dead than living" turns up again in Auguste Comte. The dead like being numerous, say the Madagascans. These Madagascan dead have good relations with the

---

[17] Philippe H. Menoud, "Le Sort des trépassés d'après le Nouveau Testament," *Cahiers théologiques de l'actualité protestante* (Paris: Delachaux et Niestlé, 1945).

[18] Emmanuel Le Roy Ladurie, *Montaillou, village occitan* (Paris: Gallimard, 1975); *Montaillou*, tr. Barbara Bray (London: Scolar Press, 1978).

[19] Camille Flammarion, *La Mort et son mystère*, vol. 3 *Après la mort* (Paris: Flammarion, 1922).

[20] Ibid.

living, advise them, and even live with them. The Madagascans have contact with their dead through their dreams, as did the ancient Greeks.[21]

The modern West has tended to evacuate death so that little remains of its cult but the visiting of graves. In primitive societies, however, and particularly in black Africa, the acceptance of death takes the form of ancestor worship. In fact, death is regarded there as a sort of promotion. To become an ancestor is to become a minor deity. Individual death has little importance in animistic Africa, since the individual survives in the tribe, in the caste, in the ancestors. Ancestor worship is a negation of death. The dead man is not dead. He is endowed with supernatural powers. He cohabits with the living, but he must remain at his place of death. So one of the most important acts in primitive society is the ritual of reintegrating the dead man in society, for he must not become a wandering soul. Death is not feared, but the dead man is always to some extent a source of fear.[22] So to be buried in the village, in order "to return to the mother through the earth," is an absolute necessity for the black African.[23] One of my pupils, Messamba Bamba, from the Ivory Coast, told me that in his tribe no distinction is made between the space of the living and the space of the dead. There is, therefore, no cemetery. Each family keeps its dead as close as possible to it, on the public square, in the hut, in the shower, or in the vegetable garden. They are present, but invisible, everywhere. On the public square, carved stones mark the place of burial of great witch doctors, musicians, or wrestlers. These gravestones are unsupported, gradually sink into the earth, and disappear after some fifty years, that is, a little more than the average expectation of life of the living. The disappearance of those stones is a sign that a generation has gone.

The tangled existence of the living and the dead is one of the themes of Thomas More's *Utopia*.[24] "They believe," he writes of the Utopians, "that the dead be presently conversant among the quick, as beholders and witnesses of all their words and deeds."

But in certain primitive societies, unlike the futurological society imagined by Thomas More, the living and the dead are undifferentiated. An unknown person is asked: "Who are you, then, are you dead or

---

[21] Raymond Decary, *La Mort et les coutumes funéraires à Madagascar* (Paris: Maisonneuve, 1962).

[22] Ruth Manahem, *La Mort apprivoisée* (Paris: Edit. Universitaires, 1973).

[23] Thomas, *Anthropologie*.

[24] Thomas More, *Utopia*, Book II, tr. Ralph Robinson (London: Burns and Oates, 1937).

alive?"[25] And Leenhardt tells of a Kanaka who arrived in Sydney and was at first terrified by the crowds of people walking about, until reassured that in that country the dead walk among the living in larger numbers than elsewhere.

From ancient China to the early twentieth century there persisted the strange custom of marriages between dead persons who had not known one another when alive and who had both been unmarried; thus a dead woman would be placed in the grave of a young man who had died before marrying. These postmortem marriages, contracted with a view to life in the beyond, also existed among the Tartars, if Marco Polo is to be believed. The Todas of southern India went even further, since they did not hesitate to marry corpses to living people.[26]

But this frequentation of the dead by the living, this communication with spirits, belongs not only to primitive societies. Victor Hugo believed in it, and practiced table turning at Jersey in 1852 in order to communicate with Léopoldine, his dead daughter. And Bergson declared, after taking part in spiritualist séances: "Survival is becoming so probable that the burden of proof will one day fall on those who deny it."

In the middle of a rationalistic, Voltairean, progressive-minded period, the dead vied with one another in leaving their graves and talking with the living. Ectoplasm (which the ancient Egyptians called, as we have seen, the "astral body") appeared in middle-class drawing rooms. Since 1848, when the first tables began to turn at Fox Farm, in the United States, ghosts began to walk, and occultism assumed the mission of proving the immortality of the soul scientifically. In 1852 an Anglican archbishop founded the Ghost Society at Cambridge. Two years later, in France, Allan Kardec published *Le Livre des Esprits*, which revealed the existence of spiritualism in France. "Incorporeal beings people space," he wrote. "They surround us constantly, and, unknown to them, exert a great influence over men."[27]

The desire to communicate with the dead, and its corollary, the fear of ghosts, seems to have disappeared from the Western world in the latter half of the twentieth century. The dead really have been evacuated. We now fear, not so much the dead, as death. So much so that we rid social life in advance of the elderly, who are marked by the stigmata

[25] Leenhardt, *Do Kamo, la personne et le mythe dans le monde mélanésien* (Paris: Gallimard, 1947).

[26] Frazer, *Fear of the Dead.*

[27] Allan Kardec, *Qu'est-ce que le spiritisme?* (1854).

of death. Thus the old have replaced the lepers of an earlier age, and, like them, are shut up in "lazar houses."

The dead are no longer feared, but we continue to shut them away in coffins, which have been nailed down or (even more securely) screwed down, and which are then enclosed in sealed, concrete burial vaults, under a very heavy stone. And all this is further enclosed in a cemetery surrounded by high walls, the gates of which are kept locked. What a mass of precautions to take against inanimate corpses! And why do we then walk around these cemeteries whispering, as if afraid to raise our voices? Are we afraid of disturbing the dead, or waking them?

At the origin of funerary rites, one observes not so much respect for the dead as fear for their survival and a desire to prevent their return. Whether we realize it or not, this fear is still apparent in our beliefs and practices.

Placing heavy stones over a corpse is a way of marking the burial place, but it is also a way of preventing it from rising.

In ancient Greece a victor would mutilate his dead enemy in order to prevent him from taking revenge or, alternatively, sought to placate him by burying him. But despite Clytemnestra's offerings, the ghost of Agamemnon continued to appear. The Greeks even thought it useful to imagine a police to look after the dead, the Erinyes,[28] while precommunist China has been defined as "a country in which a few hundred million living were dominated and terrorized by a few thousand million dead."[29]

Did they believe, as did the Tibetan lamas, that the souls of the dead could assume innumerable forms and that they pursued both men and animals to rob them of their "vital breath"? Indeed, Lamaism assumed the task of taming or exterminating these demoniac ghosts, even of enslaving them in order to force them to perform funeral tasks.[30]

All peoples, all civilizations, have taken innumerable precautions against the dead, who might come back and behave as enemies. Extreme solutions have consisted of eating the dead man, burning him, or carrying him around with one by placing his ashes in a small bag around one's neck.

In the Caribbean the dead man used to be placed in a round ditch, and food and drink were brought to him for ten days. If he showed no further sign of life, the food was then thrown on his head, the ditch

---

[28] Alfred Fabre-Luce, *La Mort a changé* (Paris: Gallimard, 1966).
[29] Ibid.
[30] David-Neel, *Mystiques et magiciens*.

hastily filled, and a big fire lit over it, around which the survivors danced and shouted.[31]

Many "dances of death," the ethnologists tell us, were a way of treading the ground to make sure that the corpse was well and truly crushed.

Some hundred burial places, dating from the early Iron Age and containing Celtic chariots, have been found in France. Generally the wheels of these chariots have been taken off so that the vehicles could no longer move.

In New Guinea, widowers go out armed with a club to defend themselves against their wives' shades.[32] But even in France, as late as the eighteenth century, those dead suspected of *coming back* and disturbing the living were disinterred after ten years and decapitated.[33] And in certain regions the orifices of corpses were sewn up to prevent the soul from returning to the body. The Anaon, or lost soul, long featured in the nightmares of the Breton people. Spells had to be used to deprive evil spirits of their powers, such as moving the hands on clocks or leaving their image in mirrors.

Sir James Frazer made a whole catalogue of the methods used against ghosts.[34] The corpse was taken not through the door of the house but through some other passage, specially opened for the purpose, which the dead person did not therefore know (South American Indians, the Ashantis of Africa, the Mois of Indochina, the Mossis of the Sudan, the Samoyeds of Siberia). Tracks were rubbed out (the Indians of Chile). The dead were blindfolded (Australian aborigines, the Banas of the Cameroons). All the openings of the body were sealed to prevent the soul leaving. The dead person's hut was burned down (Baholoholos of the Congo, Bantus, Malaccas, Navaho Indians, Lengua Indians of Paraguay, the East Indies, Malays, Sumatra). Stinking substances were burned to keep the spirits at a distance (Algonquins). Urine was poured on the threshold of the house, the ghost drank it, found it to be bad, and fled (Alaskan Eskimos). Objects belonging to the dead person were broken (Indians of the Amazon basin and of Vancouver, Australian aborigines). The dead person's possessions were burned (Tonkin). A net was held out to capture the spirits (India). A barrier of fire was lit. (Tartars coming back from a burial passed over a fire specially lit for the purpose. In China, after burials, fires were lit at the four corners of the cemetery to prevent the soul from escaping. Fires were also lit over graves in Africa,

[31] Marcireau, *Rites étranges*.
[32] Thomas, *Anthropologie*.
[33] Alfred Carlier, *Histoire des coutumes funéraires* (Paris: 1946).
[34] Frazer, *Fear of the Dead*.

[17

and one passed through the flames before returning to one's village.) A barrier of water was made. (In Ceylon, as in the Congo, one crossed a watercourse on returning from a burial, even if it meant making a detour.) The corpse was tied down (Australia, Brazil), or mutilated (North American Indians, Indians of the Chaco, Kissis of Liberia), or decapitated (Australia, Africa, Armenia), or its bones broken (Abyssinia).

In contemporary black Africa the fear of ghosts has considerably declined. Not that one no longer believes in ghosts but they have been domesticated. Since the soul, which has left the body, persists in loitering in places familiar to it, a place is made for it. Certain families in the Ivory Coast, another of my African pupils, Amon Kakou, tells me, even built a hut for the shades of their ancestors. In this way the dead are given a house, are appeased, and no longer have any need to wander.

"Some societies let their dead rest; provided homage is paid to them periodically, the departed refrain from troubling the living. . . It is as if a contract had been concluded between the dead and the living: in return for being treated with a reasonable degree of respect, the dead remain in their own abode."[35]

Primitive man, who often attributes earthquakes to the dead being startled but also makes them responsible for thunder, drought, famine, and illnesses, must therefore reconcile himself with these dangerous spirits, either by persuasion, conciliation, trickery, or force. Most mortuary rituals have no other purpose or any other meaning.

In Celtic civilization, as well as in black Africa, it was believed that a dead person without a burial place became a vampire. Egyptians, Greeks, and Romans also believed that it was a dreadful thing to deprive a dead person of burial. Were not those who were left unburied condemned to wander on the banks of the Styx? A Greek or Roman, banished from his homeland, separated from his native soil, suffered the additional torment of knowing that after his death no one would keep up the correct religious observances over his tomb. Catholic excommunication revived this ancient curse by depriving the victim of Christian burial. "Let him be cursed unto all eternity, and cursed by those who give him burial." The formula was applied literally to the emperor of Germany, Henry IV, who, after being excommunicated, was condemned to wander without asylum or help and died in exile without Christian burial. But the refusal of proper burial was not only confined to the excommunicated.

[35] Claude Lévi-Strauss, *Tristes Tropiques*, chp. 23: "Les Vivants et les morts" (Paris: Plon, 1955); *Tristes Tropiques*, tr. John and Doreen Weightman (New York: Atheneum, 1964).

The *Corpus juris Canonici* drew up a list that extended refusal of ecclessiastical burial to pagans, Jews, heretics, those placed under an interdict, blasphemers, those who looted and burned down churches, suicides, those who died notoriously in a state of mortal sin (for example those committing adultery, theft, those participating in pagan games except tourneys, those on their way back from a brothel). "One does not carry into the church those who have been killed, lest their blood pollute the floor of God's temple. . . If someone dies suddenly while indulging in such common games as ball or bowls, he may be buried in the cemetery, because he did not think that he was doing harm to anyone."[36] But two months after the fall of the Bastille, on September 29, 1789, the parish priest of Saint-Jacques-du-Haut-Pas, in Paris, was still refusing Christian burial to a worker killed in an accident and therefore without extreme unction. The population, which had acquired a taste for insurrection, while preserving a more ancient taste for funerals, entered the church, set up the black hangings, lit torches, and brought in the workman's coffin, and forced the priest to bless it.[37]

Even in the eighteenth century, actors were not buried in cemeteries. Voltaire complained that Adrienne Lecouvreur, who had been so welcome in the salons, should be excluded from the cemeteries. But it was quite common at that time that a man who died in a tavern should be thrown into the communal pit. When children died before being baptized, they were buried in the fields, like animals.

The tomb is a second house.[38] The care taken in building this house of the dead, the persistence with which this last resting-place is maintained, may prevent the dead from "coming back." To deprive a dead man of burial is, therefore, to force him to wander, houseless.

But the tomb is also a sort of antechamber between this world and the next, a place of *passage*. We have seen how the Egyptians turned their burial places into a springboard for access into the other world. The early Christians were to proceed in a less scientific way, but by building

[36] Arthur Murcier, *La Sépulture chrétienne en France d'après les monuments du XIe au XVIe siècle* (Paris, 1855).

[37] Marcel Le Clère, *Cimetières et Sépultures de Paris* (Paris: Les Guides bleus, 1978).

[38] "This house of mud where your soul has taken up residence may soon fall into ruins" (Antoine Blanchard, *Nouvel Essay d'exhortation*, 1718). Since the body of flesh is identified with the house of stone, the soul of the deceased tends therefore to wish to remain in the house. Anatole Le Braz remarks: "One must never leave the house alone during a burial, otherwise the dead man whose remains one believes one is accompanying to the cemetery, stays behind to guard it" (*La Légende de la mort chez les Bretons armoricains*, 1874).

their churches over the tomb of a martyr, they turned this mausoleum-church into the place where the living and dead would live in close contact.

The martyr's sarcophagus was to be the first altar. And in all churches the altars were long constructed in the shape of tombs. Under the papal altar of Saint Peter's in Rome, at which only the pope may officiate, lies the tomb of Saint Peter.

The mass, then, is celebrated over a tomb (or over what replaces it). When the number of churches increased to such a point that it was impossible to build each of them over the corpse of a martyr or saint, the bodies of martyrs were broken up and bits of the bones distributed throughout Christendom as relics: these were then placed under the altar stone.

There soon grew up a desire to be buried near relics. First bishops, then mere priests, arranged to have themselves buried under the church floor. Then kings and aristocrats demanded to be buried in the church. By the late thirteenth century rich commoners had also managed to get themselves buried in the "house of God." Indeed, practice corresponded closely with feudal ideology. The saint was an elected prince, whose vassal the dead Christian wished to be. The saint was buried under the altar and the bishop close to the saint, followed by the prince and his liegemen. According to one's earthly rank, one was buried in the church or around the church, under the floor of the porch, or under the eaves. The people were buried around the church, in anonymous ditches. The church surrounded by its cemetery symbolized the Christian social unit. But by the tenth century certain churches were already so encumbered with dead that they had to be disaffected and converted into cemeteries only. In the fourteenth century, charnel houses with galleries and ossuaries had to be built in the gardens adjacent to the church. When the ossuaries were full, the faithful then buried the bones, with great ceremony, in a large ditch specially dug for the purpose, each member of the congregation carrying a skeleton.

The inequality of earthly conditions certainly persisted in this arrangement of the mortuary space, with the dead bodies arranged according to their rank as living bodies: the saint in the center, the clergy next to him, then the nobles; farther away, the artisans and merchants, and at the edges the villeins and serfs. Christian democracy was a utopia that was realized only in the beyond.

As feudalism declined, the space of death changed. From the thirteenth century the rising bourgeois class introduced its dead inside the church. The clergy accepted these merchants under the floor of the nave only for increasingly large sums of money. The right to burial in the church, which had been acquired for priests and nobles, could be acquired by others through the fruits of trading and usury, in the same way that the bourgeois acquired their social responsibilities and political representation.

In this upheaval the "house of God" was to cease being the only house of the dead. Cemeteries first moved out around the church, then eventually outside the church altogether. And the souls of the poor, who found themselves once again without a house, set off on their wanderings. So a new kind of wandering appeared from the Renaissance onward that was to assume gigantic proportions in the seventeenth century: that of the souls in purgatory. In order to reduce this wandering, in order to bring these suffering souls into the house of the elect (paradise), the church, now ideologically linked to the bourgeoisie, found no other means than to sell indulgences. It even went so far as to institutionalize the will, which included an obligatory donation for masses. From now on not only did one have to buy one's place in or around the church, but one also had to buy one's place in heaven. Otherwise it was the common ditch and a wandering soul.

From the tomb-house, from the villages and towns of the dead, to the architecture of the beyond, we shall now see what a strange adventure befell the dead man. There is an architectural space of death which, until our own time, has given rise to little comment. Yet in the tissue of urban and rural space, death forms a network of places and objects, with its allegories and symbols, its signs and its reference points, forming a specific course. If death has found, during the last ten years or so, its historians, its philosophers, its psychologists, its sociologists, its semiologists, it has only too seldom been studied from the point of view of architecture, urbanism, and decoration. It seems to have been forgotten that the first known architect, Imhotep, who built King Zoser's stepped pyramids during the third Egyptian dynasty, the only architect to be deified, was above all the creator of a tomb.

I

The Houses of the

DEAD

If this house of earth and mud in which we live is destroyed, we have another house prepared for us in heaven. . . [God] intends, as Saint John Chrysostom so excellently puts it, to repair the house which he has given us: while he destroys it, and knocks it down, in order to build it anew, we have to move house. And he offers us his own palace, he gives us our own apartment, so that we may wait at rest until our old building has been completely restored.

Bossuet
Sermon on Death

I

The Tomb-House

Just as we display our wealth by acquiring, in the city, a house of our own, so we confirm that wealth by providing ourselves, in the necropolis, with a posthumous, sumptuous, and durable house.

Emile Magne

L'Esthétique des villes, Paris, Mercure de France, 1908

According to Greek authors the Egyptians called their tombs "eternal habitations" or "residences for eternity." This term *house for eternity* was taken up by the Israelites, who also called their tombs "houses for life." Nearer to our own times, Anna de Noailles compared tombs to *"maisons couchées."*

Each tomb is in effect the double of a house or apartment, and each cemetery the parallel projection of a village, town, or district. As soon as one thinks seriously of living in a place, said Pierre Sansot, the question of death arises. To this curious reflection he adds the following commentary: "Lost childhood takes root at the place where the tomb is built: a pitiful cycle of the secondary, which turns toward death while seeking its source. It is the omnipresence of that final end that produces this proliferation of movement and decoration: the tomb must be pleasant, a link, a hyphen, with the living. The erotic paintings of the necropolises, the everyday objects and food that surround the dead, the flowers of our cemeteries, the isolated graves where Corsican families take root, the whole decorum of death is associated with habitation. A person who

[25

regularly visits his family tomb extends his residence of that piece of earth."[1]

From the earliest civilizations, which emerged in Mesopotamia some seven thousand years ago, the tomb has appeared as the obverse of the house. And in the case of Egyptian civilization, rather the reverse is true: the house is the obverse of the tomb. In Assyro-Babylonian literature the grave is called "house" or "residence," "the house from which he who enters does not leave," "the house of the shades," "the house of dust." Indeed the Assyro-Babylonian burial places are conceived as veritable houses in which the dead man is supposed to go on living.[2] But it is always a house-prison, a house intended to make the dead man disappear and to prevent his return. The grave is sometimes endowed with sculpture. In the form of stelae, it even looks like sculpture. But in reality a tomb, even the most modest one, is always architecture. The stela is merely the visible part of the architectural device, which continues underground.

In most civilizations the houses of the dead are more magnificent than the houses of the living. Indeed we often know of civilizations that have disappeared, when the houses of the living have been reduced to dust, only through the houses of the dead, which have survived intact. Have not most of the riches of our museums come from robbing tombs?[3] Even prehistoric men, who did not construct tomb-houses, since they had not yet invented architecture, buried with their head, in caves that resembled their natural habitat, products of their craft, thus creating without knowing it subterranean exhibitions. They believed that they were communicating with the beyond: they were certainly communicating with posterity.

Are not our modern family vaults, places in which the members of a family, separated in life, are reunited in death, a replica of the primitive cave?

For thousands of years, when man was entirely nomadic, the house of the dead was the only house that did not move, the only one that expressed an arresting of time. And when man became a settler, during

[1] P. Sansot, H. Strohl, H. Torgue, C. Verdillon, *L'Espace et son double* (Paris: Editions du Champ urbain, 1978).

[2] André Parrot, *Malédictions et Violations de tombes* (Paris: Lib. Orientaliste Geuthner, 1939).

[3] "Practically all American archeological objects are associated with death, since they were made to accompany the deceased into the beyond" (Exhibition catalogue, *Rites de la mort* [Paris: Musée de l'Homme, 1979]).

the great Mesopotamian and Egyptian civilizations, the great architecture was that of the tomb, a tomb that was a residence in which the dead man lived and received his guests. The great Egyptian royal burial places included a reception hall for the "double." There offerings were placed for the funerary meals. There the "double" could communicate with visitors. Off this reception hall led corridors, some of which were dead ends, in order to trick thieves. Others led to a succession of rooms and, finally, to the mummy's vault. At the entrance to the corridors, a stela served as a false door. On it was written the dead man's name. In various parts of the tomb there were statues representing the dead man. Then were distributed at various points small figurines, about eight to twelve inches high, again of the dead man, representing him in various familiar attitudes. All these effigies were intended to attract the "double." The furniture, with its jewels, its adornments, its toilet utensils, the tables on which food was placed, was not there as decoration, but, again, to attract the "double." And, serving the same purpose, there were paintings on the walls representing scenes and exploits from the dead man's life, but also scenes from everyday life, depicting the grain harvest, the wine harvest, fishing, married life.

The tomb of Seti I, at Abydos, is a subterranean palace in which the pharoah could transform his coffin into a throne and preside over the assembly of his vassals and attendants, walled up at the same time as himself. In this splendid tomb are enormous halls with ceilings that seem to be supported by square pillars, carved out of the solid rock. The walls are carved and painted. There are no everyday scenes, only Seti himself, accompanied by a protective deity: Sekket with his lioness's head, Amibis with his jackal's head, or Toth with his ibis's head. Large serpents, which uncoil around the halls, rise up near doors to threaten any profaner.

More modestly, the pagan Gallo-Roman who believed that death was merely a continuation of life and that the only change would be in one's way of life, that it was a kind of removal from one residence to another, thought that one lived in the tomb as in another residence. So his dead were served with food and drink, in the same dishes and the same jugs. And children were buried with their small furniture.

Every tomb, then, consisted of an apartment, from the royal suite right down to the tiny room. The dead man continued to live in his house, a replica of his previous abode. The sarcophagi themselves often had lids that imitated a triangular or domed roof. One type of sarcophagus, known as the "palace facade" type, is intended to suggest pharaonic privilege and is offered to the dead man merely in reproduction.

On a number of lead sarcophagi, the small side is also sometimes decorated with the facade of a temple, and the large sides are decorated with
columns, a miniaturized replica of the great shrines.

In the China of the Aeneolithic period (3400 B.C.) the funerary urn
is shaped like a house. It is a "building" on four feet (piles), flanked by
two very high gables, with three "windows" in the upper part, and a
rounded roof. The decoration on Chia and Chüoch ritual bronzes indicates that the spirit of the ancestors lived in a small house, sometimes
square, sometimes circular, the shape of which was reminiscent of a tent
or a reed cabin.

Unlike the Egyptians, who hid their burial places, the Lycians of
Asia Minor built monuments, before the conquest of Alexander, which
lavished all their architectural and decorative skills on the outside. The
Lycian graves, placed one on top of another in cliffs reached by narrow
staircases or by climbing up the rock face took very few precautions to
defend the dead from looting. The ostentation of the outer surfaces seems
rather to encourage it. While no trace of decoration is to be found inside,
and the burial chamber itself is always small and intended for one oc-
cupant, the entire mountain is carved. The facades of the superimposed
tombs, carved out of solid rock, imitate wooden constructions, probably
those of the houses of the living. The dead, however, have a stone house.
And, more surprisingly still, the stone faithfully reproduces the structure of wooden construction, with carved beams and joists, and even
joints and dowels.

There are also isolated Lycian tombs which have been perfectly preserved in present-day Turkish villages and which are reproductions, in
stone, of wooden houses. "Thick ribs, or rather joists, are cut out of it
to form a cross. This word 'joist,' which applies to wooden constructions, is very suitable here: for here the stone imitates wood, and the
mason has modeled his work on that of the carpenter. . . The upper
part, the roof one might say, forms the ogive and, in its tympanum, is a
gaping opening, which, no doubt, was once blocked by a stone slab. It
was through this hole that the body was brought in."[4]

Near the township of Makry, at the end of a gulf where there was
once a port, a tomb, placed on a monolithic cube, rises from the sea to a
height of about thirteen feet. This Lycian tomb, isolated in the sea, is
reminiscent of Chateaubriand's tomb.

Viollet-le-Duc remarks that these Lycian tombs may in fact be
subdivided into three parts: a pedestal, a marble sarcophagus which

[4]Lucien Augé, *Les Tombeaux* (Paris: Hachette, 1879).

Chinese earthenware tomb model of a watchtower. Han Dynasty, 1st-2d century A.D. *(The Granger Collection, New York)*

[29

Chinese glazed earthenware tomb figure of a lion. Tang Dynasty, early 8th century A.D. *(The Granger Collection, New York)*

contains the corpse and looks like carved stone, and a superstructure which, though also carved out of marble, affects the appearance of a wooden structure. For Viollet-le-Duc, this last section is a catafalque: "The curvilinear summit simulates a material the embroidery on which is represented by very flat bas-reliefs."[5]

Viollet-le-Duc suggests that the Gallo-Roman tombs found in the Vosges near Saverne include similar catafalques.

These Gallic funerary stelae, in the form of huts or houses, are not very well known. It is true that most of them were put to different purposes by the peasants, who turned them into feeding troughs or demolished them to provide stone for roads. The most primitive form is a cuneiform stone, the facade of which is an isosceles triangle, the summit an acute angle. Ten inches wide at the base, and ten inches high, they were hollowed out through a very small "door."

One also sees proper doors with carved figures (Luxeuil museum) and twin houses. More realistic houses are to be found among these stelae: a rectangle surmounted by a triangle, walls and roofs being quite distinct. False columns flank a clearly defined door. Under Roman influence the roof became more prominent, with swellings on both slopes of the roof. The Gallic stelae, writes Emile Linckenheld, who devoted a thesis to them, sometimes imitate houses down to the smallest details (Luxembourg museum).[6] "Wasserwald cemetery has provided tombs with stone urns, with or without a stela, and also several tombs formed by a square of dry-stone walls, which corresponds exactly to the plan of Gallic houses discovered in the area. . . The stone walls around the tomb seem to represent the farm walls around the house."[7]

Emile Linckenheld tells us that among the Celts, the Leuci and the Mediomatrici left most of the stela houses. But stela houses are also to be found among the Treviri, the Remi, the Suessiones, the Sequani, the Belgae, and the Galatae of Phrygia. At the center of Gaul, where Gallic huts were round and not square, as in the East, rounded stelae are to be found.

The Gauls, like the Aryan Scythians, first made subterranean houses for their dead, dug deeply out of the ground, and covered by a heavy roof of planks, supported by thick beams. Then, in the late fourth century B.C., when incineration spread to Gaul, there appeared funerary

[5] Viollet-le-Duc, *Dictionnaire raisonné de l'architecture française du XIᵉ siècle au XVIᵉ siècle* (Paris, 1854–64).

[6] Emile Linckenheld, *Les Stèles funéraires en forme de maison chez les médiomatriques et en Gaule* (Strasbourg: Université de Strasbourg, 1927).

[7] Ibid.

monuments which contained the ashes of the dead and which reproduced the appearance of a house. A development then took place in which the subterranean tomb-house was replaced by the external stela-house.

The opening at the bottom of the stela in the form of a door is, of course, the "passage" through which the dead person may join the world of the living. If one does not want the dead person to "return," this opening is blocked, as is often the case in the stelae that have been found. The Romans said that the Celts always left the doors of their houses open so that the spirits of the dead of the house might come and go as they pleased. This custom survived in Brittany, for Anatole Le Braz tells us that, in the last century, the Bretons did not lock their doors at night in case the dead wanted to return.

The Roman civilization was to transform the Gallic stela-hut into the magnificent stela-house. The funerary mausoleums in the form of a tower, built on a square base, several stories high, like the mausoleum of the Julii at Saint-Rémy-de-Provence, are in fact stela-houses enlarged and "translated into architecture."[8]

The Gauls erected for their chiefs enormous tumuli, about two hundred feet in diameter, enclosing at their center a veritable house of between three and four hundred square feet. This house was formed of beams, with a pointed roof. One cannot help but be reminded of the Egyptian pyramids, of which these Celtic princely tombs seem to be a "barbarian" version. But, everywhere, the first tombs were tumuli. And the most admirable pyramids are themselves in fact merely gigantic tumuli, "translated into architecture."

The pre-Etruscan Italic people of the first millenium B.C. buried their dead in round huts, whereas they lived in almost rectangular houses. Did this circular hut reproduce an earlier type of house? No doubt. Had not ossuaries in the shape of rectangular houses appeared in the Etruscan

---

[8] "Among the Egyptians, the Lycians, and the Incas, the ordinary house was always precariously built, while the tombs represented the summit of their architecture. But the dead were given replicas of the ordinary houses, the size of a toy. It is thanks to this subterfuge that we know what we do of Japanese *haniwa* architecture or of ordinary Cretan, Chinese, and Egyptian architecture of several thousand years ago. This miniature house has indirectly influenced certain forms of funerary architecture. For example, the barrel-roof of Indonesian catafalques are replicas of the roofs of the nobility's houses. The tents of the Tartars no doubt served as models for such conical-roofed tombs as Döner Kübet, built in 1276, in Turkey. In turn, certain celebrated tombs have influenced ordinary building: the barns of Galicia sometimes look like royal tombs" (Bernard Rudofsky, *L'Architecture insolite* [Paris: Tallandier, 1979]).

Gallo-Roman funeral stela, father holding his son in his arms. *(Bourges, Musée du Berry, Hôtel Cujas. Photo Giraudon)*

[33

period? And the sarcophagi were often placed in tombs carved to imitate wooden houses, as we saw in the case of the Lycians.

On the pre-Etruscan civilizations of Villanova, Joseph Rykwert writes: "The biconic ossuary was sometimes crowned with a cup, as with a roof. . . Sometimes there was a hemispherical cap, which might be decorated with thatch ends, suggesting a normal roof. It is this kind of hemispherical capping that occasionally has small projecting houses as decoration. Quite early in this period these people came to use the small house model, usually about one foot high, as an ossuary instead of the urn."[9]

The Etruscan tomb was a veritable underground house, with its own door and a staircase, or a corridor sloping down to an apartment. For the covering, a real double-pitched roof was imitated, with an exposed ridge purlin. In the so-called tomb of the Capitals, three chambers open onto the rear wall. These correspond to the reception rooms of an ordinary house, and house the remains of the masters. The funerary beds faithfully reproduce the Etruscan or Greek bed, with four carved, round, projecting feet. In the position of the head was a mound representing the pillow. Conjugal tombs were placed in the middle of the room, surrounded by those of the children and children-in-law. In the rear rooms benches were placed for servants, who might have at their disposal a whole range of cooking utensils: spits, andirons, huge jars, a cauldron on a tripod. In certain Etruscan tombs a complete dinner service, which had been used for the funeral meal, has been found, giving the impression of an interrupted dinner.[10]

The Bogomil tombs of Yugoslavia, the work of a heretical Manichean community between the eleventh and fifteenth centuries, often have the form of stone houses, with pointed roofs and blind arcades carved along their sides. There are some forty or fifty thousand of these in Bosnia and Herzegovina, and they form mortuary towns much more highly populated than the present-day villages. Scattered along the roads, in the forests, among the brambles and wild vines, sometimes almost completely submerged in the ground, they have been preserved by the Islamic prohibition against tampering with graves.

In eastern Bosnia, a region covered by forests, these small, stone, funerary houses imitate planks and beams, and their roofs are carved in the form of shingles. In Herzegovina, on the other hand, where there is

[9]Joseph Rykwert, *On Adam's House in Paradise* (New York: Museum of Modern Art, 1972).

[10]Jacques Heurgon, *La Vie quotidienne chez les Etrusques* (Paris: Hachette, 1961).

An Etruscan tomb. *(Banditaccia Necropolis, Cerveteri. Photo Giraudon)*

a liking for shaded porticoes, these same porticoes have been represented on the tomb in the form of colonnades.[11]

In Madagascar, where the mortuary house has sometimes been destroyed, the Kiboris of the high plateaus spend their whole lives building a house for their dead. It was King Andriantomponkoindrindra who, in the fifteenth century, had the first small house constructed as a future tomb. Since then, the custom has survived of building tombs whose size is generally out of all proportion to the social position and fortune of their owners. "The habitation of the living man may be poor, even wretched, but the tomb on the contrary has to be vast and attract atten-

[11] O. Bihalji-Merin and A. Benac, *L'Art des Bogomiles* (Paris: Arthaud, 1963).

[35

tion. . . . The eternal abode has to stand out for its solidity and fine appearance. . . . The tomb is visible wealth, and some ruin themselves in building it."[12]

Here we find, once again, the idea diffused by ancient Egypt that the house of the living is merely a "temporary abode," as Diodorus of Sicily put it, and that one should devote all one's care to one's final resting place. One also finds here the Chinese custom by which one's life savings should be spent on the construction of the house of the dead. As a result many families were ruined by the death of one of them, and children even went so far as to sell themselves to pay for a parent's burial.

The Madagascan houses of the dead were at first simple, small wooden houses, built in the manner of ordinary houses. They had a door, but no windows. They were covered at first with thatch, then with shingles; then, in the nineteenth century, they became stone monuments with a decorated door, and in the twentieth century mausoleums of reinforced concrete, with concrete roofs. The metal door is surrounded by vases of flowers.[13]

But in some civilizations the house of the living and the house of the dead were quite simply one and the same. Or rather, to put it another way, the dead were not expelled from the houses in which they had lived. The ancient Greeks, like the ancient Romans, buried their dead under the stone floors of their houses, but this was later forbidden for reasons of hygiene. The custom of burying the dead or of preserving part of their bodies, in particular the skull, in the house in which they had lived in very widespread in a number of primitive civilizations. Some live with the dead in the house, others abandon the house to the dead. The natives of the Gilbert Islands dig graves in the earth floor of the house and open them from time to time to examine the remains. When the bodies are fleshless, they take off the skull and keep it in a box. Some even take out the entire skeleton, which they hang at the top of the house and bring down from time to time to anoint it with coconut oil.

When the colonial powers, as in British New Guinea, felt forced to

[12] Decary, *La Mort et les coutumes funéraires à Madagascar*. "On the territory of Sakalava of the former kingdom of Manabe (Madagascar) there is a wide diversity of types of tombs. The cemeteries of the former kings are made up of a line of small wooden houses, oriented on a north-south axis, with the crest of the roof dominated at each end by a triangle of wood, and the whole group is enclosed by a fence." The tomb of the last Mahafaly king, Tsiamponde, who died in 1912, over ninety feet each side, is decorated with seven hundred pairs of zebra horns from animals sacrificed for the sovereign's funeral (Exhibition catalogue, *Rites de la mort*).

[13] Decary, *La Mort et les coutumes funéraires à Madagascar*.

forbid this practice, the natives overtly buried their bodies in a proper cemetery, then secretly disinterred them and brought them back into their houses. At Makeo, on the other hand, the natives took to living for two or three weeks in the cemetery, near the relation whom they had buried, and in the end built special houses there so that they could visit their dead regularly.[14]

This custom of burying the dead in the houses of the living is obviously no more stupid than that of burying the dead in churches, as was done for almost a thousand years in the Christian West. Burying the dead in the church was to bury them in the common house, the great dwelling of the ancestors. When, from the fifteenth century, the first graves appeared in cemeteries outside the church, some reproduced in miniature the church of which they had been deprived.

In the twentieth century, in the museum-cemeteries of the Père-Lachaise type, a mimicry of religious buildings (churches, chapels) is also evident. But gradually, as it became secularized, the cemetery came to be filled once again with replicas of houses.

> The model, the referent-type, has changed: it is no longer the church or chapel which serves as a model for the mausoleum, but the ordinary, everyday house. The secular habitat [in the more modern cemeteries of Portugal and Italy, for example, the tomb] . . . has become a *third* home: the floor is covered with a brightly colored carpet, and the traditional oratory, which usually formed the inside of the mausoleum, has been transformed into a carpeted waiting room and the prie-dieux into magnificent velvet-covered modern furniture. . . In the twentieth century the mausoleum has become a house. . . properly designed villas or luxury bungalows. They have picture windows with venetian blinds. Some are surrounded by lawns and trees; others prefer a small front garden with a low wall, and railings all around to reinforce the sense of enclosure. . . In Madrid we have seen a mausoleum made of stainless steel with sliding bay windows. . . the entire structure supported at about six feet from the ground by a single steel pillar.[15]

The modern tomb, then, also mimics the house of the living. In Italy, taking advantage of sloping ground, two-story mausoleums have been built for the use of two separate families.

J.-D. Urbain also notes that the modern mausoleum is a "simulacrum of a house." An effect of life, of presence, is produced, as in that mausoleum in the Cimeterio Oriental in Lisbon, which, like others, is "the

---

[14] Frazer, *Fear of the Dead*.

[15] Jean-Didier Urbain, *La Société de conservation* (Paris: Payot, 1978).

object of frequent, meticulous cleaning: the windows are polished, the objects dusted, the floor swept, the flowers and curtains changed; sometimes even, in the silence of the cemetery, one can hear the sound of a vacuum cleaner."[16] The houses-of-the-living/houses-of-the-dead mimicry continues, then, with modern variants, which proves how powerful and persistent that fantasy is. There are now cemetery blocks of two or more stories, as at the Cimetero del Pino in Florence or the three-storied building in a Naples cemetery. In Marseille a high-rise, seven-story block provides 6,000 places. At Nice low concrete walls surrounding an entire hill offer 10,000 places. There are tower-block cemeteries equipped with lifts. In 1966 the Italian architect Nanda Vigo proposed a cemetery made up of two twenty-story towers, each some eighty feet high. They would house 14,480 persons. More recently, at Rio de Janeiro, the architect Antonio Antunès proposed a twelve-story tower for 24,000 dead, which came to be known as the "Cathedral of Silence."

Since the nineteenth century, indeed, the houses of the (rich) dead have been built by architects, just like the houses of the living. At Père-Lachaise one finds, for example, houses of the dead designed by such famous architects as Labrouste, Baltard (Ingres's tomb), Visconti, and Viollet-le-Duc. The bourgeois ideology of property, of the individual house, and the desire to keep up appearances consort well together in this survival of the tomb-house. The second home has even given rise to the buying of plots in the cemeteries of the village where one spends one's weekends. In such cases, the tomb then becomes a third home.

A long-forgotten novel, the action of which takes place entirely in a cemetery, concludes with the following dialogue, with which I shall also conclude this chapter:

"I myself have my tomb in this cemetery, and it is one of the most beautiful in the place, and I come and look at it from time, as a future tenant might come and look at the building in which he has chosen an apartment. . ."

"Oh, My friend! Fancy comparing a tomb to an apartment!"

"But there is nothing outrageous about such a comparison! From my future home, I shall have a splendid view of eternity! The apartment will not be luxuriously furnished, and I am even afraid that it may be a little cold, but the landlord will never put the rent up, and I shall have only quiet neighbors who will not disturb my sleep."[17]

---

[16] Ibid.

[17] Maurice Hamel, *Un vivant chez les morts* (Paris: Figuière, 1936).

2

Villages and Cities
of the Dead

Very often death becomes the guardian of lost cities: it goes before
them, announcing their arrival, and it is by the number of graves that
one may most surely measure the power of an empire.

Lucien Augé
Les Tombeaux, 1879

I f every modern town presupposes a cemetery, every old cemetery,
when rediscovered, indicates that a lost town was to be found nearby.
The necropolis is the reverse side of the metropolis. Which side is
which depends on one's point of view. For the cemetery, an ideal-
ized double of this city, appears at the same time as a perfect reproduction of the socio-economic order of the living.

Jean Fourastié has remarked that when the cemetery was to be found
in the center of the village, that is to say, in and around the church,
death and its rituals were to be found at the center of life. The expulsion
of the dead beyond the boundary of the village preceded in fact the
expulsion of the dead from our everyday life. From being the high place
of the spirit when it was indissolubly linked to the church, the secularized cemetery has become "a high place of the embodiment of adminis-

trative rationality."[1] The modern necropolis has achieved the perfect order that lies at the heart of the modern urban utopia. But it nevertheless expresses all the contradictions of our society, which wants to be egalitarian and consoles itself by saying that at least men are equal before death.

This is not true, however. Everybody, of course, is condemned to death, which is a sort of very relatively consoling equality. But the condemnation to death is accompanied by various tortures, from which some men are exempt, since they die in their sleep. The inequality is flagrant when one considers the time given us to live out our earthly lives and the illness and pain that precede death. The inequality is even more flagrant when we consider our posthumous space. Just as some live out their waking lives in vast houses and others in hovels, some dead have spacious tombs at their disposal and others a bare two square yards. As in the city of the living, there are good and bad parts of the cemetery, some of which are more expensive than others, better situated, or are difficult to get. Paris, for example has luxury cemeteries (Montparnasse, Père-Lachaise, Montmartre) and cut-rate cemeteries (Bagneux or Thiais).[2] There is inequality, too, in space and in duration: the common ditch or the freehold plot.

If we did not know that Philippe Julian was describing Père-Lachaise, we might think that we were reading about a nineteenth-century city:

> People generally remain in their own districts, for the demographic distribution of the cemetery is, on a smaller scale, exactly that of Paris. . . One descends to the west toward a monotonous Monceau plain of small private houses built in gray stone, and the southwest is reminiscent of the sixteenth arrondissement with its genteel streets enlivened by art-nouveau vaults. The central areas suggest the *Grands Boulevards*, and it is they which receive most visitors, whereas in the picturesque sidestreets of the oldest part, around the aristocratic, but dilapidated tombs, reigns the silence of the Faubourg Saint-Germain. . . The east is the left of the cemetery, the west the right.[3]

This odd comparison was also developed by Maurice Hamel in relation to another cemetery:

> Our garden of the dead is enormous. It extends as far as the eye can see, like a sort of hilly silent village, traversed by roads and paths, planted with various trees. . . To the right, as one descends into an area completely devoid

[1] Urbain, *La Société de conservation*.
[2] Thomas, *Anthropologie*.
[3] Philippe Julian, *Le Cirque du Père-Lachaise* (Paris: Fasquelle, 1957).

of trees, one finds the cemetery of the poor. The poor do not have a right to trees.

Is it really a cemetery? Is it not rather a city with its poor and its rich quarters, its gloomy suburbs and its grandiose avenues? Side by side with the most beautiful edifices appears a common ditch, formed by two huge trenches dug from the flanks of sterile ground. There is nothing but stark, unwelcoming solitude, while a few steps away rise Gothic chapels, sarcophagi, pyramids, obelisks, guardian spirits of death dressed more or less correctly, various symbols and attributes, for the most part monuments of pride.[4]

Conditional upon the cost of land, the surface of the tomb is obviously a function of the economic power of the deceased. But to the economic power of the owner is added the desire for ostentation, or lack of it, which is obviously a prime consideration for the "departed." Indeed there are rich individuals who are buried in a humble manner, sometimes even with a certain ostentation in the simplicity of it, and poor individuals who distinguish themselves by a postmortem ostentation that is no doubt a sort of revenge through fantasy.

As with the towers of San Giminiano and skyscrapers of New York, one often makes one's mark in terms of height. The cemetery of Père-Lachaise is dominated by a column 143 feet high erected over the grave of a certain Félix de Beaujour, who, though quite unknown, has managed in this way to get himself talked about for over a century.

Cemeteries in the Latin countries of Europe are noted above all for the abundance of their mausoleums, large and small, which follow one another as far as the eye can see along great avenues intersected at regular intervals by very straight streets. Some great mausoleums reappear in miniature versions, just as the large bourgeois villa produced the suburban house. But funerary monuments always follow a principle of relative miniaturization. The largest pyramids of our cemeteries are merely a miniaturization of those of the pharaohs; the largest tombs are merely minicastles or minichurches. Funerary architecture is always old-fashioned and naive. It is a sort of Disneyland, and its artist-inhabitants "originals" and "primitives."

The suburban ideology is very apparent, especially in the acquisition of freehold plots. After all, do not more and more of the living buy a freehold in the cemetery as they buy a second home? Like the suburban householder, the plot-owner likes enclosures: railings and walls. He also tries to obtain plots on the edge of the path, as if those further back enjoyed less pleasing views.

[4] Hamel, *Un vivant chez les morts.*

[41

Saint Gregory Cemetery, Mexico City. (*J. D. Sidaner / Editorial Photocolor Archives*)

Jean Ziegler, describing the seaside cemetery at Bahia, gives us a powerful image of that ultimate class struggle in the spatial strategy of the cemetery:

On the upper terraces rise the palaces of the dead members of the oligarchy, in all their black and pink marble splendor. They house the corpses of sugar barons, fashionable doctors, cattle breeders, and traders in black men and children. . . In the middle of the hill are to be found the tombs of the middle bourgeois, and, at the bottom, those of the smaller tradesmen, civil servants, and clerks. . . As for the corpses of the middle or petty bourgeoisie, they hardly ever travel. . . the bourgeois is buried where he has lived, at a respectful distance from the powerful. Finally, in the undergrowth, at the edges of the ravines, on arid, red earth, without enclosures or ornaments, rest the immense, anonymous mass of the people.[5]

Cemeteries by the sea, like that of Sète, made famous by Paul Valéry's poem, or like that at Menton present a curious inversion of site. The dead are usually put in the cellar (the hypogeum), while in the cemeteries by the sea they are put in the "loft." The tombs, perched on high, form a mortuary crown for the town.

Menton, like Nice, and like the towns of the Côte d'Azur in general, is a sort of mortuary antemortal town. At Menton deaths are well in excess of births. People come to die in the sun. First came the English, the Russians, and the Germans, whose rich tombs are to be found in the old cemetery. Now there are the modest, inconspicuous retired, for whom a huge new cemetery was opened by the sea. In the old cemetery the tombs are ostentatious monuments. In the second, the hill is dug out and becomes a troglodyte hypogeum. The graves are piled up, one on top of another, an extraordinary replica of the town below, of the town of the living, with its espaliers, its stepped paths, its steep flight of steps, its panoramic views over the sea, the beach, and the harbor with its yachts.

Certain towns of the living appear more mortuary than others: for example, Venice, which Albert Thibaudet called "city of euthanasia" and which Visconti's film *Death in Venice* presented as an urban space of obsessional death. Venice, city of lagoons, has the cemetery of San Michele, which, of course, is a replica constructed on its own island.

We have seen how certain cemeteries (Nice) assumed the form of a housing complex, which seems natural enough to Jean Baudrillard "at a time when high-rise blocks of flats look like cemeteries."[6] The new cemeteries of the large cities take on quite naturally the form of dormitory-suburbs. In the Paris region, Thiais is a replica of Sarcelles. Or rather Sarcelles is a replica of Thiais, since it was built twenty-five years later—Thiais, whose sinister ordering was no doubt influenced by the military cemeteries of World War I, in which the dead stand to attention, in serried ranks. Jean Cayrol refers to such cemeteries as "death's carparks."[7]

In this great segregation of the dead, there are also children's cemeteries and cemeteries for domestic pets. Stillborn children have the benefit of free burial in a special section of the adult cemetery, but their

---

[5] Jean Ziegler, *Les Vivants et la Mort* (Paris: Seuil, 1975).

[6] Baudrillard, *L'Echange symbolique*.

[7] Jean Cayrol, *De l'espace humain* (Paris: Seuil, 1968).

[43

graves are generally abandoned very soon by the parents. The child who dies at an early age is also seldom placed in the family vault, but in a children's cemetery, a sort of "ultimate crèche, ultimate kindergarten." At the Jewish cemetery in Strasbourg, three lots are reserved for children. In Italy many cemeteries have a "*Cript di Bambini*." In France most cemeteries of medium-sized towns have a corner reserved for children.

The dog cemetery set up in Paris on an island in the Seine is neither a modern anomaly nor a modern caprice, since, at Thebes, monkeys had their own necropolis two-and-one-half miles long and one-and-one-quarter miles wide, and the ancient Egyptians, who mummified animals in sandstone or alabaster funerary urns, had cemeteries for cats (at Bubastis and Beni Hasan), crocodiles (at Ombos), ibis (at Al-Ashmūnein), rams (at Elephantine), and sacred bulls. In 1907, in Brittany, the grave of a bull was discovered under a large tumulus.

In this inventory of the space of death one always comes back to Egypt: Egypt, where nothing survives of the ancient cities and palaces of the pharaohs except the tombs. The city of Memphis has disappeared, but hundreds of tombs, including the three great pyramids, still stand around the former city.

These pyramids should not be regarded only as colossal tombs. They were in fact the center of a vast monumental network comprising a high temple on the eastern face of the pyramid, a small satellite pyramid to the south of the greater one, a wall surrounding both pyramids and linking the high pyramid with a reception building at the low temple, a covered way for general access linking the low temple with the high temple. The two temples made it possible not only to celebrate funerals but also to carry out the operations of mummification and the upkeep of daily funerary worship. In addition, each pyramid possessed a landing wharf with a porch, intended at first to serve as a supply port for the construction site, then later as a reception point for funeral processions.

The royal pyramids and the monumental complex that was connected with them formed, then, a fortress around which extended the city of the dead, built on a checked pattern, the groups of tombs forming series of streets intercepting at right angles. On either side of the streets the tomb-houses contained a number of chambers, like the houses of the living, of which so little is known except from the pictures of them to be found in the city of the dead. With its royal fortress in the center, constituting a walled town in itself, surrounded by streets in a checked pattern, this plan corresponds exactly to the plan of the cities of the living, the foundations of which have been discovered in Mesopotamia. The

Egyptian cities must have resembled them and looked very similar, the double of the city of the dead.

The necropolis at Thebes was two-and-one-half miles long and one-and-one-quarter miles wide. The upkeep and administration of the dead required an enormous staff, which was managed by a special functionary. The city of the dead, then, involved the permanent presence of large numbers of the living whose sole function was to serve the dead—or to defend them. For this latter purpose, the city of the dead also included barracks for soldiers. For the building and maintenance of the tombs, certain districts consisted of villages of common laborers, masons, painters, and sculptors.

The hundred thousand slaves who worked for twenty years on the building of the pyramids at Giza must have constituted in themselves an enormous satellite town of the future city of the dead. A present-day architect, Jean-Philippe Lauer, has measured and "weighed" the pyramids, and has arrived at some stupefying calculations. The pyramid of Cheops, which consists of 2.3 million blocks of stone, is calculated to weigh 7 million tons. Its base occupies twelve and a third acres of ground. "To carry out the necessary transport in our own time, 7,000 trains, each carrying 1,000 tons, or 700,000 truckloads of 10 tons, would be required."[8]

The pyramids were built of hard limestone, granite being reserved for the corridors, inside walls, and sarcophagi. Put in place before the completion of the building, the sarcophagi were wider than the corridors, and could not therefore be taken away without being broken up. Faced with perfectly polished blocks of stone, which prevented any attempt to scale them, the pyramids offered no apparent opening. Used as quarries in the twelfth century, at the time of Saladin, the pyramids lost their facing, which must have shone in the sunlight. In this way the pyramid of Cheops lost its top 31 feet.

The first known pyramid, built at Saqqara by the architect Imhotep for King Zoser, is a mastaba, 200 feet square, which was later used as the nucleus of the first pyramid of four steps, 130 feet high, then of a second of six steps, 195 feet high.

King Seneferu, father of Cheops, founder of the Fourth Dynasty, had the first colossal pyramid built at Dahshûr, which was 585 feet high. But this "rhomboidal" pyramid seemed to Seneferu to be insufficiently strong and was abandoned by him in his lifetime for a broader-based pyramid: 715 feet by 700.

[8] Jean-Philippe Lauer, *Le Problème des pyramides d'Egypte* (Paris: Payot, 1948).

[45

The largest of the pyramids is that of Cheops: about 750 feet square and 455 feet high. From the Sixth Dynasty onward, the dimensions stabilized at 257 feet each side at the base and 171 feet high. All are at Saqqara.

Under the Middle Empire (2100 to 1700 B.C.), profanation of the tombs was already so common that the well-known entrance to the pyramid on the north side was abandoned, and access could not be made on any of the sides. Descent to the tomb was effected either on an inclined plane or by a shaft. The builders went to a great deal of trouble to make access to the burial chamber difficult. The improvement of the portcullis system made the obstacles thicker and more numerous. False corridors, which led nowhere, were dug. Sometimes access to the chamber was blocked altogether, thus turning it into a great monolithic shaft covered by enormous stones.

It has been noted that there was a correlation between the extent of the galleries and the duration of the pharoah's reign. This led to the supposition that the pharaoh began the excavation of his tomb as soon as he acceded to the throne.

On the left bank of the Nile, parallel to the river, pyramids stretch in a line nearly forty-five miles long across the desert. Mariette claimed to have discovered sixty pyramids in Egypt. These are the forty pyramids of the pharaohs and the twenty smaller pyramids of the queens, which have been explored since by archeologists, the last violators of tombs. Only a dozen still stand as imposing monuments. Many are little more than piles of stone. Others have been practically razed to the ground. Around the pyramids, holes in the ground indicate the funerary shafts where the pharaoh's servants were buried. The subjects surrounded the monarch in the grave as in life. Mummies of servants were sometimes laid on the ground, around the mummies of their masters, in the burial chamber. In the corridors mummies were also laid one on top of another, sometimes piled up to the ceiling.

The pyramids, regarded by the ancient Greeks as one of the seven wonders of the world, have long intrigued and fascinated men, who never found it difficult to explain such enormous, closed edifices. The pilgrims of the Middle Ages called them "Joseph's granaries" or the "pharaoh's granaries," believing that they had been built by the Jews during their exile, an unlikely achievement for a nomadic people. In the seventeenth century, European travelers visited the chamber of the pharaoh, inside the Great Pyramid.[9] But Bossuet, like most of his contem-

[9]John Graves, *Pyramidography* (London, 1646).

poraries, still could not believe that they were burial places: "Whatever men's efforts, their nothingness appears everywhere. Those pyramids were tombs, so the kings who built them did not have the power to be buried in them, and they did not enjoy their sepulchre."[10]

In 1726, Father Sicard, who died of the plague at Cairo, wrote the first scientific description of Thebes and the Valley of the Kings: "The sepulchres of Thebes are dug out of the rock, and at a surprising depth. . . A long tunnel, twelve feet wide, leads to chambers, in one of which is a granite tomb four feet high. . . Everything in those halls and chambers is painted from top to bottom."

But the systematic exploitation of the pyramids really began with Napoleon's expedition, in 1798. This resulted in the publication, between 1809 and 1892, of twenty-six volumes of text and eleven of plates.

Those avenues bordered with sphinxes, rams, and lions, which led to the pyramids, forming great processional ways, are also to be found in the Chinese funerary monuments of the Han period, which Victor Segalen described in 1917: imperial funerary avenues, decorated with chimeras and winged lions, statues of lions ten feet high. Those rupestrian Chinese tombs, under tumuli resembling small hills, formed "vast interior vestibules and deep corridors leading to vaults in which clay coffins and carved sarcophagi were found."[11]

The dolmens of Armorica, which date from around 3200 B.C. and are therefore contemporary with the beginnings of Egyptian civilization, represent in fact the structure of a subterranean architecture revealed by the clearing away of the surrounding ground. The stones that cover them have been removed and used for building. They have been ransacked for possible treasure. But they were originally tumuli whose outer walls must have been very high. At once burial places and ossuaries, certain dolmens were used to the maximum, the remains of earlier burials being pushed aside to make room for later ones. The very disparate funeral furniture found covers in fact a very long period, and even different races have been buried in the same monuments, as is shown by the presence of both dolichocephalous and brachycephalous skulls. Skeletons of all ages, both sexes, and even dogs, were sometimes broken to make more room in the dolmens. Eighty skeletons were removed from the dolmen of Monte-Abrao, in Portugal, sixty-two at the dolmen of

[10] Bossuet, *Discours sur l'histoire universelle* (Paris, 1681).

[11] Victor Segalen, Gilbert de Voisins, and Jean Lartigue, *Mission archéologique en Chine, 1914–1917: La sculpture et les monuments funéraires* (Provinces du Chan-si et du Sseut-tch'ouan) (Paris: Librairie orientaliste Geuthner, 1923).

Monastier, in Lozère, fifty at Port-Blanc in the Morbihan, three hundred at Sainte-Eugénie, in the Aude.

If the menhirs are not funerary monuments, the dolmens and the pre-Celtic covered avenues, on the other hand, are still pyramidal tomb-tumuli. It would seem that each dolmen must have served in the same building as the burial place for a whole family, if not for a whole village. Again, about 1800 B.C. a number of dolmens with corridors and covered ways were used as burial places.[12]

We have seen how ancient Greece and Rome first buried their dead in their houses and in the city. As a result the cities of the dead and of the living were identical. In defending one's city and house against invaders, one was also defending one's dead. One was preventing the violation of their graves. Then, for reasons of hygiene, the dead were buried outside the cities but along the roads that led to them. Apart from the tombs along roads, the Athenians also had a communal cemetery reserved for the rich, at the foot of the Acropolis, in the potters' quarter, known as the Ceramic.

Well before the Homeric period, incineration was practiced in Greece and became preponderant in the classical period. In the *Iliad* Hector's ashes are placed in an urn, which is then buried in an isolated ditch under a tumulus.

Along roads the tombs were indicated by a funerary column, a vase, a statue, either human or symbolic (sphinx, lion, bull), or a stela.

In the early days of the Roman republic only the poor and slaves were buried pell-mell in common ditches. The rich, and all those who could afford the three steres of wood required to incinerate a body, prac-

[12]Jean L'Helgouach, *Les Sépultures mégalithiques en Armorique* (Rennes, 1966). Also Fernand Niel, *Dolmens et Menhirs* (Paris: P.U.F., 1961), says that until the eighteenth century the dolmens were attributed to the Gauls. Then it was realized that there were dolmens in other than Celtic countries and that in fact they must date from the end of the Neolithic period. The two French departments richest in dolmens are the Aveyron and the Ardèche. Then come Finistère in third place and Morbihan in fourth. The region of the Ardèche, the Gard, the Hérault, the Lozère, the Aveyron, and the Lot contain over one-third of the dolmens in France. On the other hand, Brittany contains 50 percent of the menhirs in France, the two-and-one-half-mile-long group in Carnac accounting for 2,934 of them. Of the 6,840 megalithic monuments in France, 4,460 are dolmens, 2,200 menhirs, and 110 cromlechs. The highest menhir at Locmariaquer was 77 feet high (it has fallen down and smashed), almost the height of the Egyptian obelisks (82 feet). But the highest, which are almost all in Brittany, are usually only between 26 and 32 feet high. Elsewhere, they rarely exceed 16 feet. From the fifth century the church fulminated against the megalithic monuments and the devotions which still surrounded them. Hence the destruction and burial of many such monuments.

ticed cremation. Then, under the empire, the rich turned back to burial, which gave rise to the art of the sarcophagus. Rich families erected collective tombs for their freemen, and even for their slaves.

All the roads leading to Rome were bordered with tombs. The Appian, Catinan, and Flaminian ways were particularly noted for the tombs of patricians placed in several ranks along the roadside, between which tradesmen had set up their shops.

At Pompeii tombs formed an avenue from the Herculaneum Gate. "Walking from the city of Pompeii, which is itself a great burial place, to its necropolis, little changes to the view. There is the same silence, the same emptiness. . . The rich Diomedes, whose fine villa has been preserved by the ash from Vesuvius, adorned his family tomb with a frontispiece flanked by pilasters and decorated with fasces."[13]

The Roman custom of burying the dead at the roadside was to survive in the West until the eighth century A.D. The Gallo-Roman cemeteries form a cartography of villages, even of towns that have since disappeared. Only the bones and funerary objects have survived. In the department of the Aube alone, 200 ancient cemeteries with graves just under the surface of the sand have been found. One hundred and twenty-five Merovingian cemeteries have been counted in Meurthe-et-Moselle, 108 in the Meuse, 72 in the Vosges, 71 in the Doubs. At Chaussin, near Besançon, an important Burgundian necropolis has been uncovered, revealing 150 graves.

Tacitus wrote that the Germanic warriors were buried with their horses and that "their tomb is a raised mound." Indeed, bits, irons, and horses' skulls have been found in Frankish, Burgundian, and Visigothic tombs. At the cemetery of Tantonville, in Meurthe-et-Moselle, warriors' tombs form a great circle around the burial place of a chief—the ultimate feudal homage.

In Normandy, at Londinières, in the ancient region of Bray, the Abbé Cochet exhumed 400 skeletons of Frankish men, women, and children, the majority of which must have died between the ages of twenty and forty.[14] According to the custom of the ancient Teutons (such as Saxons and Vikings), the bodies were seated or bent, sometimes lying on their backs. They had been placed in wooden or stone chests, wearing their finest clothes, with long silver or copper rings in their ears, with a necklace of yellow amber around their necks, and gold rings on their fingers.

---

[13] Augé, *Les Tombeaux*.

[14] Abbé Cochet, *La Normandie souterraine ou Notices sur des cimetières romains et des cimetières francs explorés en Normandie* (1854; reprint ed., Le Portulan, 1970).

[49

Lances, axes, arrows, shields, and helmets are evidence of their warlike origins.

In the second century A.D., the height of Roman civilization in Gaul, the practice of incineration spread. Then, under the influence of Christianity, which forbade cremation, we see a period of transition from the urn to the coffin during the fourth and fifth centuries. Then burial takes over completely.

The Merovingian sarcophagi, imitated from the Roman sarcophagi, were trapezoidal troughs, wider at the head than at the feet. Certain sarcophagi had holes in the bottom to enable the liquid from decomposition to flow away. There were large Merovingian workshops where sarcophagi were made, as we know from the one found in the Yonne, at Quarré-les-Tombes, where about a thousand unused sarcophagi were found in the seventeenth century. Today only about fifty remain around the church.

The manufacture of sarcophagi was abandoned and a whole industry collapsed as a result of cultural change. Indeed, from the ninth century all cemeteries placed outside towns and villages and along roads, according to the old Roman custom, were abandoned in order to protect the graves from robbers, and the dead were now buried at the center of the town itself, surrounded by walls, which as in the earliest times of ancient Greece included both living and dead.

It was Constantine who, at Constantinople, introduced the custom of burying Christian monarchs in a church.[15] The first Christian king of Gaul, Clovis, had himself buried, in 511, with his wife Clotilda in the basilica of Peter-and-Paul on the Mons Lucotitius (the present-day Mont Sainte-Geneviève. Later the Merovingian kings were buried in the church which, in the eighth century, was to be called Saint-Germain-des-Prés.

The churches filled up with corpses: first bishops, then priests, followed in turn by nobles, burghers, and rich craftsmen. The burials were made under the flagstones, which were constantly being lifted for new burials, under pillars, and under the porch. The practice of burying under the eaves of the church roof certain important individuals who had requested this curious privilege survived until the twelfth century. When there were too many corpses under the church flagstones the bones were moved to the attics. Thus the faithful had dead both under their feet and over their heads. In order to enter the church one also had to walk over graves, which were generally anonymous, with no inscription, no monument, not even a cross, this funerary sign appearing only very

[15] Or almost in the church, since Constantine was content with the forecourt.

late in cemeteries. In the yard next to the church were buried the poor, piled up in great common ditches, fifteen to thirty feet deep, and containing up to a thousand corpses. These ditches, covered over with ill-fitting planks, gave off a terrible smell, which spread through the whole district. When the ditch was full it was covered with earth and a new ditch dug beside it. In very cold winters, wolves would disinter the corpses. Up to the seventeenth century, in all those parish churchyards, and there were a great many of them (in the Île de la Cité, in Paris, alone, there were ten churches, and therefore ten churchyards), the bones were only just under the surface of the ground and appeared mixed with stones, pebbles, and grass.

All these churchyards were very small, owing to the large number of parishes. Most of them covered no more than 1,000 square feet. The parish of Saint-Séverin, for example, had a churchyard 65 feet by 145 feet. While the largest cemetery in Paris, that of the Saints-Innocents, opened in the ninth century and in which, over eight hundred years, two million Parisians were to be buried, measured no more than 400 feet by 200 feet.

The overcrowding of skeletons in the churches and around the churches led to the creation of charnelhouses, which became particularly widespread from the fourteenth century onward. Charnelhouse and cemetery were for a long time synonymous. By extension *charnel* also meant "cloister" or "gallery" in the seventeenth century, because the dried bones of the dead were piled up in the galleries or porches around churchyards, as well as under the eaves of the churches themselves. In the fifteenth century these charnelhouses became popular (catechism classes were given in them) and were decorated with carved stones and epitaphs. In 1423, on the rear wall of the charnelhouse of the Saints-Innocents, along the Rue de la Ferronnerie, was painted the celebrated *Dance macabre*, in which thirty fleshless dead conversed with thirty living people. This *Dance macabre* remained a curiosity until 1669. It was then destroyed in order to widen the street. In the late sixteenth century the charnelhouses were given stained-glass windows. In the fifteenth century the custom of burying under the charnelhouses declined, but the popularity of these sordid places continued to grow. Its galleries were even used for charity gatherings. Communion was given there on feast days. They were decorated with tapestries, flowers, draperies. In spite of the pestilential smell, despite the constant arrival of new corpses, the charnelhouse of the Saint-Innocents was as frequented by strollers in the eighteenth century as the arcades of the Palais Royal were to be in the nineteenth.

To the two million Parisians buried in the cemetery of the Saints-Innocents should be added the million "residents" of Père-Lachaise and the 800,000 "inhabitants" of the Montparnasse cemetery. The Parisian necropolis, parallel with the city of the living, was much more highly populated. We now live over a city of the dead whose boundaries are not always recognized. A considerable number of apartment blocks, official offices, and streets in Paris have in fact been built over former cemeteries. Part of the Sorbonne was built over one of the cemeteries of Saint-Benoît. The Hôtel de Ville and one of the buildings of the Bon Marché store cover two necropolises. The Rue Racine passes over the Cimetière des Cordeliers, the Rue Monge over the churchyard of Saint-Nicolas-du-Chardonnet. The métro station Jussieu was excavated out of the churchyard of the monks of Saint-Victor.[16]

To this invisible city of the dead should be added the 1,500 acres of present-day cemetery in Paris, that is, 27 square feet per living Parisian.[17] Then, outside itself, there are the 3,000 acres of cemetery in the suburbs.[18] Thiais alone occupies 270 acres, that is, a capacity of 200,000 burial plots. With 200,000 inhabitants postmortem, Thiais has the population of a highly prosperous city of the living. The necropolis of Thiais is the most highly populated of all the urban centers of the Paris region.

We spoke above of the social segregation in cemeteries, a faithful reflection of the social segregation among the living, and even of a segregation based on age (the cemeteries for children). But once there existed, in Catholic cemeteries, a religious segregation. Since there was no other place of burial except the "Christian ground" of the churchyards, the cemeteries were reserved for Catholics alone. Pagans, heretics, the excommunicated, suicides, executed criminals, actors, Jews, and, from the sixteenth century, Protestants were all excluded. Having been excluded from the Catholic cemeteries, the Protestants first buried their dead in their own gardens, or in the fields and woods. In 1562 a Huguenot, who had been buried in the cemetery of the Saints-Innocents, was disinterred by a fanatical crowd. But, ten years later, for the two or three thousand victims of the massacre of Saint Bartholemew's Eve, a common ditch had to be found. This was dug in the Rue des Saints-Pères, outside the present number 30. This very small Protestant cem-

[16] Jacques Hillairet, *Les Deux Cents Cimetières du vieux Paris* (Paris: Editions de Minuit, 1958).

[17] On this subject Jean Giraudoux wrote in 1932: "The only free spaces there are the cemeteries, whose area almost exceeds, in Paris itself, the area of the gardens. All honor to the city which makes provision for more oxygen for its dead than for its living."

[18] For the whole of France, 30,000 hectares (73,000 acres) of cemetery.

etery in the Rue des Saints-Pères (160 feet by 80 feet) was later to receive the body of Salomon de Brosse, the architect of the Palais du Luxembourg and of the Temple de Charenton, the Protestant meetinghouse, which Louis XIV had razed to the ground after the revocation of the Edict of Nantes.

In 1576 the members of the so called reformed religion were also given a strip of land 400 feet long by 13 feet wide in the churchyard of the Trinité, which was in use until 1678. After the Treaty of Utrecht the Protestant nations, triumphing over Louis XIV, forced him to set up in Paris a cemetery for foreign Protestants, which was built on the site of the present theaters of the Renaissance and Saint-Martin. This cemetery was used between 1725 and 1762, when the more spacious cemetery of Grange-aux-Belles was opened.

The first mention of a Parisian Jewish cemetery, in the Rue Galande, dates from 1198. However, a Jewish colony had existed in Paris from the sixth century, since Childebert, Clovis's son, forbade them "to appear in public during the holy time of the Passion and to have no Christian slave or servant"—which implies that the Christians still owned slaves. A second Jewish cemetery was opened in Paris in 1223 on the site of the intersection of the present Boulevard Saint-Michel and the Rue Hautefeuille.

In the early eighteenth century the two Jewish communities in Paris each had their own cemetery. The Ashkenazim (originating from Germany and Eastern Europe) at Montrouge (it still exists, but has been closed since 1809), and the Sephardim (originating in Spain, Portugal, North Africa, and the Middle East), in the Rue de Flandre, from 1780 to 1810.

In the nineteenth century, under the pretext of religious toleration, the three "recognized" religions, Catholic, Protestant, and Jewish, enjoyed the right to use the same cemeteries, but with different sites, demarcated by walls. Thus one can still see in the Montparnasse cemetery that the Jewish cemetery is to be found on one side only of the Rue Emile Richard. Since the law of November 14, 1881, all deceased French citizens may be buried in the same cemetery, without distinction of religious or political belief, even if they committed suicide or died without baptism. But this led most of the municipalities to prevent Muslims (who did not wish to be mixed with Christians) from obtaining a separate place in the cemetery. Napoleon III had granted them one at Père-Lachaise, in order to please his Turkish allies. This "segregationist privilege" has not been withdrawn from them. There still exist special sites for Muslims in the cemeteries of Bobigny and Thiais.

The marvelous Muslim cemeteries of the East are quite unlike the sinister Catholic cemeteries of our time. Returning from Constantinople at the beginning of the century, the architect Julien Guadet remarked: "The cemetery does not arouse gloomy ideas, on the contrary: the popular walks of the city are its enormous cemeteries, superb cyprus woods from which one has a magnificent view, or where one walks about in groups along the avenues among cafes under the trees."[19]

Instead of the city of the dead and the city of the living being placed one on top of the other, or next to one another, as in the West, dead and living cohabit in the East. The Muslim familiarity with death surprises modern Christians, but it would no doubt have seemed quite natural to medieval Christians. In 1879, in Constantinople, Lucien Augé describes "men sitting on a stela, chatting as they sip their coffee, a few steps away from tombs, in the shadow of tall cypresses."[20] He takes us into the quarter around the Eyub Mosque: "The dead there are more numerous than the living." Tombs border the streets, surrounded by railings. In the middle of the cemetery is a street full of toyshops. The children come and buy jumping jacks and dolls, and chase one another among the graves, shouting and laughing.

"Often," Lucien Augé adds, "the tombs have small gardens and the butterflies flit from flower to flower amid the hum of bees. Sometimes the turbeh of some prince or sultan juts out over the path, with its boldly projecting roof supported by slim columns.[21] Certain monuments sport a round cupula, and discreetly opened windows provide a glimpse of coffins draped in black or green, surmounted by an enormous turban."[22]

Then, moving on to Cairo, Lucien Augé describes the cemeteries divided into two, by a mountain, surmounted by a citadel. To the north are the tombs of the so-called caliphs, to the south those of the mamelukes (four slim columns support a canopy over the sarcophagus).

"A few steps away, Cairo swarms and buzzes, but we find nothing but desert here; everything is silence. Everywhere wild sand in which one can walk only with difficulty, small valleys, hillocks which the capricious wind digs, raises, moves, wipes out. . . Nothing is alive, not a

---

[19] Julien Guadet, *Eléments et Théorie de l'architecture* (Paris, 1901–4).

[20] Augé, *Les Tombeaux*.

[21] *Turbeh* is a Turkish word denoting the grave of a famous person. Each Muslim prince has his *turbeh* in which he reposes among his family. The *turbeh* comprise a portico in front of the entrance and an octagonal or round hall in which the coffins are arranged. Near the green mosque at Bursa the sultan Mohamet I is buried in this way in a *turbeh*, surrounded by his family's coffins.

[22] Augé, *Les Tombeaux*.

murmur; death reigns here in absolute sovereignty. The sky is another desert, one flaming azure. . . It is in this so sadly grandiose setting that the tombs of the caliphs rise up smiling, a silent city that lives only in memory, charming, almost jolly, decorated as if for a festival. A pleasant, gentle, grace is to be found in these funerary monuments."[23]

A hundred years later, André Malraux in his *Lazare* was to speak of "Nasser's city besieging Cairo's city of the dead."[24] But if, in Cairo, the living are laying siege to the city of the dead, it is not to dislodge the dead from their roofless houses. Dead and living live happily together.

"On the left of the citadel a narrow alleyway plunges through a crowd of children, itinerant salesmen, men with nothing to do, who pay little attention to the car which might run them over. Soon the crowd thins out, then it evaporates. We come to a city wrapped in mineral silence. The houses allow no living being to enter. We are in the city of the dead. The contrast is so great with the alleyway which brought us here that one feels a strange unease, as if one had been thrown into the world of the dumb or sick. And then one notices that these blind houses have no roofs. These ghost houses are those of the dead. Men and women are buried there, but they take part in the life of the living."[25]

How? On feast days the city of the dead wakes up. Women and children arrive by train, boys on bicycle, men on foot, and they all go up to the city of the dead. The women sit in the roofless houses and cook dishes of beans on paraffin stoves. People drink coffee, sitting in their suits beside the graves. People even sleep for several days in the silent houses, disturbed only by the cries of children playing and the interminable chatter of the adults. Itinerant salesmen arrive. The city of the dead becomes a city of leisure and festival.

But we have seen how Europe also knew such urban familiarity with the dead in the days of the charnelhouses of the Saints-Innocents. We shall come back to them.

Note

The medieval custom of burying the architect in the principal church which he built is proof, if proof were needed, against those who persist in denying that cathedrals were the work of architects.

[23] Ibid.
[24] André Malraux, *Lazare* (Paris: Gallimard, 1974).
[25] Simone Lacouture, *Egypte* (Paris: Seuil, 1962).

Libergier, the architect of Saint-Nicaise, in Reims, was buried at the entrance of the great nave. We read on the gravestone, now transferred to the cathedral: "Here lies Master Hue Libergié, who began this church in the year 1267." The outline of Libergier, engraved in the stone, shows by his dress that he was a layman. He is holding in his left hand the architect's stick: the geometric rule. At his right foot is the lewis, which lifted the stones of the church. At his left foot is the square. In his right hand is the model of the church which he built and which he clutches to his breast.

Indeed it was a medieval custom to place in the hands of the statue that represented the architect a small model of the church he had designed. The identification is therefore easily made.

In the abbey of Saint-Germain-des-Prés is the tombstone of Pierre de Montreuil, the architect of the refectory of the abbey and of the chapel of the same church. His epitaph reads: "Here lies Pierre de Montreuil, perfect flower of good morals, during his lifetime doctor of stone. May the King of Heaven lead him to the heights of the poles!"

Guillaume, architect of the choir of the abbey church of Saint-Etienne in Caen, is also buried in his church: "Here lies Guillaume, most elevated in the art of stones, who completed this new work."

This medieval tradition continued with Soufflot, the architect of Sainte-Geneviève, which became the Panthéon, who lies under the huge dome which he did not live to see completed. Indeed a large number of architects were buried in churches, from the Renaissance to the eighteenth century, among the great ones of this world: Pierre Lescaut in the Saint-Germain chapel of Notre-Dame-de-Paris, Le Nôtre in the church of Saint-Roch, Blondel in the crypt of Saint-Sulpice.

3

In the Depths of
the Earth

All centuries and all peoples, then, are hidden in the earth. The Gaul
lies beside the Roman, and the Roman sleeps next to the Barbarian.

Abbé Cochet

La Normandie souterraine, 1854

The depths of the earth are the primordial space of death,
the definitive space of the body of flesh and bones. All
men, all animals, end up one day penetrating the depths of
the earth and disappearing into it. The top and the bottom
of the earth form a sort of double mirror. To the people of
the living, who bustle about on the visible surface of the earth correspond the people of the dead, who have disappeared into the bowels of
the earth and are invisible—invisible, but terribly, hauntingly present.
All underworlds, whether those of pharaonic Egypt, ancient Rome, or
Christendom, are situated in the depths of the earth. China, so vast and
so populated, imagined a hell that stretched from the center of the earth
to the pole: "Orientated to the north, buried deep down in the earth, fed
with libations filtering down through the earth, gathered together in
cemeteries to the north of the towns, the dead had to live in under-

[57

ground passages filled with water which, with growing respect and a wider view of the world, were extended to the pole."[1]

This underground world could be entered through doors: caves. A cave is both a door and an eye and therefore has always been regarded as suitable to the cult of the dead. From the caves of Dionysus, Mithra, Demeter, Attis, and Cybele to the catacombs and crypts of churches, we find the same fascination with the earth as the "universal uterus."

When Neolithic man emerged from his caves, he built his first houses in imitation of those caves by arranging uncut pieces of stone in galleries buried under a mound of small rocks. He then dug crypts, similar to his new houses, out of the hills, and buried his dead there. All the Gallic and Germanic regions are riddled with underground workings. And in the medieval West there was a proliferation of hypogeums, "very complex, highly finished underground workings. . . in general, their rooms reproduce, in section, their timber-framed and tile-roofed houses."[2]

Whether above or below the soil, then, we find this projection of the house of the living into the house of the dead. (In the chapter "The Mortiferous Architects" we shall see how modern rationality, too, was generally to conceive its plans for cemeteries as underground constructions.)

This idea of the tomb continuing the house, in the familiarity of everyday life, was perhaps carried to its furthest limit among the Etruscans. They liked to gather in the burial place all the familiars of the household. On the sarcophagus lid, the deceased, carved lifesize, were depicted leaning on one elbow, apparently observing with pleasure the women sitting on their own tombs. Seats carved out of the rock, sometimes in several rows, seem to expect visitors, no doubt those distant relations, or those freemen, whose ashes were put into urns and placed in excavated caves. The Etruscan underground tombs, carved out of rock, had a carefully concealed narrow entrance. The principal chamber was about twenty-five feet wide and six-and-one-half feet high. Often the ceiling imitated the slope of a roof, and multicolored tiles imitated dress materials.

All the Punic tombs discovered at Carthage were also underground. These were hypogeums in the Egyptian manner, reached by corridors dug out of the hillsides or by vertical shafts. The Carthaginians took such care in hermetically ceiling their hypogeums that they were redis-

[1] Marcel Granet, *La Vie et la Mort: Croyances et doctrines de l'Antiquité chinoise* (Paris: Ecole pratique des hautes études, annuaire 1920–21).

[2] Maurice Broëns, *Ces souterrains . . . refuges pour les vivants ou pour les esprits? La clef d'une énigme archéologique* (Paris: Picard, 1976).

covered two thousand years later in a remarkable state of preservation and cleanliness. "No dust, sand, or soil had got in. When, after so many centuries, we entered those funerary cells, one would have said that they had been occupied the day before."[3]

Contrary to a commonly held belief, the famous catacombs of ancient Rome were not a Christian invention. From the earliest days of the Roman Republic, subterranean galleries had been dug in the countryside around Rome in order to extract the pozzolana needed to make mortar for building. As these quarries were abandoned, the Romans turned them into burial places for those of their dead which they did not cremate. Two million pagan Romans were thus buried in the catacombs.

There had never been a specific cemetery for the Christians in ancient Rome. In the first century A.D. the Jewish communities of Rome dug their own catacombs so that their dead would not be mixed with the pagan dead. The Christians soon imitated them, and, up to the fifth century, dug for their own use over 750 miles of galleries at five levels, to a depth that sometimes reached eighty feet. With the great persecutions of the third century, the catacombs became both a refuge for the Christians and their place of worship. The first churches were, therefore, underground, a martyr's tomb serving as the eucharistic table. From its beginnings, then, the Christian church formed, by its enforced setting, a community of living and dead, which they were to become once more when the medieval churches became burial places.[4]

It is inconceivable that the Roman magistrates could have been unaware of this refuge of the Christians. But the Romans, who practiced the cult of the dead and never disturbed a tomb except after complicated expiatory ceremonies, could not imagine destroying subterranean necropolises, where so many of their own dead had been buried for centuries. Indeed the first Christians were able to assemble under the pretext of practicing funerary rites. Beneath the palaces of Rome, beneath the villas, gardens, baths, and circuses, humble men, who were regarded as superstitious and dangerous, went on digging with impunity, living the lives of moles. Beneath the radiant, splendid imperial city, they painfully built a dark, mysterious, subterranean city. Parallel to the very narrow galleries, they arranged the bodies in compartments closed by marble

---

[3] A. L. Delattre, *Les Tombeaux puniques de Carthage* (Lyon, 1890), idem, *Les Tombeaux puniques de Carthage: La Nécropole de Saint Louis* (Paris, 1891).

[4] The identification between church and cemetery from the fifth to the eighteenth century derives from the catacombs of the period of the Roman persecutions, which were both mortuary and religious townships excavated under the pagan city. Saint Jerome called the church the Basilica of the Dead.

[59

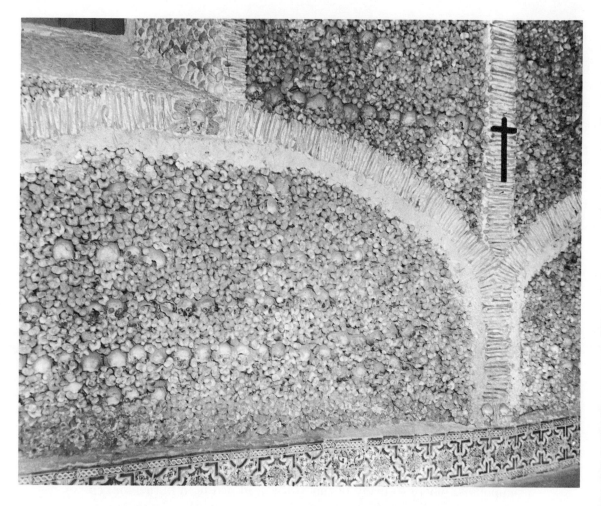

Chapel of Bones, Evora, Portugal. *(Photo H. Armstrong Roberts)*

slabs, and often with less costly tiles. With a punch, the name, age at death, and profession of the deceased were engraved, generally in Latin, sometimes in Greek, on the stone or ceramic. Small square chambers served as family vaults or sanctuaries. Occasionally there were pictures, always symbolic in nature, of fish, vines, or birds. There was never a crucifix.

Apart from the catacombs of Rome, there were also catacombs under Naples, Syracuse, Catania, Agrigente, and Palermo.

After the sacking of Rome by Alaric's hordes, who looted the catacombs, hoping to find treasure there, the catacombs were abandoned.

When Christianity became official, it separated the community of the living, who had come up to the light of day, from that of the dead, who were left in the depths of earth. The basilicas of Saint Agnes and Saint Lawrence, however, were to be built over catacombs. For certain basilicas, the ground was lowered to the level of a catacomb, where the tomb of a martyr was situated.

Then, after being forgotten, the catacombs were rediscovered by chance in the fifteenth century. Near the Appian Way discoveries were also made of Jewish catacombs and those of the followers of Mithra, whose worship, in the third century, was very widespread. During the plague of Naples, in the eighteenth century, the catacombs of that city were reopened, and the corpses thrown away by the thousand and piled up over the bones of the first Christians.

What in Paris are called catacombs are merely old abandoned quarries that the city of Paris turned into a vast ossuary in the late eighteenth century. Between 1785 and 1871 over six million Parisians, that is to say, eleven or twelve centuries of dead buried in the churchyards, were transferred to the 120,000 square feet of former quarries, which extended at a depth of sixty-five feet between Denfert-Rochereau and the Parc Montsouris. It was, then, an enormous ossuary, created in the classificatory spirit of the burgeoning industrial civilization. The bones were piled up in categories, and one can see there murals of vertebrae and femurs, skulls arranged in cornices, et cetera.

Just before the French Revolution, the Route d'Orléans subsided over a length of 975 feet, on the site of the present Avenue Denfert-Rochereau. So the city of Paris asked the architect Guillaumot to draw up a plan of the subterranean quarries of Paris with a view to strengthening them. As the Saints-Innocents cemetery had been closed on December 1, 1780, because water from the wells of the quarter had been made unfit for consumption owing to seepage from that cemetery, and as physicians and philosophers inveighed against the corruption of the air, due to the mephitic vapors given off from churches and charnelhouses, and as the Roman world was all the rage, Guillaumot was also asked to transform the former gypsum and travertine quarries into "catacombs." Guillaumot strengthened the vaults, linked the galleries together, thus turning to practical use almost 5,000 feet of corridor, and constructed a staircase and a descent shaft fifty-five feet deep at 21 bis Avenue du Parc Montsouris.

For fourteen months, from December 1785 to January 1787, the removal of the cemetery of the Saints-Innocents took place at night. Each evening cars covered with black cloth, escorted by priests in surplices

[61

chanting the office of the dead, and torch bearers, formed a procession, led by a brigade of mounted constabulary and followed by twenty-four poor men muttering prayers. Hubert Robert painted several pictures of this spectacle. Such a removal was both unheard of and incredible, the inviolability of the "last resting place" having been a Roman belief resolutely continued by the Christians. But the world had changed, and the first great enterprise of de-Christianization was close at hand. The removal of the dead preceded by a very short time the collapse of the monarchy, and the overthrow of all the values that had seemed immutable.

The removal of the cemetery of the Saints-Innocents, the most popular and most crowded of the cemeteries of Paris since the twelfth century, required 11,898 cartloads by day, 3,475 carriages at night, 1,000 cartloads of bones, 2,000 liters of vinegar, 2,500 liters of brandy, and 16,000 lanterns.[5]

Similarly, in 1787 the corpses and skeletons of the churchyards of Saint-Etienne-des-Grés and Saint-Eustache were removed; in 1792 those of Saint-Landry and Saint-Julien; in 1793, 173 coffins from the convent of Sainte-Croix-de-la-Bretonnerie and from the college of the Bernardine monks; in 1794 the dead of the church of Saint-André-des-Arts; in 1804 those of Saint-Jean-en-Grève, Saint-Honoré, the church of the White Friars, Saint-Nicolas-des-Champs, and Saint-Laurent; in 1811 those of Saint-Louis-en-l'Isle; in 1813 those of Saint-Benoît and of the Trinité; in 1826 the dead of the cemetery of Bonne-Nouvelle and the victims of the Terror from the Cimetière de Vaugirard; in 1845 the former parishioners of the church of Sainte-Geneviève; in 1850 the dead of Saint-Jacques-du-Haut-Pas; in 1857 the bones of the leprosy in the Rue de Douai; in 1859 the former parishioners of the churches of Saint-Jean-Porte-Latine, Sainte-Madeleine-de-la-Ville-l'Eveque, Saint-Leu, Saint-Gilles, Saint-Jacques-de-la-Boucherie; in 1860, 813 tombs of bones were found in the foundations of the quarter surrounding the new market hall of Baltard; in 1871 the 30 mysterious skeletons discovered without a bier in the crypt of the church of Saint-Laurent.[6]

So in the "catacombs" of Paris are to be found, in the greatest anonymity, two million dead, originally buried at the Saints-Innocents, the three hundred Swiss killed in 1792 and first thrown into the quarries at Montmartre, the victims of the September massacres, no doubt Clotaire and Philippe Egalité, and certainly Robespierre and Danton.

[5]Le Clere, *Cimetières et Sépultures de Paris.*
[6]Hillairet, *Les Deux Cents Cimetières du vieux Paris.*

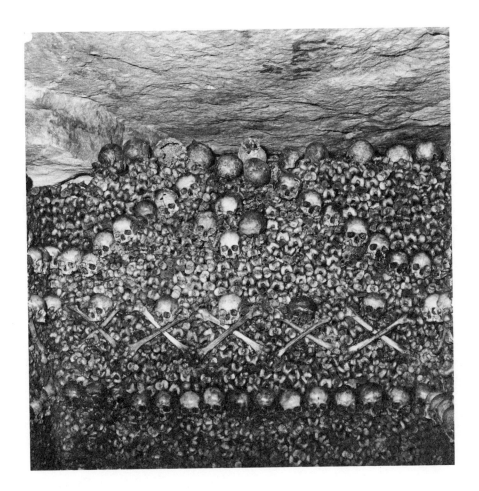

Paris Catacombs. *(Photo Giraudon)*

Inaugurated in 1786, the catacombs began to be visited only from 1800. In 1810 the prefect Frochot had them restored and enlarged, planning to give them a solemn entrance with an avenue of cypresses from the Boulevard Saint-Jacques to the descent shaft in the Rue Dareau. In 1833 the prefect Rambuteau had them closed on the grounds that they were deteriorating. On their reopening in 1859 visitors were advised "to dress warmly and to bring some provisions in case one feels weak in those cold, damp regions, or gets lost." Today entry is on the side of one of Claude Nicolas Ledoux's houses in the Place Denfert. After a fairly long descent, the ossuary opens at a stone lintel which bears this line from Delille: "Stop: this is the empire of Death."

Bones, crossed tibias, and skulls are piled six-and-one-half feet high and sometimes almost a hundred feet thick. In a crypt a stone altar has been set up in the ancient style, and a requiem mass is celebrated there on the first Sunday of November. This is a reminder of the catacombs of Rome, but also a last and certainly meager compensation for the millions of masses in perpetuity which were paid for long ago by many of these dead and which have been "forgotten" by the clergy in the most fantastic of bankruptcies in the eighteenth century, a fitting parallel to that of Law's *assignats* of the 1790s; the bankruptcy of seven hundred years of masses for the souls in purgatory.

Among his "invisible cities" Italo Calvino describes one underground city, which he calls Eusapia. "And to make the leap from life to death less abrupt, the inhabitants have constructed an identical copy of their city, underground." Underground, the skeletons continue their former activities. They sit around laden tables or are caught in dancing positions, or in any of the innumerable activities of work and leisure. And when the undertakers of the city above bring down the dead into the city below, they are received by undertakers who are themselves dead. With each year that passes it becomes increasingly difficult to tell the two cities apart, since each has taken to copying the other.

"They say that this has not just now begun to happen: actually it was the dead who built the upper Eusapia in the image of their city. They say that in the twin cities there is no longer any way of knowing who is alive and who is dead."[7]

---

[7] Italo Calvino, *Invisible Cities*, tr. William Weaver (London: Secker and Warburg; New York: Harcourt Brace Jovanovich, 1974).

4

The Spaces of
the "Crossing"

There are ninety-nine inns between us and paradise. One must stop off at each one. When one has no more money to pay, one retraces one's steps back to hell. The Good Lord comes once a week and visits the halfway inn. He takes back with him those customers who aren't too drunk.

Anatole Le Braz

La Légende de la mort chez les Bretons armoricains, 1874

The space of death is also that space of passage between the space of the living and that of the dead. Not only is it the last space of life (Joan of Arc's burning stake, Louis XIV's bed, Roland's rocks at Roncevaux, Marat's bath, Danton's scaffold, the gas chamber of the Jews at Auschwitz), but the space between life and death, the "crossing of appearances."

To gain access to the otherworld, the world of souls, there are ways and doors. It was through an ivory door that Aeneas emerged from the underworld. In ancient Rome every August 24, October 15, and November 8, the official entrance to the underground world, which was usually closed off by the "stone of the shades," was opened. The souls of the dead were then supposed to escape through the opening. This belief crops up in Ireland where, on November 1, when the souls of the dead invade the world of the living, the latter may also enter the world of the dead through temporary openings.[1]

An English humorist has said: "Don't take life too seriously: you won't get out of it alive." Again we have the idea of *exit*, and therefore of a door or staircase. One also speaks of those whom one has *lost*. Lost where? How? Hence the suggestion that the "last journey" takes the form of a labyrinth, a sudden disappearance, as at a street corner.

Every people and every religion have produced accounts of the "last journey." The ancient Egyptians provided the most meticulous account of this journey in their *Book of the Dead*, which is a sort of guide for the use of the deceased. Their sophisticated funerary ritual was intended as a guarantee that the deceased would have a happy crossing to the place of his survival. It was on the dangerous postmortem way that the wandering soul underwent a judgment, against which there was no appeal. Not to be prepared for it, not to know the intricacies of the way, was to risk being struck by a second death, a definitive one this time.

For this long voyage the Sicilians shod their deceased with strong shoes. The inhabitants of the Gironde, who believed in the virtues of their vines, preferred to put into the grave, beside the coffin, one of several bottles of wine. In old French customs, this obsession with the last journey still leads people to put a bowl of soup into the coffin, or a walking stick, a pipe and a pouch of tobacco, or a missal.

The people who liked most to talk about this journey were the Celts. According to them, the dead were taken to the beyond in a wheelbarrow, or, in the case of the better off, in a cart pulled by three white horses harnessed in a line.

As the beyond is usually situated above (heaven) or below (hell), the image of the staircase sometimes appears, but more often in the form of a ladder.[2]

In many of the tombs of ancient Egypt ladders have been found, and ladders and staircases often appear in Egyptian texts. Russian peasants used to bury their dead in graves with small ladders, either of wood or rope. This custom survives among the Slav peasants, but they are now content to put ladder-shaped cakes in the coffin.

We shall see how the space of fire (from the burning of the dead to the stakes of the Inquisition, and to modern cases of suicide by fire, like those of the Vietnamese Buddhist monks or of Jan Palach) is one of the

[1] Francis Bar, *Les Routes de l'Autre Monde: Descentes aux enfers et voyages dans l'Au-delà* (Paris: P.U.F., 1946).

[2] "How many men have never gone back up the stairs which they have come down" (Chateaubriand, *Le Génie du christianisme* [Paris, 1802]).

privileged spaces of the "crossing." But there is another, more symbolic one, which is nevertheless important in world funerary culture: the space of water.

Almost every descent into the underworld involves the crossing of an aquatic zone: river, marsh, lake, or stream. And the underworld itself is usually surrounded by a triple river. In this general space of the journey, the space of water forms a space of transition—the place "between."

Is that why water exerts such a strong fascination on suicides? Do not those sleeping waters, "symbols of total sleep, of that sleep from which one does not wish to wake," also appear as the two-way mirror of a door through which one throws oneself irrevocably?[3]

Our culture is full of famous deaths by water (Ophelia, the Unknown Woman of the Seine, Carrier's executions by drowning at Nantes), and some individuals "saved from the waters" seem endowed with strange demiurgic powers (Moses). In ancient Egypt, where Moses was found floating in a reed basket, a virgin was drowned every year in the Nile.

Peoples living near the sea, like the Koryaks of Siberia, often threw their dead into it. Others immersed them in sacred lakes, where the brine perfectly preserved the bodies.[4] Even without brine a body kept continually in water does not disintegrate but becomes waxy. Centuries later water can yield up a body that has not become putrefied.

That is why water has been attributed with so many purifying virtues, sometimes involving immersion. In Java the rich possess a funerary pool. In Japan, more modestly, a small ditch is dug beside the grave into which fresh water is poured. Washing a corpse perpetuates this rite of immersion.

When a sailor dies on a ship, his journey is interrupted. The dead man is fixed on to a plank. The body is uncovered. An officer says a prayer. Then the body is thrown into the sea and the engines start up again. Time is stopped for a moment of the ship's journey in order to begin the dead man's journey.

In the Breton romances of the Arthurian cycle, there was a stream beyond a wall of fog. One crossed a ford, and, behind, appeared the otherworld, the country of the dead, and of the fairies.

The harbor, or haven, is another image, both ancient and Christian, suggested by the space of death.

The boat has been an even more potent image of death.

Certain Celts carved their coffins out of trunks of trees planted at the

---

[3] Gaston Bachelard, *L'Eau et les Rêves* (Paris: José Corti, 1942).
[4] Or in rivers, as in immersion in the Ganges.

birth of the deceased. Delivered up to the current of a stream, the coffin became a wandering boat. In 1560 Dutch workmen found tree trunks brought down by the Rhine, each containing a fossilized man. The origin of our modern coffin may well be this archaeological hollow tree.[5]

The image of the boat of the dead is universal. It is to be found as much in the Far East as in the Far West. The Polynesians used floating tombs. But the ancient Egyptians, after burying their bodies in boats, gave their coffins the shape of boats. Did not their dead, during their perilous journey, have to cross a marshy zone for which they took a "boat of the millions" (of the millions of dead) and, in the end, it was a "sun boat" that took the blessed to share in the life of the Ra?

The boat, symbol of the journey of death, was used in Egypt for funerals. At Cheops, great "sun boats" were dug out of the rock. And at Memphis, in 1954, was found an enormous boat, 110 feet long, that had been buried for 5,000 years. "This long boat of brown wood, pointed as a pine needle, carried the dead pharaoh on his subterranean journey . . . and served his double, his Ka."[6]

At Madagascar, before the eighteenth century, the kings were buried in wooden canoes. Later they were placed in silver coffins, shaped nevertheless like canoes.[7]

In Breton legends one often hears of ghost ships, boats that come back laden with shipwrecked dead. Tristan is left to die in his boat and Yseult comes in a boat to join him in death.

The coffin is an enclosed boat. And for this final crossing of the boat, in the last journey, there also appears in Greece and Rome, China and Brittany, the disturbing figure of the boatman.

What can one do to placate this terrible boatman? The simplest means is to remember his fare. Many peoples have provided their dead with money for the cost of the journey to the otherworld. The coins the Greeks and Romans put into the dead man's hand or mouth to pay the boatman Charon are not peculiar to Greco-Latin antiquity. This custom is also to be found in Assam, Burma, and Madagascar. In the early nineteenth century a coin was placed in the hands of the dead in Angoumois, Aunis, Bourbonnais, and Morvan; whereas in Berry, Bresse, Franche-Comté, and Poitou, this coin was placed in the dead man's mouth "to pay Saint Peter for his place in paradise."

[5] Burial in a tree trunk is a protohistoric custom widely practiced among the Teutons, attested by Gregory of Tours. It may be linked to the tradition of the dead Viking warriors who were sunk with their boats.

[6] Lacouture, *Egypte*.

[7] Decary, *La Mort et les coutumes funèbres à Madagascar*.

Again, in the thirteenth century the inhabitants of the Rhone valley, above Arles, placed their dead in coffins and cast them into the river (where they became boats). For several centuries the dead traveled down the Rhone in this way toward the famous cemetery of Aliscamps. Between their teeth they held a coin intended to pay for their right to burial.

Charon seems to have disappeared with Christianity. But on Dagobert's tomb, in the Abbey of Saint-Denis, the soul of the king is represented crossing the river of the dead in a boat. In the late thirteenth century Dante reestablished Charon, with all his prerogatives, and Michelangelo was to place him in his fresco the *Last Judgment*, integrated into the Christian mythology of Christ, the Virgin, and the Saints. In modern Greece, when speaking of a dying man, one says "*Charopalevi*" (he is fighting Charon).

In fact Charon, in the form of Saint Christopher, became the nautical saint. Saint Peter also replaced him, but rather as guardian of the gate than as guardian of the boat. And where there is a gate there is a key: Saint Peter's celebrated keys have replaced the oars.

In antiquity it was said in Greece and Rome that, on the northern side of Gaul, lived a people of sailors whose trade was to bring the souls of the dead to their last resting place. In the sixth century A.D. Procopius takes up this legend and develops it: "The fishermen and other inhabitants of Gaul, who live opposite the island of Britain, are charged with taking souls across the water and are therefore exempt from tribute. In the middle of the night they hear knocking at their doors; they get up and find on the shore strange boats in which they see nobody, and which nevertheless seem so full that they are about to sink, and rise hardly an inch above the level of the water; an hour is enough for this journey, though, with their own boats, they would find it difficult to do it in a night."[8]

In these rites of passage, we should not forget extreme unction or the masses for the souls in purgatory. Purgatory is itself regarded as a space of passage, since it is a place of transit between earth and heaven. In the twelfth century the church had the idea of speeding up this time of transit by establishing a "passport for heaven"—the will or testament. The will, which existed in Roman law as a civil act, became with Christianity a sacred act, obligatory even for the poor. Whoever died without leaving a will could not be buried either in the church or in the churchyard. For the will specified the number of masses to be celebrated for

---

[8] Procopius, *The Gothic Wars* (c. 550 A.D.)

the repose of the deceased's soul—masses which had fixed prices and were paid for out of the estate. In the fourteenth century the nobility ruined itself in pious donations intended to redeem a life that was hardly pious.

Does not the modern passport, too, still have something disturbing about it? It is still an object of initiation, bureaucratized of course, but one that still opens closed frontiers. Its character as an object of initiation assumes its full value in times of crisis, war, or revolution. One has only to think of the similarities between the initiatory journey and that of the political agent working underground. Virgil accompanies Dante into Hell, like an escape agent. And how many modern underground escape agents, modern Charons, handed over their clients to death during the last war!

The underground journey, with its unknown dangers, is very like the immemorial journey of the dead. This suspended death also uses passwords, magic formulas intended to open invisible doors. Its itinerary must not divagate from strict rules. It is a journey whose every detail is laid down and during which death lurks behind every corner.

From the forced journey in tsarist Russia, so harrowingly described by Dostoevski in his *The House of the Dead*, to the journeys in the Gulag Archipelago in the U.S.S.R., such journeys are descents into hell, a hell as absurd as that of Sisyphus.

Note

We have seen how a large number of Christian funerary customs—for instance, funeral processions, the lustral water, the illumination of tombs, professional mourners, burial with precious objects, libations over tombs— are merely a transformation, if not a continuation, of ancient pagan practices.

Libations over sarcophagi led naturally to ritual meals over the tombs of the Christian martyrs, until, that is, Saint Ambrose forbade them, and substituted the symbolic meal of the Eucharist. But in the seventeenth and eighteenth centuries, in Provence, the offering of bread and milk over graves was still practiced during the year following the death of a parent (G. and M. Vovelle, *Vision de la mort et de l'au-delà en Provence*).

Christianity required a simple burial, in the ground. But Saint Cecilia was buried in a silk dress sewn with gold thread and Saint Helena was covered with gold and precious stones. "Why, then," cried Saint Jerome, "wrap your dead in gold clothes? Why does not ambition perish in the midst of grief and tears? Is it that the corpses of the rich will rot only in silk?" The Council of Auxerre forbade the decoration of the dead with rich ornaments. We know what followed.

Similarly, Saint John Chrysostom inveighed in the fourth century against the hysterical lamentations of professional mourners and threatened with excommunication those who employed them, but to no avail.

It was only in the eleventh century that the coin in the mouth to pay for the ferryman of the Styx was replaced by the host. But we have found seventeenth-century coins in the mouths of the peasants, which proves that in the seventeenth century people still set out for the great journey with money on their persons.

In the fourth century the church forbade the pagan custom of lighting fires in the cemetery and illuminating the tombs. But in the thirteenth century glass lamps were still set up in the tombs. Some funerary monuments of the Middle Ages, like the tomb of King Christian, in Denmark, which dates from the fifteenth century, even had lanterns. Were candles, perhaps, substituted for the rites of incineration? And what, exactly, is the flame of the unknown soldier?

The practice of sprinkling holy water over the coffin as one enters the church for a funeral is of pre-Christian origin. It is related to the lustral water of the Roman funerary vases, placed in tombs. In the Middle Ages this lustral water in the tombs was called holy water. One no longer places vases of water in graves (as Blanche of Castille did for her sons), but one places empty vases and urns over the graves, which continue the symbol.

5

Funerary Furniture

Of all monuments, tombs are those that present perhaps the broadest subject for the study of the archaeologist, historian, artist, even philosopher. Civilizations, at every step of the ladder, have manifested the nature of their beliefs in another life by the way in which they have treated the dead.

Viollet-le-Duc
Dictionnaire raisonné de l'architecture française

The minimum space of modern burial is a little longer and a little wider than the size of an ordinary man: six-and-one-half feet long and three-and-one-quarter feet wide, just enough to bury the standard-size coffin.

The coffin, which French gravediggers apparently call a *"paletot,"* or overcoat (cheaper coffins are called *"paletots d'été,"* or summer coats),[1] and which J.-D. Urbain calls "the last safes" are descendants of the Roman stone sarcophagus-house, which, itself, is descended from the Egyptian sarcophagus.[2]

In fact, with our wooden coffin, we have returned to the origins of the sarcophagus. At the end of the Egyptian predynastic period, the dead were buried in somewhat crudely made wooden or earthenware containers; these were followed first by wooden sarcophagi-houses, then by the famous anthropoid version enveloping the mummies.[3]

[1] Hamel, *Un vivant chez les morts.*
[2] Urbain, *La Société de conservation.*
[3] Rykwert, *On Adam's House in Paradise.*

[73

At the Carolingian period, plaster coffins appeared, in imitation of the Roman stone sarcophagi, then in the thirteenth century lead coffins. Up to the eighteenth century, in the Christian West, coffins, whether of wood, plaster, stone, or lead, were the prerogative of the rich, the poor being buried directly into the earth, wrapped in a simple shroud.

In the context of bourgeois individualism, the desire to protect the body, to delay its putrefaction as far as possible, led to an increase in the use of the coffin, just as, from the seventeenth century, there was an increase in personal funerary plaques in the churches and on monuments in cemeteries.

In England during the Elizabethan period it was fashionable in high society to offer as gifts small gold coffins the size of a tobacco pouch containing a silver skeleton. A pendant dating from 1703 represents a tiny gold coffin containing hairs. In the eighteenth century the same attitude of macabre humor is to be found in a wide range of jewelry based on the theme of the tomb.

Nearer to our own time, we know that Sarah Bernhardt liked to receive her friends lying in a coffin and often had herself photographed as a corpse. Less well known, however, is the macabre attitude of Claude Farrère, who kept in his drawing room, to his death, his future sycamore coffin, covered with marquetry and lined with lace. Or the exhibitions in 1972 of Jean-Pierre Raynaud, showing in galleries and museums coffins painted in red, blue, and yellow.

It is said that in Annam a coffin received during one's lifetime is a highly prized gift.[4] In France during the German occupation it was a gift to terrorize collaborators.

In the old days cartloads of coffins arrived each year in Shanghai harbor. They contained the bodies of expatriate Chinese who had asked to be buried in their motherland. Certain sacred cemeteries, like the Lamasery of the Five Towers in Mongolia, received coffins that had taken a year to arrive.[5]

In prehistoric times the dead took their place in the earth in a huddled-up, or foetal, position. In the earliest Egyptian wooden sarcophagi-houses, one also finds corpses in this position. It may be that this position was due to the earlier practice of burying the dead in oval jars. These jar-coffins crop up again in the Christian West during the Middle Ages. In the north portal of Reims Cathedral, the Last Judgment shows us dead

[4]Frazer, *Fear of the Dead.*
[5]Morin, *L'Homme et la mort dans l'Histoire.*

rising from a large ovoid jar in which they were forced to sit. Burial in the sitting position, though not common in the Middle Ages, seems to have been regarded with a certain prestige, since Charlemagne was buried in this position.

The leather envelope, use of which goes back to the seventh and eighth centuries, was much in favor in the Middle Ages in the Île-de-France, Normandy, and Brittany. But this envelope of cowhide sewn together, was, of course, reserved for princes and high-ranking aristocrats.

This leather envelope is midway between the shroud and the coffin.

The shroud was the first envelope. The early Christians, like the Muslims of today, were wrapped naked in a winding sheet and buried without a coffin. Ecclesiastics were the first to be buried in their clothes, no doubt believing it to be more decent.[6] This practice soon reached the upper classes in society, who also asked to be buried in their clothes. Bishops were buried in their religious vestments and knights in their armor. In the early eighteenth century, the bourgeois in turn, rejecting the nakedness of the shroud, demanded to be buried dressed. But right up to the nineteenth century all children, even the children of the rich, were buried without a coffin, the body being sewn into a winding sheet and thrown into the common ditch.

The abandonment of naked burial slowly spread from the towns to the countryside. In Savoy and the Dauphiné the shroud disappeared, to be replaced by the coffin, only between 1820 and 1900, according to the communal archives.[7] This shroud, sometimes sewn or pinned together, was quite simply a large canvas sheet, generally new, the poor using the best sheets in their cupboards. They also used shrouds of cut herbs or mattresses made of vegetable matter: moss, straw, sweet-smelling herbs. During the exhibition of Chinese art treasures, shown in Paris and London in 1973, we were able to see the shroud of Princess Tou Wan, made up of 2,156 pieces of jade sewn together with gold thread. From jade to the canvas winding sheet, from the homespun dress to armor, the first envelope was certainly varied, as varied as the second envelope, that is to say, the coffin, which could be of lead or pine.

[6] In 535 the Council of Clermont forbade the use of altar cloths and ornaments in burials. The early Christians were not buried with precious objects, but only with a lead cross placed on their breasts. The shroud was marked only by a cross painted in red.

[7] Arnold Van Gennep, *Manuel de folklore français contemporain*, vol. 2, *Du berceau à la tombe: funérailles* (Paris: Picard, 1946).

Among items of funerary architecture and furniture, two are of Roman invention: the columbarium and the cippus.

The columbarium, a vault with niches, is reminiscent of a dovecote (hence its name). It consists of rows of urns containing the ashes of the dead. Columbariums were the preserve of certain families, like the Scipios. The columbarium for Octavius's freed slaves was also famous.

The funerary cippus, a small aedicula, or miniature temple, concealed a cavity in which the ashes were placed. In certain graves a lead pipe connected the funerary urn to the upper part of the cippus. "These conduits received messages, thin plates of lead covered with inscriptions, intended for the gods of the underworld. They were rolled like cigars and dropped down the pipe. The funerary altar thus became a sort of letterbox."[8] The pipe was also used by the parents of the deceased to pour down libations of wine, blood, milk, oil, honey, and perfumes. In this way the liquids reached the ashes of the funerary urns.

Funerary towers have been found in a number of civilizations. The Persian towers of silence are well known.[9] On a circular inclined plane the dead were left to the vultures for a year, that is to say, for the duration of natural decomposition. Then the bones, cleaned by the birds of prey, were collected and placed in an ossuary. The Persians also had towers filled with ashes into which criminals condemned to death were thrown and where they perished by suffocation.

The towers of the Parsis of India, situated near towns and called dokhmans, are well known. Corpses were thrown into them and picked clean by vultures. When a tower was full of bones, it was walled up and another built.

Less well known are the square stone towers, without openings, about twenty feet square and between twenty-three and thirty feet high, which have been discovered on mounds on cliff edges in New Mexico. These ruins, which are much earlier than the Spanish conquest, seem to date from the twelfth and thirteenth centuries. Inside the towers mummies have been found, in particular that of a man with a stone ax in his skull and that of a woman with sixteen arrows in her chest and belly. These towers, whose inside walls are decorated with motifs of flowers, plants, and birds, seem to have been set fire to by incendiary arrows, some of which are still stuck in the walls.

In any case, we know that the Incas buried their dead in round or

---

[8] A. L. Delattre, *Les Cimetières romains superposés de Carthage* (Paris: 1899).
[9] The Zoroastrian towers of Iran date from much later, the seventeenth century.

square towers, since the Spaniards had some difficulty in putting an end to this practice.

In the Middle Ages children who died before they were baptized were buried in the walls of existing towers. These burial places between earth and heaven were called limbos.

Between the twelfth and thirteenth centuries, curious lanterns of the dead were built on the highest point in a cemetery; these are particularly abundant in the Limousin and the Périgord.[10] They are between twenty and sixty-five feet high, but we do not know whether they were used to illuminate nocturnal gatherings or as beacons for travelers who had got lost at night.

"The lanterns of the dead consist of a hollow pillar surmounted by a pierced lantern, surmounted by a cross. At the base of the pillar was a small door, used to insert a lamp, which was hoisted up by a pulley fixed to the top of its cavity."[11]

The funerary well is the reverse of the funerary tower. In the Roman world dead slaves were thrown into them. In the Middle Ages these wells were long used, either to throw in corpses or to fill them with bones.

In ancient Mexico, at Chichén Itzá, at the top of a temple, reached by a staircase, was a sacred well. In periods of drought the priests brought boys and girls to the temple and threw them down into the well with offerings of jewelry and gold plate. The next day the survivors were pulled out on ropes, and had, it seems, been given the gift of prophecy.

There are two specifically African pieces of funerary furniture: the stool and the basket.

One of my students from the Ivory Coast, Konan Kangah, told me that among the Baoulés, the soul of the deceased remains in the family and is incorporated in the stool, which captures the vital force when it escapes from the body. This sacred stool is kept in the house of the ancestors. Each New Year the stools are taken out and whisky or gin is offered to them.

Among Sangos a large basket covered with leather thongs contains the ancestor's vertebrae and radius. In the family home this basket-reliquary becomes the image of the protective ancestor within the home. Among the Kotas baskets also contain the skulls and bones of the ancestors, generally three, four, or five together. But the oldest family reliquaries contain between fifteen and twenty skulls.

[10] In Japan there are also lanterns of the dead.
[11] Camille Enlard, *Manuel d'archéologie française* (Paris: Picard, 1929).

The cross, the sign of death, and also the essential element of the prototype of the tomb, is a relatively recent iconography.

In fact, it only became the symbol of Christianity at a fairly late date. Until the fourth century crosses were rare in religious symbolism, the first centuries of Christianity preferring the fish, the anchor, the dove, the lamp, the lighthouse, the ship, or the palm. Then, from 313, under the reign of Constantine, crosses began to spread. Nevertheless the image of the crucified did not appear until the sixth century, in the East, and had only just taken root in the West by the Gothic period.

The cross as a symbol of death did not appear in cemeteries until the thirteenth century. And the oldest Romanesque crosses possess no ornamentation. But even these crosses were unusual and generally collective.

It was only in the seventeenth and above all in the eighteenth century that crosses began to be placed over individual graves in cemeteries. The new strata of society which, in the eighteenth century, began to individualize themselves (junior officers, smallholders, craftsmen) also began, like the nobles and bourgeois, to want their own tombs. And not only did they have engraved on their tombs the instruments of their trade (harrow, plow, netting needle, plane, hammer), but they also added an erect stela in the form of a cross. This cross, marking the grave, was the emblem of those who had never had a burial place. As a new stratum of society acquired the right to houses of their own, it also acquired a right to its own tombs.

The free-standing cross-stela is a recent funerary monument—only between two and three hundred years old. At first most of these crosses were wooden. They were surmounted by a small roof, formed of two planks, thus recalling a house. These wooden crosses decorated by a roof disappeared from France in the nineteenth century but are still common in Germany and eastern Europe.

The crosses of Ireland have a history of their own, the oldest being obviously menhirs, to which a cross and inscription were added.[12] At

---

[12] The Basque discoidal tomb was no doubt an earlier form of the carved menhir. Those to be seen today in Basque cemeteries are scarcely earlier than the sixteenth century. But the discoidal stela is earlier than the Christian era. It existed in Spain before the arrival of the Romans. The oldest ones reproduce an anthropomorphic schema: head, shoulder, bust. Astral representations are common on them. The discoidal tomb is a stylization of the human head and by that very fact a symbolic representation of the deceased. Discoidal stelae, which are common in the Basque regions, also appear, however, in Portugal, northern Spain, Etruria, and even England (Louis Thomas, *La Tombe basque* [Paris: Champion, 1923]).

Greek funeral stela, Smyrna. *(The Louvre, Paris. Courtesy S.P.A.D.E.M. Photo Giraudon)*

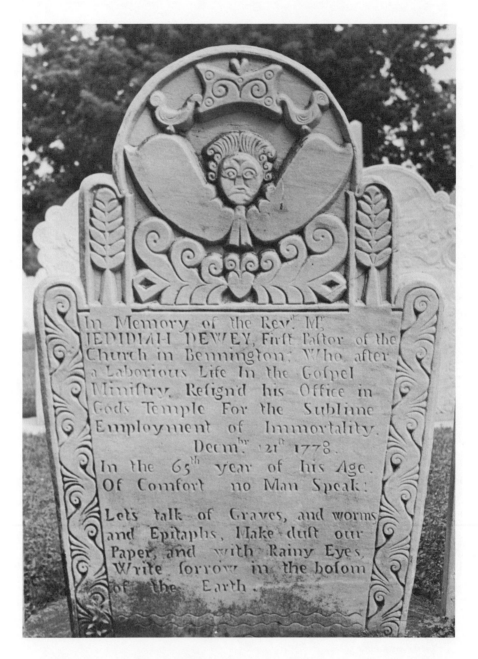

Eighteenth-century American tombstone, cemetery in Bennington, Vt.
(Photo H. Armstrong Roberts)

the end of the seventh century, pillars and stelae assumed a monumental appearance, reaching more than six or seven feet in height and ceasing to be rough blocks of stone. Perhaps under the Coptic influence, traces of which are also to be found in France, in Merovingian art, and no doubt under the Visigothic influence from Spain, the Greek cross within a circle appeared and occupied the entire top of the stone. The Maltese cross was also quite common. The great stelae, divided into several panels, "rather like a page of manuscript. . . [formed] massive strapwork crosses rolled into spirals at the ends."[13]

In the tenth century the attacks of the Scandinavians halted the building of Irish crosses, which reappeared in the eleventh century.

"To the quite simple crosses of their models, the Irish added a luxuriant decoration generally adapted from the repertoire of pre-Christian curvilinear ornaments, with which were mixed, here and there, helices, swastikas, and Greek-key patterns. Sometimes the ends of the cross form a simple roll; this was a theme that was not unknown on the Continent, but it was seldom so exuberant."[14]

The Breton calvaries appeared much later, between the early sixteenth century and late seventeenth century.

The coffin has become in our time a very expensive piece of furniture, which is itself protected from rotting in a brick vault. In Portugal and Corsica there are even mausoleums that make it possible to exhibit the coffin behind a window.

The modern coffin possesses certain accessories, some of them functional, such as the four handles for the bearers, others decorative, such as screw-covers and linings, hygienic, such as antiseptic salts, or bureaucratic, such as engraved plaques. For long-distance transport, wood an inch thick is required. Otherwise, the coffin may be of any kind of wood, the rarest being obviously for the rich, and pine for the poorest.

In older times the corpse was exhibited at the door of the house. Then the corpse continued to be exhibited, but in a coffin. Up to the mid-eighteenth century, most makers of wills asked to be borne uncovered for the tour round the town, rather than "closed up in a chest." Or they asked to be borne in an open chest, the coffin being closed only at the moment of burial.[15]

[13] Françoise Henry, *L'Art irlandais* (Paris: Zodiaque, 1963).
[14] Ibid.
[15] Michel Vovelle, *Piété baroque et déchristianisation en Provence au XVIIIᵉ siècle* (Paris: Plon, 1973).

Stone cross of Mulredach with scriptural scenes, Monasterboice, Ireland, tenth century. *(The Granger Collection, New York)*

The announcement of mourning, nailed to the door, then replaced the exhibition of the coffin which, itself, replaced the exhibition of the body.

The corpse is whisked away, shut up as soon as possible in the coffin which, itself, is shut up in a vault. The vault, acquired by the bourgeoisie in the nineteenth century, became widespread in the twentieth. This "super-coffin," this "coffin of coffins," is an index of the "fever of preservation. . . it is no longer enough to protect the corpse, we now have to protect what protects the corpse." [16]

And every vault is surmounted by a monument, manufactured by

[16] Urbain, *La Société de conservation.*

large funerary enterprises that keep a tight hold on the market. Like new private houses, most tombs are bought from a catalogue. And, like residences, trains, and planes, these industrialized tombs are given flashy names: in France these might be Elysée, Grand Trianon, Petit Trianon, Capitole, Chambord, Chenonceaux, Chinon, and so on. The catalogues of "funerary art" also offer twenty-one types of stelae, thirty-eight types of grave, seven colors of stone (red, labrador, black, grey-Touraine, and so on).[17]

The myth of marble seems invincible despite widespread use of granite and a timid appearance of concrete and metal.

The cross, which has become a symbol of death, even more of Christianity (a cross in front of a name signifies a deceased person), is practically the general emblem of the grave in Western Europe. Certain atheists—they do not appear to be many—hold nevertheless to a stela in the form of a rectangular parallelepiped. A new type of stela has appeared in Yugoslav Macedonia: the red, five-pointed star signifying that one is a communist, just as the cross once indicated that one was a Christian, the star of David marked a Jewish grave, and the crescent a Muslim grave in Europe.

There is a proliferation of inscriptions and various objects on the tomb. The most redundant is the false coffin reproduced in granite on the tombstone. And on this false coffin is a false representation of the drapes that conceal the real coffin during the funeral service.[18] One can also see in our cemeteries false sarcophagi surmounted by recumbent figures.

The photographic portrait, more recently in color, has replaced the plaster cast and the aristocratic recumbent figure.

One of the symbols of the space of the "crossing," the door, often appears engraved or carved on tombs. There is the false door, shown half open. But it is symptomatic that, in this modern furniture of death, everything is artificial, including the books, open or closed, with their pompous phrases, picked out in ceramic. Also in ceramic are the enormous mottoes, the mortuary crowns which resemble buoys (death is a shipwreck), and the pillows.

Statuary became very widespread in the nineteenth century. It is much less common today. It no doubt seems rather affected to order one's bust with a view to one's tomb. However, in nineteenth-century cemeteries and right up to World War I, busts of men were very numer-

17 Ibid.
18 Ibid.

ous, while busts of women rare. Women always appeared in such inscriptions as "wife of . . . " and so on. Phallocracy also appears to be triumphant postmortem. There is plenty of female sculpture in cemeteries, however, but it is more in the nature of decoration: weeping figures, Venuses or Dianas.

Animal sculptures appear, of course, largely for their symbolic value: the dog for fidelity (but may it not also be the guardian of the tomb?), the dove for gentleness or purity (usually on the graves of young girls), the eagle and lion for courage (always on men's graves).

There are a great many angels, and, over children's graves, cherubs. There are also sphinxes, index finger on lips (silence, people are asleep here!).

There are a great many sculpted or engraved medals, lyres, flames. These flames, these torches, so frequent in funerary symbolism, unconsciously recall the ritual fires lit around the remains of the dead by the Gauls and Teutons.

This kind of funerary monument, however ridiculous it may be, appears nevertheless as an unquestionable democratic conquest. From the monument for the king to the monument for all, the development of the funerary site corresponds to other mass phenomena. The right to a burial vault parallels the right to housing. The urban cemetery-museum grew up with the claim to political rights.

Let us consider this conquest of individuality, and later of individualism, from the point of view of the grave, from the Middle Ages to our own time. First there is the simple, open burial of the early Christian period. Only martyrs and saints were given a tomb. Around them spread the anonymous community of bodies. Then the flat grave (with its stone) appeared: this had no antecedent in antiquity, where a monument, if only an inconspicuous stela, always rose above the level of the ground to mark the grave. The flat grave, a medieval creation, is a sort of compromise between the open grave and the timid desire to affirm one's identity.

The flat grave also corresponds to the ideology of humility that spread from the early Christian period. Integrated into the ground, the flat grave was walked over by the living. Better still, it was always situated in places of passage: in the courtyard in front of the church, the porch, the nave. By the late fifteenth century the paving stones of churches were composed entirely of juxtaposed gravestones.

The second stage of individuality brought in the inscription on the gravestone, which identified the deceased; this was followed by his effigy, his outline, engraved on the gravestone, which lasted up to the mid-seventeenth century.

This outline, which was at first engraved, eventually became a life-sized carved image of the dead person—the gisant, or recumbent figure.

The gisant appeared in Western Christendom in the twelfth century on the mausoleum of Philip I, who died in 1108, and was buried in the church of Saint-Benoît-sur-Loire. The king is represented lying down, dressed in his royal robes, crown on his head, and falconry glove on his hand. The gisant, on his stone litter raised above the ground, is the dead person exhibited on his funeral bed frozen for eternity. Viollet-le-Duc stressed that the gisants of the twelfth and thirteenth centuries kept their eyes open and that their gestures and attitudes were those of living people.[19] About the mid-fourteenth century, he adds, sculptors gave gisants the appearance of sleep, but never the signs of death. This observation is taken up and developed by Philippe Ariès, who writes that the earliest gisants do not represent the dead: "They have their eyes wide open, the folds of their clothes fall as if they were standing and not lying down. . . They are *beati*, blessed, glorious bodies, eternally young. . . the Elect waiting in repose."[20]

From the fourteenth century, the eyes of the gisants are closed in Italy and Spain. The folds of the clothes fall. The head lies on a cushion. The blessed becomes simply a dead person. The way is open to the decomposed corpse, and the carved skeleton of the fifteenth and sixteenth centuries.

The gisant, which seems to be so closely bound up with medieval iconography, is not however a creation of the twelfth century. As with so many other features that appear essentially Christian, it is a resurgence of pagan antiquity. There were, in fact, Roman gisants. But if the medieval gisants had the rigidity of corpses, the Roman gisants were always lying in the familiar attitudes of sleep, or sitting and awake, like the Etruscan gisants, or semirecumbent on dining couches, like a guest at a meal. In Asia Minor sarcophagus lids also comprised a life-size statue of the dead person, with legs crossed, and wrapped in a huge cloak.[21]

In the sixteenth century the semirecumbent figure, or the figure leaning on an elbow, which appeared in Christian Europe, was inspired by Etrusco-Roman statuary.

On the other hand, the image of the praying figure, common in the

---

[19] Viollet-le-Duc, *Dictionnaire raisonné de l'architecture française*.
[20] Ariès, *L'Homme devant la mort*.
[21] Franz Cumont, *Recherches sur le symbolisme funéraire des Romains* (Paris, 1942).

Seventeenth-century American tombstone, New York City, 1681. *(Photo H. Armstrong Roberts)*

sixteenth century, is specifically Christian. In such figures, the dead person is represented on his knees, in prayer.

The praying figure replaces the recumbent figure, which disappeared in the early seventeenth century. The juxtaposition of the gisant (below) and of the praying figure (above) is to be found in the tombs of the Valois in the basilica of Saint-Denis.

In the seventeenth century, allegorical figures accompanied the statue of the dead person and his sarcophagus, figures that were to become more and more common in the eighteenth century.

Manufactured in series in the seventeenth century, the tomb with praying figure was to disappear at the end of the eighteenth century.

Another funerary theme, which lasted from the twelfth to the sixteenth century, was that of the weeping figure. In the twelfth century, when the sculptures of the paleo-Christian sarcophagi were being discovered, these weeping figures were carved in relief on the side of tombs. Then they became independent sculptures. For the tomb of Philip the Bold, Duke of Burgundy, which may be seen in the church of Saint-Benigne at Dijon, Claus Slutter carved forty-one weeping figures (of which only thirty-four have survived).

The royal mausoleums of the Renaissance, in the form of ancient triumphal arches, gave rise among the most common of mortals (yet nevertheless the more exceptional of common mortals, very rich merchants and bourgeois) to shrines in the form of catafalques that covered the funeral effigies. Then these grew larger until they formed small buildings in the form of chapels surmounted by ogival arcades. The floodgates were then opened to the rhetorical, declamatory tomb, with its proliferation of symbols, allegories, and dramatic figures. In the century of the opera the tomb became a theatrical representation with an abundance of declamatory statues representing death, angels, skeletons, and such accessories as hourglasses, scythes, and torches. At the same time these burial places assumed a sinister character, which the sleeping gisants or praying figures had not possessed. Great effort, in fact, went into surrounding them with emblems that recalled pain, annihilation, night, oblivion, nothingness.

In the nineteenth century, in the great cemetery-museums, built near the centers of the larger cities, the tomb ceased to be the megalomaniac representation of a single man and became a family tomb, a bourgeois form of expression certainly, but was not the basilica of Saint-Denis also a family tomb (that of the Valois, then of the Bourbons)? This bourgeois family tomb was, then, in imitation of the nobility, the expression of the homogeneity of a family and a name. The bourgeoisie, which had acquired political power, now manifested through its tombs its own dynastic ambitions. It was no longer the soul that was indestructible, but the family, the name. In Montparnasse cemetery there is even a family vault for a hundred places!

In 1815 the Greffulhe family built at Père-Lachaise the first of these funerary chapels, which was to give rise to a whole series of neo-Gothic, neo-Greek, neo-Egyptian mausoleums. Eclecticism, which was fashionable for the architecture of the living, could not spare the dead.

The family tomb led to the cemetery-towns. And for a long time it was to be the only expression of city life. The upkeep of tombs and their decoration in the cemeteries is very recent as a popular phenomenon. It

[87

was even more exceptional in the countryside, until the late nineteenth century.

The tomb-chapel, an innovation of the nineteenth century, is a mini-church, a private church without a tabernacle and without a priest, a simulacrum of a church, with nevertheless an altar preceded by one or two prie-dieux. In general, as it was also the fashion for the living, this construction is neo-Gothic in style and bears on its pediment the name of its owners: Family *X*.

The architecture and statuary that proliferated in the European cemeteries of the nineteenth century, in imitation of Père-Lachaise and of the Italian *campi santi*, borrowed their repertory from church tombs and from antiquity: pyramids, obelisks, sarcophagi, columns, urns. Pastiche reigned supreme as in all the architecture of the time.

6

The Cemetery as Museum

My favorite walk, especially when it is raining, when it is pouring with
rain, is through Montmartre cemetery, which is near where I live. I
often go there, and I have many friends there.

Hector Berlioz
February 22, 1863

Our period is, as we know, a museum period. We turn everything into a museum: old stones, old districts, old towns,
and even the contemporary arts. The cemetery, of course,
has also become a museum, as is shown by the publication
in the very serious Blue Guides of a guide to the *Cimetières et
Sépultures de Paris*.[1] In the introduction its author, Marcel Le Clere, writes:
"The finest portraits of David d'Angers are to be found in Père-Lachaise,
while Montmartre Cemetery possesses the most magnificent funerary
sculpture of all time: the gisants of Cavaignac by François Rude." And
Marcel Le Clere calculates that there are about a thousand "interesting"
sculptures in the Père-Lachaise. Few art museums possess as many.

The cemetery as a place-to-visit, the beginnings of our present-day
cemetery-museums, was an innovation in the nineteenth century. Like
museums, cemeteries are governed by a functionary called the "*conser-
vateur*" (curator).

---

[1] Le Clère, *Cimetières et Sépultures de Paris*.

[89

THE HOUSES OF THE DEAD

The beginnings of our cemetery-museums are to be found in the Italian *campi santi*.

In 1225 fifty ships of the Republic of Pisa returned to the harbor of their city laden with earth dug up in Jerusalem. The *campo santo* thus created made it possible to lie in truly holy ground without having to make the final voyage to the Holy Land. In 1280 Giovanni Pisano built in white marble the sacred wall forming an enclosure 433 feet long and 148 feet wide, pierced only by two gates. Inside, sixty-two bays, arranged in a full curve, looked out on to the central courtyard. Frescoes were painted on them in the fourteenth and fifteenth centuries: these include scenes of the wine harvest and drunkenness by Gozzoli and a dance of death by Orcagna. Long saturated with corpses and monuments, the *campo santo* of Pisa was finally closed to further burials and became a museum.

Though still open to new dead who can pay the very high price of a place, the cemeteries of Père-Lachaise, Montparnasse, and Montmartre in Paris have also become museums.

But, like the *campo santo* in Pisa, these cemeteries have become museums only after the event. On the other hand, there are cemetery-museums created as such, for example, the *Famedio*, a communal pantheon built in 1869 by influential Milanese, at the entrance of Milan's monumental cemetery.

Certain churches, too, which are, or have never been anything other than, storehouses of illustrious corpses have also become cemetery-museums: Westminster Abbey in London, the Panthéon and Invalides in Paris, the chapel of the abbey church of Saint-Denis, the memorial of Louis XVI, the chapel of Notre-Dame-de-Consolation.

On April 4, 1791, the Constituent Assembly, having decided to give a national burial place to its great men, assigned them the church of Sainte-Geneviève. The first "secular saint" of that truly universal religion which, at the time, was called "morality," was Mirabeau. A year later it was realized that Mirabeau was no longer worthy of such an honor, and he was expelled to the cemetery at Clamart. The same thing happened to Marat, who after Thermidor was not thrown into the common pit, as was commonly said, but buried in the cemetery of Sainte-Geneviève, which has since disappeared under the library of the same name.

Voltaire and Rousseau were transported to the Panthéon with an enthusiasm which is entirely justifiable. But Descartes was rejected by the Council of the Five Hundred. Subsequently the Panthéon was to receive Lazare Carnot, Marceau, La Tour d'Auvergne, Victor Hugo, Emile

Zola, Painlevé, Braille, Berthelot, Langevin, Jean Jaurès, Jean Moulin, et cetera.

While the cemetery of Père-Lachaise has continued to exert an attraction over the dead, whether famous or not, the Panthéon attracts fewer bidders than one might suppose. Famous soldiers prefer the Invalides. And some of its guests, like Voltaire and Jaurès, who would have preferred to have been buried in natural surroundings, are there against their will.[2]

The First Consul wanted to turn the Invalides into a military pantheon. With this in mind, on September 21, 1800, he had the remains of Turenne, whom the Revolution had taken out of Saint-Denis and who had long served as an object of curiosity in the museum of the Ecole des Beaux-Arts, installed there.

In fact, the Invalides is to the new dynasty of the Bonapartes what Saint-Denis was to the Valois and Bourbons. For lack of descendants, Napoleon I is accompanied only by his son ("L'Aiglon," the young eagle, which Hitler "handed back to France" in 1940), his brothers, Joseph and Jérôme, and Marshals Bertrand, Duroc, Mortier, Jourdan, Bessières, Oudinot, Moncey, Exelmans, and d'Ornano.

The embalmed, intact body of Napoleon I was brought back from Saint Helena in 1840 and buried for twenty years in the Chapel of Saint Jérôme. A competition was set up for a tomb. One project, by Hector Horeau, consisted of a pyramidal pedestal fifty feet high and a statue of the emperor twenty feet high in coronation robes. But this project, and another by Labrouste, were rejected in favor of Visconti's antique tomb, made of Finnish porphyry given by the tsar, raised on a plinth of green granite from the Vosges. The project was carried out in 1861. Liankey, Foche, Bugeaud, Rouget de l'Isle, Gallieni, Mangin, and, from World War II, Marshals Leclerc and Juin have also been buried in the Invalides.

The Invalides has become, then, an "imperial" cemetery, but only against the wishes of Napoleon I, who intended that his dynasty would continue that of the Bourbons, and, by a decree of February 20, 1806, had ordered the building of a burial vault for himself and his descendants in the royal basilica of Saint-Denis.

Monarchs are usually buried in cemetery-museums. All the kings of France, except three, from Dagobert to Louix XVIII, were buried at Saint-Denis; similarly, the Spanish kings were buried at the Escorial,

---

[2] The marquis de Villette had Voltaire's heart embalmed, and erected at Ferney a pyramidal monument designed by Houdon. Then he succeeded in having the ashes transfered to the Panthéon.

Napoleon's Tomb, Les Invalides, Paris. *(Photo Ewing Galloway)*

the emperors of Austria in the church of the Capuchins in Vienna, and the tsars of Russia in the cathedral of Petropavlosk.

Whereas the Communist revolution piously preserved all the tsars in their rows of coffins, content to massacre the living czar, the Revolution of 1789 set about trying to eliminate all trace of the monarchs of the past. On October 6, 1793, on a proposition introduced by Barère, the Convention voted not only for the destruction of the mausoleums of Saint-Denis but also for the exhumation of the skeletons of twenty-five kings, seventeen queens, and seventy-one princes and princesses, which were thrown into two great ditches and covered with chalk. The lead roof was removed, the stained-glass windows taken out, the iron railings of the choir dismantled, and Suger's and Pierre de Montreuil's building was left a virtual ruin. The Bourbons' burial vault was opened up by workers armed with picks. The fifty-four lead coffins (each with a wooden coffin inside), and the lead vessels containing the entrails of the monarchs, were removed, melted down, and turned into bullets.

Twenty-four years later, in 1817, Louis XVIII set about restoring Saint-Denis, reconstructing the destroyed tombs, and replacing such bones as could be recovered. There were plenty of documents about the siting of the tombs. But Louis XVIII, allowing for future religious and funerary ceremonies, did not want the church to be too encumbered. So instead of restoring the church to its original state, only thirty-eight out of sixty-seven tombs were restored in the church itself. The others were taken down into the crypt and placed in chronological order. But one may well wonder whether the work of the restorers was the result of postrevolutionary black humor or incredible incompetence. For they placed in the crypt a tomb supposedly belonging to Clovis I, who had been buried in the church of Sainte-Geneviève, and had therefore never had a burial place at Saint-Denis. A memorial was erected to Joan of Arc, whom the kings had never thought fit to honor with such proximity. Over the tomb of Saint Louis, they placed a statue of Charles V. To the sculptured body of Turenne, they added a marble head topped by a wig in the style of Louis XIV, taken from the tomb of the duc de Noailles. Finally, Dagobert's tomb was presented sawn in two. A contemporary, the Baron de Guihermy, wrote an amusing account of this archaeological potpourri:

> The scholars, architects, or other specialists, entrusted with the task of classifying the tombs and statues brought back to Saint-Denis, seem to have been preoccupied by a matrimonial fantasy of the strangest kind. Having listed all their characters, they decreed that each marble king would have the right to a wife of the same material to share the boredom of the grave with him. The personal position of all the princesses represented by the statues to be replaced, their previous commitments, their legitimate affections, presented no obstacle to the classification proposed. The princes of the second order were condemned to handing over their wives, whether they liked it or not, to the kings, except in cases when, the sharing out having been concluded, there were any ladies left over. As a result of this arbitrary measure there resulted some odd incests of stone, and adulteries of marble of the worst kind. It was a scandal to make the venerable pillars blush. One cannot imagine what archaeological immoralities were committed beneath the darkened vaults of Saint-Denis.[3]

What Louis XVIII began, Charles V and Louis-Philippe continued. Under Louis XVIII two white marble monuments representing Louis

---

[3]Quoted by Georges d'Heilly, *Extraction des cercueils royaux à Saint-Denis en 1793* (Paris: Hachette, 1868).

[93

XVI and Marie Antoinette, in court costume, kneeling on a prie-dieu, were added to the pre-Republican monuments. Then a huge group was erected to the duc de Berry, assassinated as he left the Opéra, on February 13, 1820. Finally Charles X gave his brother the last available place in the crypt and erected to him "a pitiful monument, made up, like the others, of bits of marble and statues, on which was placed a marble bust of the king which. . . had no doubt been intended to decorate the wedding hall of some town hall."[4]

Finally, on July 27, 1847, Montalembert spoke in the Chambre des Pairs on the scandal of the appalling restorations which had been carried out at Saint-Denis over the past thirty years.

> The dishonor of this church has become the laughing-stock of artists and travelers. . . It has been the victim of a double restoration, or what I shall call a double degradation: the degradation of the exterior and the degradation of the interior. . . Hitherto we have seen churches fall into ruin by age and neglect; but that churches should be ruined by the work of restorers is a phenomenon peculiar to our own time, and the special glory of our official architects.
>
> Thanks to the restorers, the interior of the church of Saint-Denis is now no more than a frightful hash of monuments, debris of every period, and of every kind, jumbled together in total confusion; it is now no more than a wretched museum of bric-a-brac, swarming with innumerable anachronisms. . . The last king to have had a mausoleum at Saint-Denis was Henri II. Now one can see those of Henri III, Henri IV, Louis XIV, and even Louis XV. Louis XV's tomb is built out of debris from the former tombs of the duchesse de Joyeuse, the comtesse de Brissac, and of the wife of a sculptor called Moitte. Bits from the three have been brought together to form a tomb for Louis XV. This is what is called restoration.

Taking up his great-uncle's idea, Napoleon III decreed in 1859 that Saint-Denis would be the burial place of the new dynasty. Viollet-le-Duc, called in as restorer, replaced the tombs in their original positions. At the end of the Second Empire, Georges d'Heilly could write enthusiastically: "When complete, M. Viollet-le-Duc's Saint-Denis will certainly be the finest title to glory of that learned and skilfull architect. . . It has involved not only rebuilding, but replacing the tombs where they were, the columns where they were removed, the statues where they had been broken. It has involved above all removing the clumsy embellishments added by previous governments. . . To destroy and to restore

[4]Ibid.

has been the starting point of the immense work undertaken by M. Viollett-le-Duc. Go to Saint-Denis today and see for yourselves this intelligent, magnificent restoration."[5]

Yes, go and see for yourselves, but this cemetery-museum is more a museum than a cemetery, since most of the tombs are cenotaphs. From the two common ditches in which the remains of twelve centuries of monarchs had been buried, only broken bones were removed. The bones of Hugh Capet, Francis I, and Louis XIV were probably mixed in walled-up boxes in 1817. But the tombs of Henry II and of Catherine de Médicis by Germain Pilon, and that of Francis I, by Philibert Delorme, are high points in the history of statuary.

The earliest kings of France (or rather of the Franks) had been buried in the church of Saint-Germain-de-Prés. Childebert, Fredegond, Clotaire, and Childeric are still there. No doubt they were so old that the revolution spared them.

On the site of the cemetery of the Madeleine where, in a common ditch, had been buried five hundred Swiss massacred during the attack on the Tuileries on August 10, 1792, then the guillotined body of Louis XVI (his head placed between his legs), and, last, 1,343 guillotined on the Place de la Concorde, including Marie Antoinette, Charlotte Corday, Philippe Egalité, Hébert, Mme Roland, Mme du Barry, a cemetery closed by saturation on April 19, 1794, Louis XVIII had a chapel of expiation built, in memory of his brother and sister-in-law. At the present day, at 36 Rue Pasquier (8th arrondissement), this cenotaph erected by Fontaine, between 1815 and 1826, comprises a garden where roses of the species preferred by Marie Antoinette are still exclusively grown.

At the other end of Paris, near the Place du Trône (later nicknamed the Place du Trône renversé) where, between June 14 and July 27, 1794, 1,356 other persons, mainly aristocrats, were guillotined (La Rochefoucauld, Montalembert, Montmorency, Noailles, Broglie, Clermont-Tonnerre, Grimaldi, Chimay, La Trémoille), and citizens of less exalted lineage (André Chénier, General de Beauharnais, Joséphine's husband, the sixteen Carmelites of Compiègne, about whom Bernanos wrote his magnificent *Dialogues*, and Léonard, Marie Antoinette's hairdresser). The former convent of Picpus was then turned into a cemetery to receive this influx of decapitated nobles, who were stripped of their clothing and piled up in a bleeding, naked mass in a common ditch.

In 1803 the princess of Hohenzollern-Sigmaringen, and other relations of the victims, bought together the ground which has become the

---

[5] Ibid.

private cemetery of Picpus, reserved to the descendants of those who were guillotined. A son-in-law of the duchesse d'Ayen, La Fayette, for example, was buried there.

In the crypt of the Carmelites' chapel at 70 Rue de Vaugirard, Paris VIᵉ, one may see behind glass the bones of the 117 ecclesiastics beaten to death with staves, hammers, and axes, on September 2, 1792, and then buried in a pit, mixed with manure and broken plates.

At 23 Rue Jean-Goujon, Paris VIIIᵉ, one may also visit the Chapel of Notre-Dame-de-la-Consolation, built on the site of the sinister Bazar de la Charité, where, on May 4, 1897, 143 people were burned alive in an accident caused by the beginnings of cinematography.

The church of the Sorbonne is also a cemetery-museum, since it contains not only the mausoleum of Richelieu, in the center of the choir, but also in the crypt, the bodies of ten teachers and two students, martyrs of the Resistance, and the urn containing the ashes of five pupils of the Lycée Buffon, shot by the Germans on February 8, 1943.

Until 1792 the church of the Sorbonne was above all the private cemetery of the Richelieu family, since the cardinal had been buried there among twenty-seven members of his family. But in 1793 the body of Richelieu was removed from his tomb and decapitated (under the Great Revolution, not only the living, but also the dead, and even statues, like those of the kings in the porch of Notre Dame, were decapitated). In 1866 a descendant of the revolutionary who had appropriated Richelieu's head restored this macabre inheritance to the government of the Second Empire, which replaced it in the mausoleum, decorated with statues by Girardon depicting the cardinal seated, like an Etruscan, but supported by a woman in mourning.

We often forget that the Louvre and the British Museum are also cemetery-museums, since we can see there, in particular, the mummified bodies of Egyptians, not to mention innumerable empty tombs and funerary objects. While the Musée de l'Homme, in the Place du Trocadéro, in Paris, is really one of the few cemeteries where (apart from the catacombs) one can see so many skeletons and mummies.

Does it not offer to our view Descartes's skull, the skeleton of the dwarf Nicolas Ferry, just under three feet high, who was the jester to Stanislas Leczinsky, the skeleton of a giant from Indre-et-Loire, just over seven feet tall, a hunched-up mummy of an Indian woman from Bolivia, a Cro-Magnon skeleton, a Pithecanthropus mandible, reduced heads of Jivaro Indians, the mummy of a Nubian foetus, a gallery of heads of all races and all times, a mummy from Aqsum dried in its open sarcophagus, the mummy of a Bolivian child, the entire skeleton, and the section of the cranium, of a modern man.

The Musée de l'Homme is a museum of bones, an ossuary-museum. But in the register of cemetery-museums visited not for their dead, but for their tombs, the three Parisian cemeteries built in the nineteenth century—Père-Lachaise, Montmartre, and Montparnasse—are unbeatable, except perhaps by the Italian, Spanish and Portuguese cemeteries of the same kind.

Much has been written about Père-Lachaise, a magnificent park with 12,000 trees (200 to 300 thujas, 500 elms, 200 sycamores, and lime trees, cherry trees, cypresses, cedars, ash trees), its 300 to 400 cats, its birds (blackbirds, magpies, jays, nightingales, woodpeckers, tits), its eroticism: "a bastion of roguery, humor, and sexuality," writes Michel Dansel, who adds, "the largest, most historical, most religious, most romantic, most airy, most bizarre, and most erotic of promenades which overlook Paris."[6]

Between 1820 and 1870 the highest and most famous strata of society were buried there. As a result, Père-Lachaise contains "the greatest number of famous people per square mile" and is visited by 800,000 tourists each year.[7]

From the beginning the cemetery of Père-Lachaise was conceived as a museum of death. Indeed, after the indifference to burial places of the Revolutionary period, the Consulate had to reinvent a funerary ceremonial without borrowing from the religious ceremonies of the Ancien Régime. So Frochot, prefect of the Seine, was given the task of building a model cemetery. In 1804 Frochot bought on behalf of the city of Paris the estate of Mont-Louis, which belonged to Baron Desfontaines but which had previously been the property of the Jesuits. The architect Brongniart, who had designed the Bourse in Paris, was given the task of transforming the site into a necropolis. Brongniart's first project was imbued with the spirit of Ledoux and of the rationalism of the Enlightenment. It consisted of an enormous peristyle, a semicircular covered gallery, with a basement of vaults, which would be decorated with sculpture. This, he said, would encourage a revival of the skills and inventiveness of sculptors. He believed that each rich family would buy one or two arcades and would decorate their interiors. Thus each burial place would

[6]Michel Dansel, *Au Père-Lachaise, son histoire, ses secrets, ses promenades* (Paris: Fayard, 1973).
[7]Ibid.

vie with its neighbors. This museum-cemetery was not accepted, and Brongniart, moving from the mineral to the vegetable, conceived a new plan, which respected the undulations of the 108-acre site, including the existing drives, especially the avenues of lime trees and chestnuts. Brongniart moved away from the idea of the architectural cemetery to that of the cemetery-park, which was to be so widely imitated in the future.

On May 21, 1807, the opening of the first "modern" cemetery took place, and that same year Napoleon decreed that henceforth no burial would be permitted in churches, Protestant chapels, synagogues, or within the boundaries of towns and townships. Furthermore, each religion was to have its own burial places.

The first individual to be buried at Père-Lachaise was a modest police employee. Frochot, who wanted to "launch" his cemetery and encourage a rich clientele to be buried there, offered freehold plots, an innovation that met with little success since, in the first year, only thirteen families bought such freeholds. Frochot then had a quite new advertising idea: to exhume the famous and to rebury them with great pomp in Père-Lachaise. Thus, in 1817, the presumed bodies of Héloïse, Abelard, Molière, La Fontaine, and Beaumarchais were transferred to the new cemetery.

We know that Héloïse and Abelard had been put into a common grave at the convent of the Paraclete. In 1630 one of the abbesses concluded that the reunion in the same grave of a nun and a monk was indecent, and had the skeletons separated and buried in two separate tombs. Under the Revolution the remains of Héloïse and Abelard were bought by a doctor at Chalon-sur-Saône, who in 1900 gave them to Lenoir. Lenoir put them in his museum of national antiquities. Then, under the Restoration, he was commissioned to build a tomb for them, using stone from the chapel of the Paraclete. As for Molière, buried more or less secretly at night in 1673, in the cemetery of the church of Saint-Eustache, his presumed bones had been exhumed on July 6, 1792, on the orders of the Legislative Assembly and also placed in Lenoir's museum. The same year La Fontaine had been exhumed from the churchyard of Saint-Joseph's. Both were taken to the cemetery of Père-Lachaise and buried side by side.

Between 1820 and 1830 the architect Godde built the principal gateway and chapel. Mont-Louis was then referred to as the eastern cemetery, but Parisians soon began to call it Père-Lachaise. He was certainly a strange celebrity, that Reverend Friar François d'Aix de la Chaize, friend of Fénelon, confessor to Louis XIV from 1675 to 1709, who, like his fellow Jesuits, had only an apartment at Mont-Louis. This all-powerful libertine priest, who was on such familiar terms with the king, was still associated in the popular mind, long after his death, with a park in which he had actually spent very little time. On March 22, 1822, Baron Desfontaines, who had sold the site of Mont-Louis to the city at a price of 1.02 francs per square meter, was reinstalled (dead) in his former estate by his widow, who must have bought back a plot at 250 francs a square meter. This gives some idea of the galloping speculation in land which was to contribute so much to the enriching of the Parisian bourgeoisie under the Restoration and the Second Empire. A rise of 24,500 percent in eighteen years was quite a good investment! The operation had come off. The high society of the west of Paris had in the end adopted this cemetery in the east. In order to grant it an additional distinction, Louis-Philippe wanted to give it the character of a posthumous reward: he had buried there the national guards who had died defending the throne in 1832, and, in 1838, he gave a gratuitous concession to the Sisters of Charity, who had died as victims of their devotion.

In 1848 the success of Père-Lachaise was so great that there were already fears that it was getting too full. A new project for a grandiose *campo santo* was put forward, unsuccessfully, by M. de Saint-Yon. In 1856, in an attempt to attract the sympathy of the Turks at the time of the Crimean War, Napoleon III gave the Muslims a separate enclosure, complete with a mosque.

During the Commune the heights of Père-Lachaise served as the last bastion against the assault of the Versailles. Between May 21 and 28, 1871, the last *Communards* were tracked down to the funerary chapels, where they had taken refuge. The 147 last combatants were all shot along the eastern outer wall of the cemetery, which has since come to be known as the *"mur des Fédérés."* In all 1,018 corpses of *Communards* were buried in the cemetery, on the same spot as they had been shot dead.

The Third Republic, after abolishing the common ditch in 1874, repealed the granting of separate spaces for the different religious communities: the walls of the Jewish cemetery were knocked down in 1882; the Muslim cemetery was abolished in 1885 and the mosque demolished. On the other hand the columbarium, built by Formigé, was opened with great pomp in 1887. Composed of two underground stories and two stories opening on to the garden, this columbarium comprised 25,000 compartments, 15,000 of which are at present occupied. It is equipped with two gas ovens and two oil-fired ovens, the former being used only for the remains of hospital dissections. Volunteers for cremation were at first slow in coming, since the first incineration did not take place until

April 17, 1889. At present, among the well-known individuals whose ashes are preserved in the urns of the columbarium, we find Isadora Duncan, Loïe Fuller, Paul Dukas, Max Ophuls, and Monthéus.

In 1895 Bartholomé's monument to the dead was completed; it is a fine example of the conventional statuary of around 1900, but it in no way detracts from this museum-cemetery in which, although statuary abounds in number and picturesqueness, it is less represented by genius.

Between 1804 and 1872 close on a million Parisians were buried at Père-Lachaise.[8] To wander up and down the avenues of the former Mont-Louis is to turn the pages of a *Who's Who* in stone. The politicians of the nineteenth century are almost all there, adversaries brought together: Talleyrand, Ledru-Rollin, Saint-Simon, Louis Blanc, Barras, Sieyès, Raspail, Blanqui, and, closer to our own time, Léon Jouhaux, Thorez, Cachin. M. Thiers, who had the *Communards* shot, has a chapel of his own, the walls of which are regularly covered with such graffiti as "Murderer of the people," "Leader of the dogs and pigs," "Swine." Since 1968 it has even been the object of several plastic bomb attacks. On Raspail's tomb a woman wrapped in a shroud holds out her hand to her husband, depicted behind bars. Those of Napoleon's generals and marshals excluded from the Invalides also find their last meeting place here: Murat, Ney, Junot, Lefebre, Masséna, Davout. Romantic literature has its representatives: Gérard de Nerval, Nodier, Musset, Béranger, Michelet. Alfred de Musset lies here, of course, under his willow, and Vallès, Rémy de Gourmont, Auguste Comte, Alphonse Daudet, Balzac, Drumont, Villiers de l'Isle-Adam, Moréas, Courteline, Oscar Wilde, Proust, Gertrude Stein, Barbusse, Sully Prudhomme, the comtesse de Noailles, Jules Romains, Radiguet, Colette, Apollinaire, Eluard, Merleau-Ponty. . . The statue of Oscar Wilde has the form of a winged sphinx, but since two English women knocked off its male organs, a sexless sphinx. Raymond Roussel has to himself a vault of thirty-two compartments, a solitary chess-player facing death.

Among the painters and sculptors are Ingres, Gustave Doré, Corot, Daumier, David d'Angers, Géricault, Delacroix, Pissarro, Seurat, Barye, Modigliani, Marie Laurencin. Statuary shows Géricault lying on his tomb, the upper part of his body raised, brush in his right hand, a palette in his left. *The Raft of the Medusa* has been carved in bas-relief. Delacroix specified in his will: "My tomb will be in the cemetery of Père-Lachaise, on the heights, in a place somewhat removed. There will be neither emblem, bust, nor statue; my tomb will be copied very exactly from

---

[8] According to Michel Dansel, 928,341 (ibid.).

antiquity, or from Vignole or Palladio, with very pronounced swellings, contrary to everything that is done in architecture today." A curious architectural aberration to place Vignole and Palladio on the same footing! Delacroix's sarcophagus, made of Volvic lava is, according to his wishes, copied from antiquity since it reproduces Scipio's tomb.

Although Chopin's heart is in the church of the Holy Cross in Warsaw, his body is at Père-Lachaise, beneath the white marble muse, whose toes and hands are periodically mutilated. It is not sure whether the perpetrators of these acts are admirers or vandals, especially as Chopin's tomb is often used as a letterbox for lovers' meetings.[9]

In addition to Chopin, there are Reynaldo Hahn, Cherubini, Rossini, Bizet, Chausson, Lalo, Enesco, and Poulenc. And the three great French pianomakers: Pleyel, Gaveau, and Erard.

There are Champollion and Monge, Parmentier and Cuvier, the crook Stavisky and the author of the *Internationale* (Eugène Pottier), Méliès and Félix Pottin, Nadar and Haussmann, Edith Piaf and Sarah Bernhardt, Talma and Jules Berry, Rachel and Pierre Brasseur, Pierre Overney and Gabrielle Russier.

The most colossal mausoleum at Père-Lachaise, and also one of the oldest, houses Elizabeth Demidoff, née Strogonoff, who died in 1818. Its three stories are punctuated around their periphery by wolves' heads. At its summit an Ionic temple rises over the princess's sarcophagus.

The most florid tomb is that of the spiritualist Allan Kardec, under his pseudodolmen. The tomb which, since 1973, has attracted young people the most, particularly hippies, who visit it on pilgrimage from every part of the world, is the tomb of the "pop" musician Jim Morrison, who died a victim of drugs.

Two other "modern" cemeteries were built in the nineteenth century, also under the administration of prefect Frochot: that at Montparnasse in 1824 and that of Montmartre in 1825. The forty-five acres of the Montparnasse cemetery was erected on the site of three farms. Between 1824 and 1874 397,023 Parisians were buried there. The most astonishing tomb of that cemetery-museum is no doubt that of M. and Mme Pigeon, represented life-size in bronze, lying in a middle-class bed. Two remarkable contemporary sculptures are Brancusi's *The Kiss* and a work by Hans Arp over the tomb of his dealer, Pierre Loeb. Sainte-Beuve, Barbey d'Aurevilly, Huysmans, Maupassant, Paul Bourget, Proudhon, François Coppée, and Baudelaire are buried in the Montparnasse cemetery. There are also the authors of two famous dictionaries—Littré and

[9]Ibid.

Larousse—and the publisher Hachette. Music is represented by César
Franck, Vincent d'Indy, Chabrier, and Saint-Saëns. Charles Garnier and
Bouguereau, Bartholdi and Rude, Houdon and Dalou, Bourdelle and
Brancusi, Boucicaut the founder of the Bon Marché store, and the Four
Sergeants of La Rochelle.

For the Montmartre cemetery the architect Molinos proposed placing
mausoleums in underground galleries. In the end the Montmartre cemetery was built in the same spirit as Père-Lachaise and Montparnasse,
that is to say, a majority of vaults, with an exuberance of statues, which
was encouraged by the obligation to buy freehold sites.

There are fewer writers in Montmartre than in Père-Lachaise, but it
contains nevertheless Théophile Gautier, Dumas fils, Heine, Stendhal,
Edmond and Jules de Goncourt, Renan, Alfred de Vigny (in his army
greatcoat), Labiche, and Feydau. Its composers include Léo Delibes,
Offenbach, and Berlioz, who was so fond of strolling there, and its painters
Greuze, Fragonard, and Degas. But it also has Charles Fourier and God-
efroy Cavaignac, Mme Récamier and the Dame aux Camélias, whose
tomb is always plentifully adorned with flowers, Sacha Guitry and Louis
Jouvet, Nijinsky and Clouzot.

The museographical, decorative installation of the dead leads to a historical scene-setting that is both grandiloquent and naive. We have seen
how the tombs of Molière and La Fontaine were coupled at Père-Lachaise,
just as the tomb of Turenne forms the pendant to that of Vauban in the
Invalides. There is the same postmortem dialogue between Racine and
Pascal in the church of Saint-Etienne-du-Mont, between Boileau and
Descartes in the church of Saint-Germain-des-Prés. We make the dead
act out a scene suited to their historical role. Lenin at Moscow in his
glass coffin, Chateaubriand on his island near Saint-Malo, Brecht in his
steel coffin in East Berlin, Pasteur in the Institut Pasteur, Braque at
Varengeville, Le Corbusier at Cap-Martin, Anne of Brittany in Nantes
Cathedral, Montaigne in the chapel of the Lycée of Bordeaux, de Gaulle
at Colombey, all have become signs, symbols. Similarly, Pétain is in
reclusion at Saint-Martin-de-Ré, though an attempt was made to steal
the corpse and bring it (again symbolically) to Douaumont—and the
tomb of Jan Palach, an object of pilgrimage in Prague, has been removed
by the Czech authorities.

At Palermo, in Sicily, a mother, who erected a chapel to the memory
of her son, who had been run over by a bus, thought fit to preserve the
lethal vehicle in the monument as a relic and added to it an altar, complete with religious objects, portraits of the dead boy, images of the pope,

and candles. This is how popular cults begin. "To start a cult, one needs only a burial place, and a guardian."[10]

Is this chapel, which may be thought naive, in fact more so than the church at Brou, entirely conceived as a shrine to the memory of the beloved prince? Or than the very many unintentionally funny tombs, like that of the engineer Apollinaire Le Bas, who, because he had calculated the erection of the obelisk of Luxor, felt obliged to have himself buried under a pyramid decorated with the building plans of the operation; or that of Chappe, who, on a mound of rough stone, erected a telegraph pole, with movable arms, which, at a distance, might be thought to be a television aerial; or Georges Rodenbach's tomb, representing a young man raising a granite gravestone and offering a rose to the passerby; that of the liontamer Pezon seated astride the lion which devoured him; or on the tomb of Louis Vigneron, known as the human cannon, his circus cannon,[11] or that of the engineer, John Wilkinson, who, in 1779, built the first iron bridge in England and was buried in a cast-iron bier; or the tomb of that former wine merchant, in the cemetery at Rochechouart, Haute-Vienne, representing an enormous barrel on its wagon, made of colored concrete, with electricity and a telephone installed inside; or the tomb of the manufacturer of Venetian gondolas, who had his gondola factory represented on his tomb; or the former deportee, who had his gravestone decorated with barbed wire? One could extend this list indefinitely, carrying it right back to antiquity, since in Rome, near the Portus Maximus, the baker Eurysacius had a tomb built in the shape of an oven.

Whether mausoleums or humble graves, the burial places of our "modern" cemeteries in the Latin countries are encumbered with crosses, "souvenirs," and objects of every kind: menhirs, grottoes, sphinxes, snakes, violins, garden chairs, beds (of roses), a planisphere, a van, a motorcyclist at the wheel, a motorbike, a life-size boy scout, a football, an enormous heart (in place of the usual cross), a derailed train and its pileup of carriages, a ship on the verge of shipwreck, a woman feeding birds, an airplane nose diving, a child pushing a wheelbarrow of flowers, a shepherd leading his flock.[12] In short, a whole neurotic accumulation of

---

[10] Marcireau, *Rites étranges.*

[11] All these tombs are in Père-Lachaise.

[12] André Chabot, *Le Petit Monde d'outre-tombe.* (Paris: Cheval d'Attaque, 1978) an album of photographs of 340 contemporary funerary statues and monuments, most of them taken in Père-Lachaise, in the Cimetière de Montmartre, and in cemeteries in the south of France. Unfortunately, the captions, which are supposed to be humorous, are appalling.

Tomb, Mahafaly, Madagascar. *(Albert Moldvay / Editorial Photocolor Archives)*

images, signs, fantasies. But this pathological delusion, which led nineteenth-century man and which leads modern man to set off for the otherworld *accompanied*, while marking as clearly as possible the place at which he has entered the earth in order to cross the "mirror of appearances," merely continues a thousand-year-old tradition. Since no one has received an answer to his interrogation of death, modern man finds himself in his agony at the mercy of the same delusions as our most distant ancestors. Archaeologists are still perplexed by the huge bronze vase found in the Gallic burial place of the dame de Vix: a vase containing 224 gallons, weighing 458 pounds, and measuring 5 feet 4 and a half inches high. Why was such a huge vase, which, no doubt, though we do not know how, had come from Corinth, placed in that Celtic tomb? For what symbolic purpose?

What appropriation does it simulate? Closer to our own time, the tombs of Martinique dating from the early twentieth century, are just as perplexing. Entirely covered with black and white ceramic tiles, they bear a strange resemblance to the paintings and interior decoration of the house of Jean-Pierre Reynaud. This ceramic emphasizes the idea of the field closed for eternity, of the sealed tomb, but also expresses a curious desire for cleanliness, for hygiene. This model kitchen and spotless bathroom aspect, which one finds in the cemeteries of Martinique, is all the more curious in that the houses of the living do not share this aesthetic at all.[13]

Strange, too, and like no other, are the Madagascan tombs, bristling with forked posts and piled high with ox skulls. Carved posts also represent naked men and women, with out-sized sexual organs. The Madagascan tomb, a family property, like the west European vault, is the collective residence of the ancestors. Certain tombs are built for ten, fifty, and even three hundred dead. The bucrania, placed at regular intervals in rows on all four sides of the tomb, were those of the dead man's oxen sacrificed at his death. The Christianity imposed by the French colonists abolished the sacrifice of oxen and, by the same token, the bucrania. But at the top of some recent gravestones are large pieces of white material intended to serve as clothes for the dead who come at night to sit on the stones.[14]

And here we emerge from the museum and enter once again the world of active myth, in the symbolism of the dialogue between living

[13]"Interface: tombeaux à la Martinique," *Créé*, no. 29 (June 1974).

[14]Decary, *La Mort et les coutumes funéraires à Madagascar.*

and dead, though this dialogue is not always absent from our own cemetery-museums. Is this not shown by the fresh flowers that appear on the grave of the Dame aux Camélias, in Montmartre cemetery? As also do the vengeful inscriptions on the tomb of M. Thiers.

7

War Memorials

Consider the thousands of millions of francs expended on the thirty-six-thousand war memorials, of which thirty thousand at least are an insult to the memory of those to whom they were erected. What prescience was displayed by that far-sighted diplomat who proposed as the test of the first article of the Treaty of Versailles: that all war memorials should be erected in the defeated countries.

Jean Giraudoux

When one speaks of war memorials, one thinks of the memorials erected to the memory of the soldiers killed in the 1914–18 war. Indeed it was a phenomenon unique in both extent and duration. Between 1920 and 1925 the municipal councils of every commune in France, with the agreement of the families of the victims, had a memorial erected.[1] These 36,000 monuments, built in five years, that is, over sixteen a day, are the only secular edifice to compete with the church. That is to say, both are the object of a cult. At both, ritual ceremonies take place at certain fixed dates. As a collective cenotaph, the memorial of World War I has become the emblem of the nation, of the republic. Ancestor worship, which had disappeared from the Christian West, revived around these memorials. This is particularly clear in the list of names, so moving in small villages,

[1] With the exception of one of Thierville, in the department of the Eure, the only French village to have suffered no loss of life either in the 1914–18 War, in that of 1870, or in that of 1939–45.

[107

Monument to the Russian soldier of World War II, East Berlin. *(Photo SEF / Editorial Photocolor Archives)*

where one can no longer see clearly the extent of the massacre since the same surnames recur in the wars of 1870, 1914, and 1940. For on the monuments of the 1914 war were added the names of the victims of the other wars: that of 1870 and the more recent ones of 1939–45, Indochina, and Algeria. The memorial to the dead of the 1914 war has become, therefore, quite simply, the memorial to the dead of all wars.

Conceived at first as monuments to victory, they soon became monuments to suffering, to the memory of those who had gone off and had not come back, to the unlucky comrades, to the sons and fathers snatched from their land. The Panthéon of great men in Paris is little more than a curiosity. The Arc de Triomphe, at the Etoile, the supreme war memorial, is, despite the daily ritual of relighting the flame on the tomb of the unknown soldier, above all a tourist site. The war memorial assumes its full significance only in the villages, townships, and small towns, in places where a community life still survives, where the names on the memorial have faces for those who read them. Every public festival sees them bedecked with decorations; not an anniversary passes without its bouquets of flowers. Usually they are surrounded by a small garden, carefully maintained by the municipality. Many of the memorials are identical from one village to another, quite simply because they were manufactured. Depending on the resources available, the commune bought a bronze soldier or merely surmounted a stela with a Gallic cock or a bare stone, the obelisk of the poor.

Giraudoux's irony—and resentment—in the lines quoted as epigraph are easily explained by a regret that almost none of those memorials is the work of a significant modern sculptor. But if they had been, these monuments would no doubt have become museum objects. The tourist circuits would have included a visit to a particular memorial by Brancusi in a particular village, another memorial by Lipchitz, or Zadkine, or Maillol elsewhere. Though the creations of jobbing workmen, they have been transformed into popular sculptures, corresponding to the majority taste of the population. Their aesthetic is certainly a decline from the flourishing academic statuary of Père-Lachaise. But they also express a taste for melodrama, for the fine gesture, for the bawdy song. There is a certain old-fashioned vulgarity about them that betrays their plebeian and petty-bourgeois origin. In particular, one sees this in the taste for accumulation that is also to be found in, say, concierges' lodges or in working-class gardens: old shells used as fences, heavy chains.

The modern sculptor Olivier Descamps has made a remarkable analysis of what he rightly calls a "quite exceptional manifestation of public art."[2] Before 1920, he reminds us, the public monuments of agricultural villages had only three themes: the fountain, the crucifix, and the Virgin. The municipal councils of the postwar period found themselves caught between the religious convictions of most of the families, and the secular ideology of the Third Republic. The state wanted monuments that in no way suggested religious practice. The sculptors approached, all establishment artists (Prix de Rome, art-school professors), had to invent a new mortuary iconography that owed nothing to Christianity. And so, twenty years after the separation of church and state, there reappeared pagan forms of mortuary art: the menhir, the obelisk, the pyramid, the draped urn, the broken column, and, of course, the Gallic cock, replacing the cross. The sculptors applied realism in representing the detail of weapons and uniform and arrived at a sort of stereotyped portrait of the sacrificed soldier.

[2] Olivier Descamps, *Les Monuments aux morts de la guerre 14–18 chefs-d'oeuvre d'art public* (Paris-Lyon: Cahiers d'art public Francis Deswarte, 1978).

Olivier Descamps stresses that the memorials of World War I were "the first public monuments that dared to use the products of modern industry": fences made of old shells, for example. "Whereas the history of art constantly insists on the genius required of Marcel Duchamp to exhibit a bottle dryer and a urinal in an art exhibition, how is it that the introduction of industrial objects into public art passed unperceived? . . . The rules of the Beautiful have evolved since 1920, and the statues have aged, but the shells have changed neither in form nor in material, and Dynamics Bound has kept intact its charge of naive and desperate poetry."[3]

The war memorial is, of course, a secularization of the Calvary, and one finds in it those martyrs' palms previously taken over by Christian iconography. But it is true nonetheless that the war memorial in each village is the only monument that is as living, and as frequented, as the church. Quite often, indeed, in certain regions where almost total de-Christianization has practically disaffected the church, the war memorial remains the only place which is the object of a regular cult. This creation of a monument, a secular and republican symbol, which the First Republic tried obstinately, but unsuccessfully, to bring about, was perfectly achieved by the Third Republic, and, fifty years later, has lost none of its meaning.

World War I also brought about the creation of specifically military cemeteries, with their endless rows of identical crosses. As the only egalitarian cemeteries, they have revived, though this was no doubt not their intention, the character of the old *campi santi*. But in their impeccable symmetry of identical graves they also suggest the discipline of the serried ranks of the army.

World War II gave rise, on the contrary, on the sites of great battles, to the creation of an audiovisual spectacle, with real weapons, and real uniforms. War as if you had actually been there! But none of these museums has anything but historical interest, while the ossuary of Douaumont, without music and without photographic slides, pulls at your heartstrings.

Our "society of spectacle" could not fail to turn the sites of great battles into shows. Up to the nineteenth century all great battles that left a region littered with dead sowed terror all around, for, very often,

[3] Ibid. It should be noted that Duchamp's bottle dryer dates from 1914 and his urinal from 1917. There is, therefore, no influence on Duchamp of the art of the war memorial. But it is also true that Duchamp in no way influenced the aesthetic of the war memorial. Nevertheless, Duchamp's ready-mades and the anonymous fences made of shells both came out of World War I.

plague or cholera followed. The soldiers, stripped of their uniforms, were buried on the spot in common graves, and the officers were buried in the nearest church. After the battle of Sedan, in 1870, the population of the Ardennes appealed for help to the Belgian government, which immediately sent a chemist to the battlefield. The chemist quite simply spread tar over the corpses and set light to them.

In certain French departments, notably in the Loiret, monuments were erected after 1870 to the victims of the recent war. But these monuments were placed on the sites of the battles. They usually consisted of small obelisks, bearing the names of the victims, which anticipates directly therefore the memorials of World War I. But, situated well away from the villages, often in the middle of fields, they did not become active symbols.

According to Ariès, the first monument to dead soldiers was erected at Lucerne, to the memory of the Swiss guard murdered in Paris on August 10, 1792. And the second, again according to Ariès, appears to be the monument that the Restoration had constructed at Quiberon to the memory of the émigrés who tried to land in Brittany in 1795 and were shot and buried on the spot.[4] There, again, however, ancient necrological customs preceded ours, and we have merely reinvented what had already existed in the Athenian democracy. For its soldiers who died in battle, Athens erected monumental stelae around the anonymous graves of the assembled warriors. On them one could read the names of the tribes and even sometimes those of the combatants themselves. "To this day the plain of Marathon is dominated by a steep artificial mound that covers the burial place of the dead heroes."[5]

The nineteenth century also created, in Paris, two monuments to the dead that have become virtual "museums," as they have lost their primary significance.

Between 1808 and 1836, following plans put forward by the architect Chalgrin, a triumphal arch was erected on the Place de l'Etoile, which is, for several reasons, a funerary monument. First, it is a monument to Napoleon's generals, auxiliaries of death indeed: a commission entrusted with the task of examining the names of the generals that might be inscribed on the triumphal arch came up with 660, plus the names of 128 battles. It is also a monument to the dead, on account of the illustrious men who made a final halt here: Napoleon led the procession in 1840, followed by Thiers in 1877, Gambetta in 1882, Victor Hugo in 1885,

---

[4] Ariès, *L'Homme devant la mort*.
[5] Le Clère, *Cimetières et Sépultures de Paris*.

and, after some delay, Rouget de l'Isle in 1915. Last, it is a monument to the dead by virtue of the unknown soldier who was buried beneath a bronze gravestone on January 28, 1921. Twelve coffins from the most lethal battlefields were presented to a soldier who had been blinded in the war, and he chose one at random. Since November 11, 1923, each evening a flame is rekindled to the memory of the million and a half dead of World War I.

If the presence of the tomb of the unknown warrior still gives the Arc de Triomphe de l'Etoile an obviously funerary character, the Colonne de Juillet, in the Place de la Bastille, has lost all mortuary significance. Yet 509 names are inscribed on it. They are those of the citizens who died during the revolution of 1830. Hastily buried after the street fighting, in front of the colonnade of the Louvre, in the Champ-de-Mars, and in the garden of the Bibliothèque Nationale, they were exhumed on July 28, 1839, and placed in a circular vault, corresponding to the basement of the column erected by the architects Alavoine and Baltard, surmounted, at a height of 165 feet, by Dumont's statue *Genius of Liberty*. After the bloody days of February 1848, the provisional government laid down that the dead of the new revolution would be placed beneath the Bastille Column. A hundred and ninety-six coffins were placed there on March 4, 1848. There they joined the remains of hundreds of prisoners of the Bastille, buried in surrounding ditches. Among these bones were no doubt those of Bernard Palissy.[6]

---

[6] Bernard Palissy (c. 1510–1590) was a French potter, enameler, writer, and scientist. Arrested in 1589 as a Huguenot, he was imprisoned in the Bastille and probably died the following year (Translator's Note).

8

The Vegetal Setting

of Death

Why cypresses in cemeteries, wreaths of flowers at burials, chrysanthemums on All Saints' Day? The vegetal setting of death also has its own long history and, again, our customs are merely reminiscences of Greco-Roman antiquity.

Evergreen conifers and wood so hard that it was almost rot-proof were quite naturally chosen as symbols of immortality. The cedar, whose longevity is exceptional, the box tree dedicated to Pluto, god of the underworld, the cypress, whose branches were used on Greek and Roman funeral pyres, soon became trees and shrubs dedicated to death. Chaldeans, Syrians, and Assyrians regarded the pyramidal cypress as sacred. The Muslim world and even China adopted the cypress as a tree of death. Quite naturally, the Romans planted cypresses in Provence, where they proliferated, spreading out well beyond the mortuary setting. In northern Europe the yew and the box took on the same significance as the Mediterranean cypress. Thousand-year-old yews are still to be found in northern cemeteries. Escaping this custom, Alsace adopted the fir, Poitou the walnut tree, and Wales the rowan, once the sacred tree of the Druids.

Arnold Van Gennep makes some sarcastic remarks about the weeping willow, which he says is both a romantic invention and a joke.[1] But although in Western Europe the weeping willow appears mainly in the cemetery-museums of the nineteenth century, the willow, which is common on the banks of the Nile, was already being used by the pharaohs to weave funerary wreaths. So, whether or not a joke, this tree seems to have found its way to the environment and setting of death at a very early date.

Greek and Roman cemeteries, which were sometimes funerary gardens, were decorated with beds of roses and other flowers used as ritual offerings. Cypresses and box trees were planted in rows between the tombs.

As for chrysanthemums, so indissolubly linked today with November 1, which the church made the feast of All Saints and which has become secularized into the feast of all the dead, their use is relatively recent. They seem to have first appeared on the Toulouse markets about 1830, and it was only after 1880 that they became commonly used as flowers in cemeteries. Is it a coincidence that Pierre Loti's *Madame Chrysanthème* was published in 1887?

Viollet-le-Duc tells us that in the course of his excavations he often found under the remains of persons buried between the twelfth and fourteenth centuries "still clearly visible litters of herbs and flowers, in particular roses, easily recognizable by their spiny stems."[2]

This custom, which comes to us from Roman civilization, goes back as far as ancient Egypt. Garlands, with leaves of willow and delphinium, decorated the mummy of Ahmos, the founder of the eighteenth dynasty (1700 B.C.). Flowers were found in all the ancient Egyptian burial places: rosemary, reseda, mint, stocks, laurel, olive, myrtle. There were so many yellow flowers among them that we may conclude that this color was associated with mourning in Egypt. The lotus, the emblem of resurrection, is to be found only in the form of painting or sculpture on the monument, not as real flowers in the grave.

[1] Van Gennep, *Manuel de folklore*, vol. 2.
[2] Viollet-le-Duc, *Dictionnaire raisonné de l'architecture française*.

But the practice of placing flowers in graves goes back well beyond ancient Egypt since a recent excavation in a cave in Iraq has revealed eight Neanderthal skeletons that have retained traces of pollen, analysis of which suggests that they must have been laid out on a litter of flowers.

It is hardly surprising that the Catholic Church tried to steer its faithful away from a practice so strongly imbued with paganism. In the second century B.C., Tertullian criticizes the use of flowers and wreaths. But in Romanized and Christian Gaul cypresses were planted in the cemeteries of the south, yews in those of the north. Sulpicius Severus speaks of a pine near an ancient temple which the Christians of Saint Martin's time still visited and worshipped. The cemetery yew remained for so long a sacred tree for country people that they were still recounting on the island of Bréa, in the nineteenth century, how parishioners spent their time in purgatory "in the branches of the beautiful cemetery yew trees." And H. Bourde de la Rougerie, who reports this fact, adds to it an episode in the struggle waged by the bishops against the pagan trees of cemeteries.[3] In 1636 the bishop of Rennes ordered that all the yews be "uprooted and removed from the cemeteries because the people of the fields make evil use of them." There followed a general uprooting of trees from the Breton cemeteries, but there was a good deal of resistance by the peasants to the bishop's orders. At Plouasne, for example, they nearly killed their rector when he tried to implement the order, and he had to barricade himself in the sacristy.

Yews were replanted in the Breton cemeteries in such large numbers that Anatole Le Braz remarked in the last century that a yew was growing out of the mouth of every corpse.[4]

During the period of the Church Triumphant, that is to say, the seventeenth and eighteenth centuries, all planting was forbidden in cemeteries. A decree of the Paris *parlement*, of May 21, 1765, forbids "the porter and anyone else to plant any tree or shrub in the said cemeteries." This rejection of pagan customs was backed up by arguments based on hygiene. It was believed, in fact, that trees impeded the circulation of

---

[3] H. Bourde de la Rougerie, *Le Parlement de Bretagne, l'évêque de Rennes et les ifs plantés dans les cimetières, 1636–37* (Rennes, 1931).

[4] But, as we know, medieval cemeteries usually had only a single cross and practically no monuments. Similarly, although trees were planted in them, there were always very few of them, usually a single yew in the middle of the cemetery and another at the church door. The former cemetery of Saint Paul, where Rabelais is believed to have been buried under the shade of a walnut tree (others say a fig tree) and which in the Middle Ages possessed an avenue of trees, is cited as an exceptional case.

air. In the late nineteenth century the church, which had finally admitted trees into cemeteries (because they were now regarded as purifiers of the air), turned its attacks on funeral wreaths, a pagan rite if ever there was one. An article by Georges Gibault, librarian of the Société nationale d'horticulture de France, makes a vigorous defense of flowers and wreaths in the name of "the interests of flower growers, florists, and an entire industry which supports thousands of individuals."[5]

These funeral wreaths are a custom that was practiced by the Egyptians, the Etruscans, the Greeks, and the Romans. The Greek wreaths, woven to the size of a head, were first made up of a simple branch of foliage tied together at its ends. Then flowers were inserted into it. Special books were written in Greece on how to weave wreaths for various purposes—civic, naval, triumphal, mural, obsidional, and so on. Plutarch speaks of the funeral wreaths at the obsequies of King Numa, second king of Rome. Alexander laid a wreath on the grave of Achilles, and the emperor Augustus did likewise on Alexander's grave. Roman funeral beds were strewn with flowers and decorated with wreaths. On the head of the dead man a crown of natural flowers, or a gold crown imitating foliage, was placed. All these crowns disappeared, of course, in the cremation, but we know that they were made up of amarant, immortelle, asphodel, violets, narcissi, ivy, myrtle, laurel, and olive. In Roman antiquity roses were also scattered on graves. The Egyptian sarcophagi have yielded a great many natural wreaths, perfectly preserved, concrete expressions of Egyptian funerary ritual: "You live for eternity. . . Receive this fine crown of justice."

The first Christians, whether under the worst persecutions or at the time of Constantine, adopted the palms and wreaths of pagan ceremonial. But did not Saint Paul speak of the crown of glory reserved for the elect? And did not the fathers of the church, taking up a comparison of the Greek philosophers, compare life to a chariot race in which the crown awaited the victor? So on the first Christian tombs were hung, or represented, wreaths or crowns of laurel, flowers, precious metals, in imitation of those metal crowns found so often in Etruscan necropolises. The idea of a crown was often associated with that of martyrdom ("he won the martyr's crown," Acts of the Apostles). The leaf of the date palm, handed out to the victors of pagan games, even became the em-

[5] Georges Gibault, "Les fleurs et les couronnes de fleurs naturelles aux funérailles," *Revue horticole*, November 16, 1902. We are also referred to an article by the same author: "Les fleurs et les tombeaux," *Jardin*, 1902.

blem of the martyrs so often put to death in the circus. Saint Jerome speaks of the violets, roses, and lilies scattered over the tombs of their wives by widowers. And Saint Gregory of Tours describes the crowns fixed on the tomb of Saint Martin. In speaking of the tombs of the early Christians, Father Ménestrier says: "Lamps were lighted over these tombs, crowns were tied to them, flowers were thrown on them, and though pagans used similar ceremonies, the Christians were never accused for all that of doing anything that smacked of paganism."[6]

Father Ménestrier pleads for more pomp and circumstance in funerals of which, in the seventeenth century, he was one of the great organizers, and expresses regret that crowns and wreaths had become no more than symbolic, and made only of marble.

Wreaths of natural flowers reappeared in the nineteenth century with the fashion for wreaths of immortelle (a play on words, as in the case of the weeping willow), made up of dried flowers. Ollioules, near Bandol, in Provence, became the center for the growing of immortelle, in the 1820s, and for the production of funeral wreaths. In 1834 the consumption of immortelle in Paris was already considerable. Whereas, traditionally, the wreath never exceeded the diameter of a head, huge wreaths of natural flowers for funeral processions became fashionable in the late nineteenth century. Vegetal decoration then assumed megalomaniac proportions in the funerals of well-known persons. On June 20, 1877, the hearse of Queen Sophie of Holland was covered with natural flowers woven together into garlands. On September 8 of the same year Auguste Thiers's hearse disappeared beneath flowers, palms, and greenery. Huge wreaths of natural flowers were carried by delegates from the towns of France. *L'Illustration* mentions a large wreath of violets on which was inscribed, in white roses: "From the youth of Paris to Monsieur Thiers."

Finally, at the funeral of President Carnot certain wreaths were thirty-two feet in circumference. Georges Gibault cites this funeral as a "triumph of floral art. It was estimated that the cost of the flowers ordered for this national act of mourning amounted to the sum of three million francs."[7]

Certain twentieth-century cemeteries have an architectural composition made up of vegetal screens and clipped bushes, like the cemetery of the village of Boiscommun, in the Loiret, with its odd plantings reminiscent of the *jardin à la française*. Two great avenues bordered with clipped trees intersect perpendicularly, and the small paths are flanked

[6]C. F. Ménestrier, *Des décorations funèbres . . .* (Paris: 1683).
[7]Gibault, "Les fleurs et les couronnes de fleurs."

by clipped box trees. While in the cemetery at Forcalquier, which is visited as a kind of "green museum," its vegetal walls are over sixteen feet high.

Cypresses, yews, and box trees form part of the now almost obligatory setting of the cemetery. Flowers in vases or pots decorate the graves, but they are so often stolen that the cemetery administrators have had to forbid the carrying of suitcases or bags.

9

The Architecture of the Beyond

Man is instinctively that improvising architect who is as much concerned with his installation in the beyond, his residence in eternity, as with his temporal habitation.

Robert Auzelle
Dernières demeures, 1965

Descriptions of hell, heaven, and purgatory are fairly vague as to the architectural setting. There, too, one has the impression that what one is seeing is a mirror image of the architecture of the living. Hell is a double—or rather it is our earthly hell transposed. "What need have we to look for hell in another life?" asked Jean Jacques Rousseau, for whom the devil was Voltaire. And Schopenhauer remarked, "Where did Dante find the elements of his hell if not in this world."

Virgil and Dante visit hell as poets. Their journey, guided by the initiatory cartography of ancient Egypt, has nothing surprising about it. It is as if they were still on earth and in the society of their time. One knows very well, however, that they are making it up, that they are telling a poetic story. But, on the other hand, the theosophists believe that their incursions into the beyond are real. We shall see with Swe-

[119

denborg and other travelers who claim to have come back from the otherworld that it differs even less from our everyday life.

Hell, there can be no doubt, is as old as the world. Heaven, on the other hand, is a more recent creation. In the most distant antiquity, hell, or rather the underworld, was the place where the dead, all the dead, resided.

The universal practice of burial led quite naturally to the thought that the dead lived in the bowels of the earth. The sun that each evening sank on the horizon traveled through its vast cavities. Thus each night it visited the residence of the dead and emerged again each morning in the East. Like Greece, Japan had its Orpheus legend. Izanagi also descended into the underworld in order to bring back his wife.

Homer, on the other hand, situated the kingdom of the shades at the ends of the earth, beyond the ocean. And the Pythagoreans shifted the residence of the dead to the moon.[1] This belief in the moon as residence of the dead persisted for a long time, as we can see in the frequent appearance of crescent moons on Gallo-Roman tombs, and Christians were vigorously opposed to this practice.

Primitive Egypt had no hell. It was only about 1600–1000 B.C. that this punitive beyond, which must have inspired Plato and which was then to pass into Christian doctrine, emerged. The idea of two residences of the dead, one of punishment and the other of reward, only appeared slowly therefore. Before its deportation to Babylon (seventh century B.C.), the Jewish Sheol, like the Mesopotamian Aralu, was also simply a residence of the dead without punishment.

Nevertheless, the idea of a terrible hell soon became as universal as the idea of God and was to be found among the Chaldeans, Babylonians, Etruscans, the Celts, the Teutons, Oceanians, Black Africans, and pre-Columbian Americans. Thus all men have projected into an elsewhere the hell that was in themselves, just as God is a projection of the divine in us. Hell is a transcription of our ancestral terrors, and paradise a fixation of our utopias.

Some hells are more terrible than others. For Origen (third century A.D.), hell was scarcely more than a benign and temporary correction chamber. The Sheol of the Hebrews was only a sort of subterranean area, a dark tomb rather than a place of torment. On the other hand, Greeks and Romans made such horrible descriptions of hell that Epicurus made fun of them, and many philosophers relegated these visions to

---

[1] Cumont, *Recherches*.

the world of fable. Why is so little credence accorded to hell in the Christian West today? Is it because the daily descriptions by the media of earthly hells make the tortures of the medieval hell anachronistic? The Nazi concentration camps, the Soviet Gulag, torture in Latin America, the famine of Sahel, genocide in Cambodia are so many visions of a photographed, filmed hell. What need have we to imagine another hell?

Hell, situated at the center of the earth, is a brazier, a cauldron of boiling oil. This burning liquid, these lakes of fire, depicted in medieval iconology, already existed in the hell of ancient Egypt. The damned burned there without being consumed. This infernal fire is also to be found in Plato and again in the *Aeneid*, written twenty or so years before the birth of Christ. "Aeneas looked behind him, and, to the left, at the foot of a rock, he saw a broad enclosure formed by a triple wall, surrounded by torrents of flame from a fast-moving river." Saint John's Apocalypse describes "a lake of fire and sulphur." The fathers of the church spoke of the "hard and bitter," "cruel, inextinguishable, unbearable" fire of hell, and Saint Thomas Aquinas practically turned it into a dogma. The Buddhist hell describes similar scorchings and burnings.[2]

The Zoroastrian hell, on the other hand, is cold.

The Breton legends collected by Anatole Le Braz also describe a frozen hell—like the Lapp hell in its frozen lake. The Chinese hell is subdivided into eight hot hells and eight cold ones. There are 28 hells in the Sanskrit *Law of Manu* and 256 in the *Majjimanikaya*.

Brahmanism has twenty-one hells, Buddhism forty. Mictlam, the Aztec hell, is situated in the north. The soul sets out for it accompanied by a dog god, Xolotl, who, like Cerberus, is also guardian of the beyond. This Aztec hell is a dark, subterranean pit where night is eternal.

For hell and the underworld have this in common, that they are a furnace and that, despite the flames, the darkness is total. The Greek Hades and the Hebrew Sheol confirm this—and Saint Theresa of Avila even more so: "The entrance seemed to be by a long narrow pass, like a furnace, very low, dark, and close. The ground seemed to be saturated with water, mere mud, exceedingly foul, sending forth pestilential odors and covered with loathsome vermin. At the end was a hollow place in the wall, like a closet, and in that I saw myself confined. . . Those walls, terrible to look on themselves, hemmed me in on every side. I could not

[2] "Doctor Swinden in his researches into the fire of hell, claims that hell is in the sun, because the sun is a perpetual fire" (J. Collin de Plancy, *Dictionnaire infernal* [Paris, 1863]).

breathe. There was no light, but all was thick darkness. I do not understand how it is; though there was no light, everything that could give
pain by being seen was visible."[3]

Hell is subterranean. Saint Thomas Aquinas devotes an article of his
Summa Theologica to proving it. The posthumous Taoist world is also
underground but in the form of "an immense cesspit."[4] One descends
into hell, just as one ascends into heaven. The Sheol speaks of the "depths
of the abyss," the same abyss described in *The Divine Comedy* as conical
and created by the fall of Lucifer.

The descent into the underworld has given rise to a whole literature,
rather like travelers' tales. "An immense, deep pit under the earth, lower
than the sea and the foundation of the mountains," the Old Testament
tells us. After the funeral the spirit of the dead Egyptian went to a
mountain where the entrance to the underworld was to be found. He
descended into it by a route similar to that taken by the sun each evening. But what the spirit of the dead man found in the bowels of the
earth was an exact replica of the Egypt on the earth's surface. A river,
father of all the gods, subdivided the underworld into twelve regions,
like the pharaonic empire. In the Egyptian underworld, a cartographical
replica of Egypt, the domain of night was divided into hours, and the
gates that led from one hour to another were identical with those of the
fortresses of earthly architecture. A corridor led between two walls studded with spikes. Just as the funerary statue, a replica of the living body,
constituted its double, the life of the beyond was absolutely identical
with earthly life, the only difference being was that it was eternal.

The Coptic books, which, as much as those of Plato, provided Christianity with a hell in the image of that of ancient Egypt, placed hell at
the same place as the tomb of the god Sokar (god of the Sparrow hawks),
and at an enormous depth. The spirit of the dead man needed a whole
day to reach the bottom.

Like Orpheus, Jesus descended into the underworld after his death
on the cross, "broke the locks, threw down the gates, tied up Satan and
delivered the souls."[5] This belief of the primitive church became a dogma
in the ninth century at the instigation of the Frankish church. These
men of war turned Christ into a warrior whom none could oppose. Christ
brought Satan down and freed the Just imprisoned in hell. He reopened

[3] *The Life of St Teresa of Avila*, trans. David Lewis (London: Burns and Oates, 1962).
[4] Paul Ghisoni, *Eschatologie infernale* (Paris: La Colombe, 1962).
[5] Jean Monnier, *La Descente aux Enfers*, D. Theol. diss., Faculté de Théologie protestante de Paris, 1904.

the gates of paradise that had been shut by Adam's sin. In the iconography of the late Middle Ages, Christ carries his cross like a weapon, a halberd with which he brings the Devil down. "Christ is greeted on his return from hell as the inhabitants of a besieged city greet the banner of their liberator."[6]

Hell, a dark cave beneath a mountain, became in the thirteenth century a fortress, the "devil's castle." The kingdom of hades was given a drawbridge. It was surrounded by an outer wall bristling with towers and battlements from which the devils sounded their horns.

Dante, a man of this time, had no other way of describing hell. Deep ditches surround an isolated city whose walls seem to be made of iron. He arrives at the foot of a tower, has to cross muddy water in a boat which, of course, is that of Charon.

The medieval hell, however, usually keeps the image of the cave, also to be found in Greco-Roman antiquity, as the entrance to the underworld. Sometimes flames, pouring furiously out of it, are added. The Greco-Roman hell is more welcoming. Although the number of fires increases on the infernal journey, the entrance to hell is rather bucolic. It is a normal cave in which we see Aeneas and the Sibyl enter without fear. The Sheol was enclosed by gates secured by bars. Seven gates defended the Sumerian Aralu. The figure seven had already made its appearance for the Semites, who placed paradise in the seventh heaven. The Muslim hell also has seven doors, and each of the elect has seventy robes at his disposal.

The Greek Hades is closed by an iron gate and a threshold of bronze. The Styx is a river that winds round hades nine times. The boatman, Charon, ferries the souls in a barge after taking as his fee the coin placed in the mouths of the dead.

All infernal architecture comprises an outer wall and a solemn gate. "Opposite was a huge gate and pillars of solid steel. . . an iron tower rose up into the air," writes Virgil. "We arrived at the foot of a huge castle, seven times surrounded by high walls, whose approaches were defended by a fine stream. We crossed it as one does on firm ground; I passed through seven gates," writes Dante.

The image of the house, which as we have seen is always associated with that of the grave, disappears entirely from hell. There then appears that of the prison, with a gate, that is both open and shut. In Virgil's hell furies shout and scream in iron chambers. The Islamic hell is "a

---

[6] Ibid.

subterranean prison, hermetically sealed, divided into several increasingly low catacombs."[7] Seven gates enclose special categories of damned souls. But all are bound, in flames or in boiling water, and can drink only fetid water. The tortured souls are tormented by innumerable animals. There are camels, goats, and cows, but they have been transformed into monsters. Serpents and scorpians bite and sting the inmates.

The Christian hell is also described as "a dungeon filled with the deepest darkness." Saint John, in the Apocalypse, peoples it with dragons, serpents, and worms. Fire and worms are curiously associated in the horror of the Christian hell. "The worm of the wicked shall not die, their fire shall not be quenched," says Isaiah. "In the Gehenna a fire, where the worm of the damned does not die," says the gospel according to Saint Mark.[8]

In the mystery plays of the Middle Ages, hell's mouth was always marked by Herlequin's cope. The Herlequins were a family of medieval devils that were to reappear in a rather more civilized form in the commedia dell'arte under the name of Arlecchino. The seducer Harlequin is still an image of death. He is an avatar of Persephone, goddess of the underworld.[9]

The Homeric hades did have its tortures, since those of Tantalus, Sisyphus, and the Danaidae are described. But those which appear in the *Aeneid* and which were to seem so terrifying to Augustus' sister, Octavia, that she fainted when Virgil read his descent into the underworld to them, come directly from the Egyptian model. The journey of Aeneas and the priestess Sibyl is "exactly the Latin counterpart of the journey which the dead of Egypt made to descend to the places of justification and eternal happiness."[10] The Elysian fields, of which Virgil speaks, are called Fields of Yalu in the Egyptian *Book of the Dead*. And Virgil has these Elysian fields crossed by the river Po, just as the Fields of Yalu were crossed by the Nile. Virgil no doubt drew directly on Egyptian mythology, but Virgil's ideas are all to be found in Greek authors, especially in Plato, who seems to have been an initiate of Egyptian esotericism. Saint John's Apocalypse also derives from the beliefs and poetry of ancient Egypt—through Virgil, certainly, a Latin author with a huge audience at the very beginning of the Christian period, but also through Christian Egyptian anchorites who, unconsciously, were to

[7] Soubhi El-Saleh, *La Vie future selon le Coran* (Paris: Vrin, 1971).

[8] Abbé Louis Brémond, *Le Conception catholique de l'enfer* (Paris: Bloud et Barral, 1900).

[9] Menahem, *La Mort apprivoisée*.

[10] E. Amélineau, *L'Enfer égyptien et l'enfer virgilien: Etude de mythologie comparée* (Paris: Ecole pratique des hautes etudes, annuaire 1914–15).

propagate ancient Egyptian ideas on the beyond. In its beginnings, however, Christianity was of Greek obedience and was to describe its hell more in the image of Hades than of Tartarus. The damned were to appear later, when the idea of judgment superseded that of sleep.[11] The early Christians slept while awaiting an imminent resurrection. As the "great evening" dragged on, some policing organization had to be set up while awaiting the Last Judgment.

In a mythology that is very garden-oriented—it all begins in the Garden of Eden, and the Fall of Adam is accompanied by the loss of a gardener's sinecure and the obligation to plow the fields and tend the animals—two gardens are to emerge in Christian mythology: the garden of torment and the garden of delights.

Let us deal first with the garden of delights.

Paradise comes from a Persian word meaning "pleasure garden." Moses describes paradise as a garden with shady trees and delicious fruit. Mohammed describes it in the same way, adding that it is irrigated by four rivers. These shady, cool, watered gardens occur quite naturally to the utopian imagination of desert peoples, made hot and thirsty by sun and sand. The primitive people of Greenland, however, situated their paradise at the bottom of the ocean, beyond the visible icecaps. It was perpetual summer there, and reindeer and dogs were in abundance. The early Christians, all Mediterraneans, also saw their paradise, of course, as a place of coolness. But also, quite naturally, as Christianity reached the northern regions of Europe, coolness is replaced by eternal summer.

Paradise not only transcends a climatic aspiration, it also transposes the ideals of the dominant classes, such as masculinity. Aristotle saw no other posthumous life for the Greek slave than a servile one. The Muslim paradise abounds in houri servant girls. Christianity, on the other hand, as an expression of the dominated classes, claims the immortality of the poor and the equality of all the Elect. Although, in the underworld of antiquity the occupations of the beyond continued very precisely those of this world, in the Christian beyond everything changes. But although the images of hell, taken over in their entirety from those of ancient philosophy and esotericism, are precise, the new vision of the

[11] Early Christian iconography depicts the Elect, and not the damned. The portrayal of the Last Judgment, with its separation of the good and the wicked, does not appear until the twelfth century, in the church of Sainte-Foy-de-Conques. The Gothic style, which marks the triumph of monarchy, introduces the law court. Christ the King, seated on a judge's throne, is surrounded by angel-soldiers. The weighing of souls may also be related to the calculating spirit of a mercantile civilization, a new power with a great future before it.

[125

Christian paradise remains vague. Angels, taken from the winged devils of antiquity, play on the harp and trumpet. The Elect sing and dance in light. There is no work, no care, no sexuality. But anyone can get tired of singing and dancing forever.

Saint Paul said to the Philippians: "Our city is in heaven." But nineteen centuries later Jacques Maritain, after questioning himself like so many other theologians as to the architecture of the celestial Jerusalem, concluded: "Heaven is unimaginable."

Camille Flammarion, both an astronomer and an occultist, reflecting on the expression "to be in heaven," replied like a good astronomer: "The earth is in the heavens. Therefore we are in heaven. There is neither up nor down in the universe." And the devotee of the occult sciences added: "The dead who communicate with us speak neither of heaven nor of hell, nor of Islamic gardens, nor of the Greek Elysian fields, nor of the Hindu Nirvana."[12]

So where do they speak from? Where do they come from? Where are they? Just as Theresa of Avila had the advantage over Virgil that she had actually seen hell (or thought she had), Emmanuel Swedenborg also describes his journey to paradise:

> I have seen the palaces of heaven which were so magnificent that they cannot be described. Above, they glittered as if made of pure gold, and below, as if made of precious stones. . . Neither words nor knowledge are adequate to describe the decorations that adorned the rooms. . . the temples in the spiritual kingdom seemed to be of stone and those of the celestial kingdom of wood. The reason for this is that stone corresponds to truth in which are those in the spiritual kingdom, while wood corresponds to good in which are those in the celestial kingdom. As there are societies in heaven and the angels live as men they have also dwellings and these differ in accordance with each one's state of life. They are magnificent for those in a higher state of dignity and less magnificent for those in a lower state.[13]

As we see, in the eighteenth century the Christian paradise had become much less egalitarian. But what concerns us in Swedenborg's account is the reappearance of houses, which no one had ever seen in hell.

---

[12] Flammarion, *La Mort et son mystère*, vol. 3. "If we pass from astronomy to astrology, we observe that the heavens are divided into twelve *houses* and that the eighth is the house of death" (ibid).

[13] Emmanuel Swedenborg, *Heaven and Its Wonders and Hell from Things Heard and Seen* (London: The Swedenborg Society, 1958).

"They have dwellings which are called heavenly habitations and these surpass earthly habitations in magnificence. . . In them are chambers, inner rooms and bedrooms in great number. There are also courts and around them gardens, flowerbeds and lawns. Where they live in societies, their houses are near each other, one alongside another, arranged in the form of a city, with streets, roads and public squares exactly like the cities on our earth."[14]

This represents a return, therefore, of the phenomenon of the mirror, of the double. We saw how the city of Babylon was the exact reproduction of the paradise of the Sumerians.[15] In the nineteenth century the similarity between paradise and bourgeois life appeared among certain English romantic authors, like Elizabeth Stuart, who imagined the life of the inhabitants of heaven with drawing rooms in which poor girls were allowed to play the piano.[16]

The house, the *domus*, is also at the heart of the Albigensian paradise as described by the shepherds of Montaillou. "For the people of Montaillou, heaven would be one huge *domus*. . . 'There every soul will have as much wealth and happiness as every other; and all will be as one. And all the souls will love one another as if they loved the soul of their father or their children.' 'Great and rich ladies' continued to ride in carriages over hill and dale, just as they did in life; but the carriages were drawn by demons instead of mules. . . the Jews were segregated in the other-world."[17]

Note that Christian egalitarianism is not dead since middle-class ladies invite poor girls into their drawing rooms to play their pianos. But it survives only in the form of charity. We are nevertheless far removed from the paradise of ancient Egypt, where the privileged dead of the

[14] Ibid.

[15] As in the Madagascan civilization, certain sites were used as cities for the spirits of the ancestors. Ambrondrombe was, for example, an Elysium in which the dead talked to one another, sang, danced, reared animals, cultivated the land, made war. In New Guinea, after a period of wandering, the spirits of the dead went to reside in the country of the dead. The life there was exactly like that of the living, except that the dead led a happy life, without any famine or other misfortunes. The villages of the dead were identical doubles of the villages of the living. But the male and female worlds were radically separated, invisible to one another.

[16] Ariès, *L'Homme devant la mort*.

[17] Le Roy Ladurie, *Montaillou*. Another house-grave-soul association: in the Cathar regions the Inquisitors destroyed the village house of the guilty person and, if he was dead, his grave; "this was done in order to deprive him, by the same occasion, of rest in the beyond" (tr. Barbara Bray).

pyramids had at their disposal steps enabling them to rise to heaven, whereas the poor can expect only an agricultural survival. "May my body germinate!" demanded the fellah buried in a field.[18]

The Talmud places paradise in the seventh celestial sphere. Seven hundred angels guard its two gates. Four rivers flow through it: a river of milk, a river of honey, a river of wine, and a river of incense. Six hundred thousand angels move around it among 800,000 trees. They eat succulent dishes at tables made of precious stones.

This flowing of milk, wine, and honey is to be found again in the Muslim paradise, with the addition of aromatic fountains of camphor and ginger. In the Koran paradise is often identified with a garden: "garden of delights," "garden of Eden." It is a sort of ziggurat of a hundred stories constructed by God with bricks of gold and silver. The highest story is the residence of God. Eight gates provide access to the various levels: the gate of prayer, the gate of holy war, the gate of alms, the gate of the well-watered ground, the gate of repentance, the gate of those who subdue their anger, the gate of submission to the will of God, the gate of those who have no need of preliminary judgment. The principal gates lead to others. "They are of unbelievable splendor, quite transparent, they even speak and understand what one says to them."[19] But one must shake a ring for them to be opened.

In order to penetrate into the "sublime garden" one needs a passport. Poor believers enter 40 to 500 years before the rich. It is eternal spring there. From time to time gentle rain falls. The only animals are the horse and the camel.

The blessed are all thirty-three years of age (the age of Christ at his death) and all are beardless. They are dressed in green, perfumed satin, and wear bracelets of silver, gold, and pearls. Resting on carpets or sofas, also green in color, they drink a wine that does not intoxicate. Polygamy exists in the Islamic paradise. But in addition to their legitimate earthly wives, the Elect also have at their disposal houris as concubines and handsome young men as servants. The houri lives in a pavillion hollowed out of a single pearl and furnished with seventy beds, seventy sofas, and seventy carpets. The houris, "coquettes with large eyes and well-formed breasts," do not menstruate, are never pregnant, never spit,

[18] This osmosis between human body and the earth as foster mother is also to be found in the yam fields of Morobe province, New Guinea, which had once been necropolises. The dead were temporarily laid there in deep ditches, in the middle of the plot, so that the humus, drained from the body, would make the yam fields fruitful.

[19] El-Saleh, *La Vie future selon le Coran*.

never wipe their noses.[20] There is neither sleep nor procreation in the Muslim paradise, but an astonishing erotic activity. The blessed spend most of their time deflowering the houris.

It is hardly surprising that Arabic is the only language spoken in this paradise.

"Who loves his neighbor and does good for the love of God will have a palace with transparent walls," says the Koran. Some of these palaces are made of gold and silver, others of rubies or topaz. We are a long way from the everyday Muslim household. The Muslim paradise is not a double of earthly life, but a fantastic invention. The Christian paradise, with its blessed in white robes, hands joined and eyes raised to heaven, is far from being as attractive.

Neither the Old nor the New Testament is very precise about the siting of purgatory. The Greek fathers of the church saw it as a dark prison. The Latin fathers of the church described it as a furnace. The Council of Trent refused to settle the matter. Thomas Aquinas in his *Summa Theologica*, attributes it with a probable site: "a low place next to hell," with the same fire doing double duty for damnation and purification, with hell below. Other theologians think that purgatory is situated above the earth, between us and heaven. J. Collin de Plancy provides a curious rejection of this idea: "Those who say that purgatory is separated from hell only by a large spider's web or by paper-thin walls which form its outer boundary and vault say things which the living do not know."[21]

The Curé d'Ars, on the other hand, returns to the purgatory depicted in the iconology of the martyrs: cauldrons of boiling water, sawn off limbs, entrails pulled out by iron hooks, tables fitted with sharp blades, red-hot braziers.[22]

It has often been said that purgatory was only the invention of the Catholic Church. It is true that only Catholics have given it the importance that it achieved in the seventeenth and eighteenth centuries.[23] But there did exist a sort of purgatory in the Greek underworld; Plato, for example, fixed a stay of one year in a special hell for certain sins. Virgil describes a place for children who died young, which the Middle Ages

[20] Ibid.

[21] Collin de Plancy, *Dictionnaire infernal*.

[22] J. Goubert and L. Christiani, *Les Plus Beaux Textes sur l'au-delà* (Paris: La Colombe, 1950).

[23] It was on All Saints' Day or the day after that prayers for the souls in purgatory were then said. The separation between All Saints' Day and All Souls' Day dates from the nineteenth century.

turned into limbo. The Jews, like Plato, accepted a purgatory of only one year. The Muslims call *araf* a place of waiting for men whose good and evil deeds counterbalance one another, while the Buddhists' hells, like their paradises, are merely superimposed purgatories, where the soul becomes gradually purified. But within Christianity neither the Orthodox nor the Protestants accept the notion of purgatory. After death the soul simply waits for the Last Judgment.

Purgatory began as a hypothesis, then, in the later Middle Ages, became descriptive. About 1264 Jacques de Voragine, in *La Légende dorée*, provides the iconographical themes that were to become widespread, especially after the fourteenth century. Purgatory appears as a pseudo-hell in which the naked souls are plunged into flames, or into a lake, or, again, shut up in a roofless dungeon. In his picture the *Coronation of the Virgin*, at the charterhouse of Villeneuve-sur-Avignon (1453), Enguerrand Charonton places to the right of hell the small dwellingplace of limbo and purgatory with its mitred, crowned, or bareheaded representatives plunged in flames less violent than those he attributes to hell.

In that same fifteenth century, a fresco in the chapel of Notre-Dame-de-Benva, at Lorgues, in the Var, shows "a small dungeon with a barred window, but with no roof, which allows one, by an effect of perspective, to appreciate the piling up of the naked bodies of the penitents who fill it."[24] The souls are looking up toward heaven at the angels, who bring them water and small loaves. The souls are climbing up a staircase towards the celestial Jerusalem where other angels are giving them clothes.

In the sixteenth century, in response to Protestant denials, the Council of Trent made purgatory an article of faith: "There is a purgatory, and the souls which are detained there are aided by the appeals of the faithful, and above all by the holy sacrifice of the mass."

A veritable inflation of masses for the repose of the souls in purgatory was to follow in the seventeenth and eighteenth centuries. Very soon, years in purgatory could be bought off. Some testators paid for a thousand masses for the repose of their souls. In 1650 Simon Colbert, councillor at the Paris *parlement*, paid for ten thousand masses for himself. In 1690 the marquise de Solliers requested 2,000 masses, including 1,000 on the day of her death. But how could one be sure that those masses bought in advance would actually be said thirty or forty years later? Testators were "obsessed by the fear that the clergy, the church councils,

[24]Gaby and Michel Vovelle, "Vision de la mort et de l'au-delà en Provence d'après les autels des âmes du purgatoire, XVᵉ – XXᵉ siècle," *Cahiers des annales* (Paris: Armand Colin, 1970).

130]

and the legatees of their gifts would not exactly fulfill their obligations. So they publicly displayed the terms of the contract in the church, the gift that they had made, and precise details of the masses, services, and prayers due."[25] But it got to the point that so many masses had been credited that priests, whose sole income derived from this source, did nothing but say uninterrupted series of masses every morning. However, certain religious communities, completely crushed by the weight of these masses to be said, asked for "reductions of masses." Indeed in the end there occurred a sort of "spiritual bankruptcy," the number of masses to be said for the souls in purgatory exceeding the capacity of the number of priests available.

Belief in a purgatory, long confined to Catholic poets and theologians, did not pass into popular ideology until the mid-seventeenth century, overthrowing the traditional Christian images of sleep and rest by the introduction of this temporary hell which could be avoided by buying indulgences. No purpose was served by praying for those sinners who were in hell, since no mercy could be granted them, or for the saints who were in heaven, since they would never attain greater delight; but the souls in purgatory, on the other hand, might shorten their pseudo-damnation by means of our prayers. The crier of pater nosters, who ran at night through the streets of the town ringing a small bell, announced the time and intoned: "Awake, awake, ye sleeping people. Pray God for sinners. Requiescant in pace."

Purgatory is an antechamber of heaven, but the room known as an antechamber exists on earth only in aristocratic and upper bourgeois architecture. Ordinary people have only a bedroom—hell or heaven. Hence a long resistance among the lower classes to the idea of purgatory, which was introduced in fact among the peasants only by the resurgence of the pagan belief in "restless ghosts." In the eighteenth and nineteenth centuries prayers for the souls in purgatory became one of the most popular devotions, and a chapel was reserved for this purpose in churches, with an explanatory picture.

The altar of the souls in purgatory was often painted black, highlighted by decorations in gold thread. It was flanked by twisted or fluted columns, surmounted by Corinthian capitals. Sometimes the decoration showed skulls and crossed bones, an hourglass, a book, a scythe, a rake, a recumbent figure, a bearded Old Father Time brandishing a scythe. Sometimes there were images of the raising of Lazarus and of the agony of Saint Joseph (the image of the good death), watched over by the Vir-

[25] Ariès, *L'Homme devant la mort.*

gin and Saint John and visited by Christ. In the fifteenth century, and again in the seventeenth, devils were depicted, but these were suppressed by the Counter-Reformation. Altarpieces tended to depict delivery rather than suffering and, in the eighteenth century, there was a preference for images of beautiful penitents chastely seminude.

In the nineteenth century all these narrative altars were destroyed and replaced by altars of black and white marble, with incrustations, decorated on the central panel by a black Maltese cross, or by a veiled urn, or the traditional skulls and crossed bones.

In the romantic period there appeared the purgatorial cave with multiple entrances.

It is more than curious, even incredible, to see that in his *Salon de 1761*, Diderot lovingly describes what, for him, is an ideal purgatory—an ideal purgatory in painting, that is. As for G. Briard's picture *Passage des âmes du purgatoire au ciel*, executed for the sepulchral chapel of Sainte-Marguerite, Diderot remarks that it would have required a Rubens to paint such a subject. He adds:

A bold, vivid head would have covered the fiery pit at the bottom of his picture. The pit itself would have occupied the whole breadth and depth of the picture. In it one would have seen men and women of all ages and of all conditions; every kind of pain and passion, an infinity of various actions, souls borne up, others which have fallen, the former with arms outstretched, the latter with arms close to the body; one would have heard a thousand cries and moans. Heaven, depicted above, would have received the delivered souls. They would have been presented to eternal glory by angels, which would have been seen rising and descending, and plunging into the pit, impervious to the devouring flames.[26]

It may be surprising that Diderot, an avowed atheist, should be preoccupied with the description of souls in purgatory, but still more surprising is his own burial in the chapel of the Virgin in the church of Saint-Roch.

What is purgatory like? A seventeenth-century hermit placed it in the middle of the Etna volcano. A number of saints have applied themselves to describing its internal arrangements, declaring that it is not a single place and that it is subdivided into several distinct dungeons, according to the gravity of the sins to be expiated. Saint Francis, for example, divided it into three parts. The souls of the upper part suffer only the penalty of exile from heaven. In the middle reside those souls

[26] Denis Diderot, *Salon de 1761*.

who have committed less serious sins. This region is itself divided into three zones: the first is a frozen lake, the second is filled with a mixture of pitch and boiling oil, the third consists of molten metal. Thirty-six angels have the unpleasant task of plunging the souls alternately into the frozen lake and the bath of boiling oil. The lower purgatory, which is situated, of course, in the vicinity of hell, is itself divided into three parts. The first for the secular committers of grave sins, the second for the religious, the third (the most intolerable) for sinning priests and bishops.

The Abbé Louvet tried to calculate the number of the Elect. First setting aside 800 million pagans, who could not be other than damned, then 120 million heretical Christians and 80 million schismatics, who could hardly claim heaven, he finally arrived at the figure of 200 million Catholics. "They are the chosen people." But he was troubled by the fact that three-quarters of the total number of Catholics were living in a state of mortal sin. "Oh God, where are your Elect?" he cried in desperation.[27]

In the 1900s Angelo Solerti applied himself to reconstituting by means of models the three worlds of the beyond described by Dante. Purgatory thus appears as an immense pyramid, or rather as a steep, irregular mountain. Ledges mark the poet's stopping places. In fact, the mountain was surmounted by a sort of ziggurat, a sort of artificial construction consisting of eight circular terraces: seven for the deadly sins, and one, the upper platform, for the earthly paradise. The sixth circle, that of greed, is characterized by its trees, whose branches are watered by cascades falling from the rocks above. This mountain, situated in the middle of the sea, at the antipodes of Jerusalem, is therefore an island. In fact, it is a version of the tower of Babel, with its series of more or less narrow ledges and vertical walls. In 1902 a dispute broke out between different commentators on the shape of Dante's purgatory. V. Russo claimed that Dante's purgatory is twice as high as it is wide. Not at all, retorted Agnelli and Piranesi, who saw it as having "a base so wide that it is no longer a mere *isoletta* but a continent."[28]

Popular belief remains faithful to the image of the dungeon and, in the nineteenth century, added sculptures of the Virgin and Child receiving the prayers of a soul wearing a nightdress in the midst of flames.

Despite the challenge to the notion of purgatory made by certain

[27] Abbé Louvet, *Le Purgatoire d'après les révélations des saints* (Paris, 1883).

[28] H. Hauvette, "La forme du purgatoire dantesque," *Annales* de la faculté des Lettres de Bordeaux, Apr.–June 1902.

churchmen in the eighteenth century,[29] the devotion to the souls in purgatory reached its peak at that time and continued into the nineteenth century. The Curé d'Ars talks about it constantly. Catherine Emmerich had a vision of it. Marie de la Providence founded her "*auxiliatrices du purgatoire*," who devoted themselves to the comfort of the suffering soul. Mélanie, a shepherd girl from the Salette, described the soul in purgatory as "perfectly resigned, informed by the divine will." And Saint Thérèse of Lisieux took upon herself the mission of "delivering all the souls in purgatory."

Although the scientists and rationalists of the late nineteenth century attacked this cult, denouncing the 90,000 francs a day, or 32 million francs a year, earned by the clergy of France for masses said for the souls in purgatory, an enormous literature on purgatory was nevertheless published by the "good press"; there was even a journal called *L'Echo du Purgatoire*. There was an *Association de la bonne mort*, which published a *Manuscrit du Purgatoire* written by Mother Marie de La Croix under the dictation of a nun in a Norman convent between 1873 and 1890.[30]

Strangely enough, so widespread a cult disappeared almost immediately after the war of 1914–18. The altars of the souls in purgatory disappeared from all the churches, often to be replaced by plaques to the war dead. The monument to the dead has replaced the monument to the souls. All that now remains is a simple collection box in a few churches, "for the souls in purgatory."

[29] The Curé Meslier wrote: "Purgatory is the brazier which heats up the pastor's pot, of which his flock provide the wood."

[30] Gaby and Michel Vovelle, "Vision de la mort."

II

FUNERALS

or the Grand Finale

IO

Death as Urban Spectacle

In the words of a historian of funerary practices in the Middle Ages, Bernard, the cemetery was "the noisiest, busiest, most animated, most commercial place in the rural or urban center." The church was the "common house"; the cemetery the open, also common space, at a time when there were no other public places except the street, no other meeting place, since the houses were generally so small and over-crowded.

Philippe Ariès
L'Homme devant la Mort

From the fifteenth to the nineteenth century death in the West was a spectacle, made a spectacle of itself. From the "mystery" of dying in bed to the great operatic ceremonies in the cathedrals, of which in the seventeenth century Bossuet was the prima donna, by way of the funeral corteges which parodied the parades of princes, from the death agony to the grave, there unfolded, one after another, a whole series of representations.

"Beautiful deaths" were high points in the collective memory. Greuze painted some of these for the edification of bourgeois families. Everyone is seen to be playing his proper role in a drama in which the participants are letter perfect. Sudden death, which, since there is no longer a spec-

[137

Jean Baptiste Greuze (1725–1805), *The Guilty Son. (The Louvre, Paris. Photo Lauros-Giraudon)*

tacle of death, we tend to desire, was for a long time feared. It did not enable one to play one's role in the required rituals. The woodcuts of the fifteenth century depict a crowd around the deathbed. Angels and devils stand ready to do battle. There are diabolical creatures, some with birds' beaks, others with dogs' and horses' heads, others half-wolves, half-fish. And there is Saint Peter with his keys, the good thief, Mary Magdalene, Saint Paul struck down from his horse, God the Father, God the Son, God the Holy Ghost, and, of course, the Virgin Mary. All these protagonists are fighting over the soul of the dying person. This scene survived into the late nineteenth century, except that good and evil spirits are replaced in the family bedroom by friends, and even by strangers. For a veritable crowd invades the bedroom of the dying person. Passersby, alerted by the bustle around the house come in, inquire, discuss the circumstances, and want to see the dying person who is at the center of the assembly. He is the hero of the day, the star. The house of the dying person is the place of a great ceremonial. The last act of the play which is being played out is lived through collectively. Everyone, beginning with the dying person himself, tries to make it an exemplary public act.

To this small theater of individual death are added the great representations of collective death. From time immemorial war was one of these representations. From the death of the gladiators and Christian martyrs in the Roman arenas to the Revolutionary carts of 1793, from the single combats, tourneys, and duels to public executions, there has been a constant attempt to arrange other spectacles of death when war was absent.

Between the wars, between the epidemics, which were even more deadly than battles, death and corpses have constantly made their presence felt in everyday reality. At the present time, in a village of about a thousand inhabitants, one may expect ten deaths a year, but in the eighteenth century there would be some forty, that is to say, four times more burials. Almost every week the church bell rang out, the house of the dying person was filled with onlookers, and mournful processions passed through the streets. "Death was then at the center of life, just as the cemetery was at the center of the village."[1]

In the cities it was worse. Paris, constantly the scene of enormous funeral processions, was awakened every morning at four o'clock by a bell announcing the cart which carried the dead from the Hôtel-Dieu to the cemetery at Clamart. In the streets passersby stopped to look at the dead exhibited before their houses, a custom borrowed in the seven-

[1] Jean Fourastié, *Machinisme et Bien-être* (Paris: P.U.F., 1951).

teenth century from ancient Rome, where the dead were exhibited for seven days in the vestibule of the *domus*. In seventeenth- and eighteenth-century Europe the duration of lying in state was proportionate to the wealth and power of the dead person. This explains the revival in techniques of embalming.

With private townhouses draped in black to the roof, cypress-shaped lamps, skulls on the black hangings, coaches with horses caparisoned in black, hundreds of torches borne by lackeys, poor people engaged for the occasion, hooded monks, death was a spectacle and was seen as such.

After the horrors of the Hundred Years' War, which was accompanied by famine and plague, there appeared in the fifteenth century a morbid iconography that was to survive until the eighteenth century: it was known as the *danse macabre*.

The *danses macabres* painted in Paris at the charnelhouse of the Saints-Innocents, in Amiens Cathedral, in the ducal chapel at Dijon, at the charnelhouse of Saint-Maclou in Rouen, and so on, were a common subject throughout fifteenth-century Europe. Naked dead attack the living with the tools of the gravedigger. Grimacing, grinning skeletons, with strips of flesh hanging off their bones and crawling with vermin, lay in wait for the living, dragging them into the dance. All trades, all social classes were represented. The *danse macabre* spared neither king nor peasant, neither bishop nor poor monk. All were dragged into a saraband of bones.

With the Renaissance, the taste for the macabre became still more widespread. An exhibitionism of pain and tears, especially in the processions led by the monks of the Sainte-Ligue, with people wailing and swooning. In 1596 four thousand Marseillais set off "wearing sackcloth, which revealed only their weeping eyes, their moaning mouths, and their backs marked by whiplashes. In the great days of the Sainte-Ligue in Paris, not a week passed but the flagellants stirred up the population with their cries and gesticulations."[2]

To the art of dying well was added a veritable devotion to death. Like Girolamo Savonarola, many Catholic preachers exhorted the faithful constantly to keep in mind the idea that they might die at any moment. To maintain this sense of death, the preachers advised attendance at deathbeds and funerals as often as possible. "If you are weak," said Savonarola, "you should have death hung in your house, and carry in

[2] Robert Mandrou, *Introduction à la France moderne, 1500–1640* (Paris: Albin Michel, 1961).

your hand a small bone skeleton, and look at it often. . . Look sometimes at your flesh and your hands, and say to yourself: 'These hands and this flesh must become dust and ashes; they will soon rot and decay.'"[3]

This love of the macabre did not disappear in the seventeenth century, because painting and the theater were particularly given to depicting graveside scenes. In the eighteenth century the macabre became erotic. Love stories between the living and the dead were an attraction, and Sade went so far as to describe sexual intercourse with the dead.

In Italy the *danse macabre* was replaced by the triumph of death. The *danses macabres*, which enjoyed enormous iconographic success in France and Germany, did not really take root in Italy. The Italians preferred the theme of the encounter between the living and the dead, which was especially popular in the fourteenth and early fifteenth centuries. Three dead men meet three living men, or three open biers bar the way to three knights. But these dead are neither putrefied nor worm-eaten. They are skeletons. And these skeletons owe nothing to Greco-Roman mythology. Skeletons certainly appear in ancient iconography, but they are exceptional. In the fourteenth and fifteenth centuries, however, they abound. They are shown on horseback and even riding oxen. Only the scythe is borrowed from Chronos, who, himself, acquired it from the Egyptian god Typhon.

The first representations of the triumph of death appeared during the great plague of 1348, when three-fifths of the Italian population died, including Petrarch's Laura. Highway robbery, rapine, and murder followed the plague. As the Italian cities collapsed and mercenaries turned lookers pillaged the countryside, white-clad penitents, barefoot, a red cross on their hoods, wandered along the highways in processions, sleeping on the ground, fasting, whipping themselves, and singing psalms.

As with the *danse macabre*, no one, whether prince or beggar, escaped the triumph of death.

The triumph of death, drawn on its chariot, was nevertheless a parody of the entries of princes or the funerals of aristocrats: a skeleton slowly drove a huge chariot drawn by oxen.

In 1511, for the carnival, Piero di Cosimo organized a cavalcade of death through the streets of Florence. A huge black chariot, dotted with bones and white crosses, drawn by oxen, conveyed a very tall figure of Death, scythe in hand, surrounded by closed tombs. When the cortege stopped at a station, the tombs opened and characters wearing material on which bones were painted emerged and sang, accompanied by muffled,

[3] A. Tenenti, *La Vie et la Mort à travers l'art du XVᵉ siècle* (Paris: Armand Colin, 1952).

raucous trumpets. Before and behind the chariot rode horsemen dressed as skeletons on emaciated horses. The entire procession sang the *Miserere* in trembling voice. This spectacle filled the city with terror and wonder.[4]

This Petrarchan theme of the triumph of death was a survival from antiquity, though; for the Quattrocento the stress lay on the notion of triumph. In the triumph of death the men of the Renaissance responded above all to the spectacle, to the pomp of the accessories. "The theme is in the air," one might have said. "It inspires artists who are given the task of organizing princely entertainments, entries, weddings, commemorations of victories, and even the ordinary scenes of the carnival. . . Anything is a pretext for entertainments and processions."[5]

On February 25, 1443, Alfonso of Aragon, entering Naples, was dressed as a conquering hero of Roman antiquity, arriving in a golden chariot decorated with historico-mythological allegories. In 1500, for the triumph of Cesare Borgia, eleven chariots were followed by processional corteges. For the marriage of Francesco de' Medici and Bianca Capello the bridal chariot was drawn by elephants.

So why not the triumph of death since in fact death is the greatest conquering hero of all? So the practice of triumphal decorations at funerals spread throughout Italy. In the 1450s the theme of the triumph of death appeared on furniture, on marriage chests, and in miniatures. In 1488 it became a favorite subject of engravers.

We shall see later how these funeral spectacles, and the architectural imagination of funeral decoration, developed. But from the fourteenth to the eighteenth centuries, it seems that the least macabre place was the cemetery. Cemeteries were in fact public places, always full of bustling, animated crowds, where people seemed concerned with everything except death. The cemetery was a public place, open to all comers, a center of communal life.[6] Markets, fairs, and pilgrimages were held there. Shops were permanently open there, despite the prohibition of the Church. The village bakehouse was built in it. Harvesters and other workers got themselves hired there. Tumblers, mask showmen, mimes, popular musicians, and charlatans attracted idlers there. People walked about and danced there. In the towns the market halls were usually next to the cemeteries, as was the case in Paris, where the Champeaux were

[4]Liliane Guerry, *Le Thème du triomphe de la mort dans la peinture italienne* (Paris: Maisonneuve, 1950).
[5]Ibid.
[6]It should be remembered that cemeteries looked rather like waste ground, since there were neither tomb-monuments, crosses, nor trees.

next to the Saints-Innocents, or the Saint-Germain fair next to the graveyard of Saint-Sulpice.[7] At the cemetery of the Saints-Innocents were permanent shops and stalls for drapers, haberdashers, booksellers, and public writers. Hence the terms *drapers' charnelhouse* and *writers' charnelhouse*, which one often encounters in the literature of the time but which had nothing macabre about them except the names. The ground floors of the ossuaries were almost always used as shops, even as ballrooms. Even as late as 1750 the girls of the parish of Saint-Eustache who were preparing their first communion seemed to have found it quite natural to attend their catechism lessons in the graveyard.

The cemetery soon became a place of prostitution and theft, and in 1186 Philippe Auguste had the Saints-Innocents closed; in the seventeenth century the church ordered the building of walls for all cemeteries in order to prevent fighting, theft, prostitution, markets, and grazing. But in the eighteenth century the diocese of Tours still had to forbid the use of cemeteries as a place for threshing the wheat, or as grazing land, a public walkway, a fairground, or rubbish dump.[8]

As holy ground, like the church of which it was an extension, the walled graveyard became a place of asylum. Fugitives not only hid there, but some of them took up permanent residence there in the rooms over the charnelhouses. Others even went so far as to build their own houses there. Women hermits had themselves walled up in churchyards, as did Jeanne La Vairière, in the Saints-Innocents, in 1442. These voluntary recluses lived side by side with involuntary ones: prostitutes and criminals condemned to be walled up forever. Last, the cemetery was used for trials at the foot of the cross. Joan of Arc was tried at Rouen, in this way, in the churchyard of Saint-Ouen.

What a contrast with the deserted acres of our present-day ceme-

[7] In the eighth century the Parisian graveyards around certain churches were already saturated, and the dead from the Hôtel-Dieu, the plague victims, and bodies found in the street were buried in the Champeaux (small fields). A "paupers' ditch" was dug that was to stink out the quarter for ten centuries. At first reserved for the parishioners of Saint-Germain l'Auxerrois, the cemetery of the Saints-Innocents, which succeeded the Champeaux, was next to Philippe Auguste's new Halles, or market. It stretched from the Rue Saint-Denis to the Rue de la Lingerie and from the present Rue Berger to the Rue de la Ferronnerie, where Henry IV was to be assassinated. It was reached by four carriage-gateways. It was in the *charnier des lingères* (linen-maids' charnelhouse) that, in 1424, the frescoes of the *danse macabre* were painted. Closed in 1780 and the bones transferred to the catacombs, the Cimetière des Innocents was replaced by a market which in the mid-nineteenth century was absorbed into the Halles, or central market.

[8] Robert Favre, *La Mort au siècle des lumières* (Lyon: Presses Universitaires, 1978).

teries, peopled only with monuments, like so many museums of tombs, museums of the dead! Like the church, the churchyard was a public place, an urban space in which the community assembled. When the rising bourgeoisie began to build townhouses everywhere, they never took on the popular character of the church and churchyard. As so often, secularization, by bringing order and virtue with it, also gave rise to boredom. However, another urban space, the public square, flanked by galleries of shops, was to take over the animating function of the cemetery when, walled and closed, it was to become exclusively a space of death. With the destruction of the cemetery of the Saints-Innocents, the courtyard of the Palais-Royal was to take over all its functions, except that of burial. And one may well wonder whether it was the charnel-house or the cloister that inspired this new form of urban architecture in the eighteenth century.

In any case, in the mid-eighteenth century cemeteries cease almost everywhere in France to be places of public intercourse, meetings, and festivities. Innumerable edicts forbade people to dry their clothes there or to thresh the wheat, to hold fairs or markets, to graze cattle, to play tennis or bowls, to dump refuse, to open taverns, to organize dancing and assemblies. One can see by this list that there was a wide range of activities in this public space. But it also expressed a familiarity with death.[9] In wishing to inculcate in its followers an abstract notion of the sacred, the church was laying the ground, without intending to, for the great, present-day disaffection of both the sacred and the cult of the dead.

On the eve of the French Revolution, even though it had been enclosed with walls for five centuries, the cemetery of the Saints-Innocents, in Paris, still preserved many of its old frivolous activities. Louis-Sébastien Mercier describes the "writers' charnelhouse" in the following way: "Without the secret correspondence of hearts, which is not subject to vicissitudes, they would go and increase the already prodigious number of skeletons, piled up above their heads, in barns overburdened with their weight. When I say overburdened, I am not using a figure of speech. These accumulated bones take one by surprise; and it is in the midst of the worm-eaten remains of thirty generations, of which nothing is left but powdered bones, it is in the midst of that fetid, cadaverous odor,

---

[9] F. Lebrun, *Les Hommes et la Mort en Anjou* (The Hague: Mouton, 1971), writing about the cemeteries, says that people "talked loudly before going into the sanctuary where the merchants laid out their wares, certain of finding customers, and where children and adults ran about, playing, even dancing between the graves, where no one would be offended at seeing cows and pigs grazing."

[145

offensive to the sense of smell, that one sees some women buying dresses and ribbons, and others dictating love letters."[10]

And even in the nineteenth century, hardly a hundred years ago, we see in 1874 the inhabitants of Brussels going out at Easter to a suburb where the fair of Dieghem, near Shaerbeek, was held in the local cemetery. Chickens, pigs, and other farmyard animals were sold by auction to the profit of the patron saint of the parish. The day ended with dancing and drinking among the graves.[11]

But cannot this dancing, which we know to have been held in the cemetery since the Middle Ages, even if it has become profaned, be linked to the very archaic rites of the dances of the dead, practiced by primitive people, of which the *danses macabres* are a sort of Christian parody?

Saint Vitus's dance is itself the consequence of those graveyard dances, since Saint Vitus, having seen Christians dancing in a graveyard, cursed them and condemned them to dance forever.

[10] Louis-Sébastien Mercier, *Tableau de Paris* (Paris, 1781).
[11] Max Gossi, *Le Catholicisme et ses cimetières* (Paris-Brussels, 1874).

I I

Funeral Decoration

The funeral practices of other nations are full of oddities in which im-
piety often borders on the ridiculous.

Arthur Mercier

La Sépulture chrétienne en France d'après,

les monuments du XIᵉ au XVIᵉ siècle, Paris 1855

The pomps of death terrify more than death itself," said
Bacon. But do not these rites of death spring from fear
of death, are they not intended more to conceal it than to
exalt it? Was not the first of all funeral rites, burial, originally
a simple way of getting rid of the corpse, of no longer having
to see it, of making it disappear? And was not mourning, whose duration
corresponds to that of the putrefaction of the body, a way of avoiding
contagion by isolating the family?

The winding sheet, the coffin, the catafalque are so many successive
masks. In his struggle against nature, man has failed to tame death, but
he has at least transformed it, denatured it, by a whole series of rituals.
He has turned it into a spectacle.

"The envelope of the dead person has become, at least since the fourteenth century, a theatrical monument of the kind that were erected for
the setting of the mystery plays and great entries."[1]

[1] Ariès, *L'Homme devant la mort*.

The clothing of the corpse is itself a travesty. The mask of pain is replaced by a mask of serenity. Eyes closed, hands joined, the corpse simulates sleep. As for the visitor who approaches the funeral bed, his features set, his gestures restrained, observing, in the absence of any prayers to be said, a minute's silence, it is as if he himself "pretends to be dead."

Up to the nineteenth century, in the countryside death was announced by the ringing of a bell. The shutters were closed in the house of the deceased and candles were lighted. The pendulum of the clock was stopped, since life had stopped in the house. Mirrors were turned to the wall "to prevent the soul of the deceased being reflected in them." The water from buckets and basins was thrown away ("the soul of the deceased has sullied it by washing in it"). Beehives were covered with black cloth "to prevent the bees from dying that year." If the deceased was a miller, the sails of the mill were placed in the form of a cross. The deceased was dressed in a clean cap and shirt, and his ordinary clothes were given as payment to the woman who laid out the body. In the eighteenth century many testators asked to be buried in a coffin, which implies that it was not common practice. Indeed each church had at its disposal a "coffin of the poor," used only for the procession, the poor person being taken out of it once the procession had arrived at the cemetery and buried straight into the earth.[2]

There were seven different classes of burial. The first class involved the removal of the body by all the clergy wearing copes, and a solemn procession; the second, a high mass with deacon and subdeacon, and fine ornaments; the third a procession without copes; the fourth an ordinary high mass; the fifth and sixth low masses; the seventh for children under twelve.

Mourning dress, hangings, catafalques, the presence of the poor emphasize the hierarchy that was only really felt in the towns where the house of the deceased and the church were draped in black.

The custom of draping the house of the deceased goes back to the Middle Ages and survived up to the seventeenth century. The antechambers were draped in black, the other rooms in gray. All mirrors and pictures were veiled. This draping of the house or apartment sometimes lasted for a year in the bedroom; mirrors were hidden for six months. The draping of the house was superseded by the mere draping of the door of the deceased's house, or of the porch of the building, a custom that has survived to our own day.

[2] Lebrun, *Les Hommes et la Mort en Anjou.*

The custom of wearing black during the period of mourning, which is of relatively recent date, only became widespread in the sixteenth century. Two years of mourning were required for a widow, but only one for a widower. This misogyny is to be found in all funerary customs: although the practice of burying the wife alive, with her dead husband (practiced by the Scythians, according to Herodotus), or of burning her alive on the husband's funeral pyre (India) were widespread, in no culture has it been a practice for the husband to be buried alive in order to rejoin the soul of his dead wife.

Under the Ancien Régime every French citizen had to wear mourning for a king's death. In the Middle Ages this period lasted for a year; in the eighteenth century, for six months.

Printed funeral invitations go back to the seventeenth century, but the names of members of the family did not appear on them until the mid-1780s.[3]

Last, the hearse dates only from the early nineteenth century, middle-class and plebeian biers being still carried on foot under Louis-Philippe. The hearse, of course, marks class differences in terms of decoration: hearses of the first class were drawn by horses caparisoned in black and silver, whereas the hearses of the poor carried no ornament. The motorized hearses of today are white for children, nuns, and Muslims, and are less frequently black, gray and violet being preferred for the trimmings. In any case the days of funeral "pomps" have gone. With the abolition of classes of burial, death has become democratized. The great veils worn by widows have disappeared, as have cleaners' signs: "Mourning clothes cleaned in twenty-four hours." Only the undertaker's showrooms, transformed in fact into "thanatological services," shops for arranging the funeral formalities before the body is sent to the "funeral complexes," survive. Deaths in hospital, which are more and more numerous, are hastening the decline of funerals at home. The family reunions around the funeral bed, a great episode of everyday life in the seventeenth and eighteenth centuries, are becoming rarer. Mourning is practically unworn. Death is dodged.

What a contrast with the triumphal death of the classical age, a death which, it can be said, "was intensely lived"![4] In the centuries of opera, a death was also a supreme opera, whose various settings we shall examine.

Up to the thirteenth century the face of the deceased was left uncov-

[3] Carlier, *Histoire des coutumes funéraires.*
[4] Michel Vovelle, *Mourir autrefois* (Paris: Gallimard-Julliard, 1974).

ered until the final closing of the sarcophagus. From the thirteenth century, the deceased disappeared completely, sewn up in a shroud. Then he was buried in a wooden chest, which in French was called the *sarceu*, which derives from "sarcophagus." *Sarceu* became *cercueuil*, coffin.

In the fifteenth century the nobility did not care to appear before their survivors other than masked. So the corpse was concealed, and a figure, made of wood or wax, in the image of the deceased, was exhibited on the funeral bed. Then it was thought that the coffin itself was too sharp a reminder of the deceased, and it was covered with material, the *pallium* (pall), first of precious cloth, then a special black ornament, decorated with macabre motifs. Last, the coffin and pall in turn disappeared under a monumental catafalque, a sort of architectural reconstruction, no doubt unconscious, of the primitive sarcophagus-house.

"In the seventeenth century the Jesuits, the great theatrical producers of the baroque age, were to turn it into a huge operatic machine, constructed around a theme and an action, animated with moving characters, commenting on the Last Things."[5]

In this setting the skeletons of the *danse macabre* reappeared, but domesticated. They sprang up at the most unexpected places in the nave and altar, a sinister counterpoint to the triumphal splendor of the funeral. "The allegorical skeleton became active. He raised the catafalque, and seemed ready to set in motion what had hitherto been above all a motionless spectacle. . . In a service to the memory of the duc de Beaufort, in Rome in 1669, designed by Bernini, there was a symbolic pyramid raised in the air by two skeletons.[6]

Under the Ancien Régime, court entertainments were called the *menus plaisirs du roi*. These "minor pleasures" included the funerals of the royal family. Revived under the Restoration, they gave rise to so many jokes that Louis XVIII changed their title to "material of the entertainments and ceremonies of the crown."

These funeral ceremonies were so long that the use of embalming for kings, princes, and the French and English aristocracy became necessary.

As soon as the king had died, his body was washed, embalmed, and enclosed in a bituminous wooden coffin, placed in a second lead coffin, which was then placed in a third oak coffin. A veil of black velvet covered it, embroidered at the four corners with the French royal coat of

[5] Ariès, *L'Homme devant la mort*.
[6] André Chastel, "L'art et le sentiment de la mort au XVIIᵉ siècle," *Bulletin de la société d'étude du XVIIᵉ siècle*, no. 36–37 (July–Oct. 1957).

arms. In earlier times a mold of the king's face was used. Cast in wax, this mask served as the effigy, which was alone visible, exhibited for eight to ten days on a funeral bed over which an embroidered canopy was placed. This effigy, which was very true to life and life-size, wearing the royal tunic and cloak, with collar around the neck, crown on head, lay on the bed.

At this point a strange episode in the royal funeral ceremonial took place, all the stranger that it survived into the eighteenth century: the table was laid and the king's clothes laid out as if he were still alive. On the table, drawn up in front of the lying in state, meals were served each day, according to the usual court ceremonial. Fingerbowls were presented at the king's chair as if he were still sitting there. The persons present in the funeral chamber were those who usually approached the king at meals: princes, princesses, prelates, officers. After this simulated meal, the victuals were distributed to the poor.

Just as curious was the custom by which the new king, from the death of Charles V onwards, did not accompany his predecessor's funeral procession. This is all the stranger in that the accompaniment of a dead monarch's body by his successor seems to have been a sort of rite frequently practiced. David followed Abner's coffin. Tiberius attended Augustus's funeral, Caligula that of Tiberius, Nero that of Claudius. Chilpéric and Clotaire I accompanied the body of their mother Clothilde of Tours to the church of Sainte-Geneviève in Paris. The funeral of Philippe Auguste was followed by his two sons. As for Saint Louis, his son Philippe III himself carried his body on his shoulders and made the journey, barefoot, from Paris to Saint-Denis. On the route taken, small monuments were erected at the places where he stopped to rest, small towers surmounted by statues, which were destroyed in 1793.

The conveyance to Saint-Denis was carried out by the *hanouards* (carriers or breakers of salt) who, after having had the privilege of salting and boiling the dead kings, inherited that of bearing the sovereign's coffin. Over the coffin was placed the effigy, sheltered by a canopy of gold brocade.

The convoy arrived at Saint-Denis at night, received in torchlight by the abbot and all the monks. Carried into the *chapelle ardente*, or taper-lighted funeral chapel, built between the high altar and the altar of the martyrs, the royal coffin remained there for forty days. Morning, noon, and night, the bells rang out announcing the king's death. Offices were said continually night and day. And the table continued to be served. At the table, laid at dinnertime, a place of honor was reserved for the king. When all the dishes had been served, a herald repeated three times: "The king has been served." After a pause, he added, in a lugubrious tone: "The king is dead."

On the day of the burial the coffin was taken down into the royal burial vault. A handful of earth was thrown on the coffin, and all the royal insignia followed pell-mell into the vault: escutheon, coat of arms, gauntlets, military ensigns, cloak, sword, sceptre, hand of justice, crown. The new king stayed in the Louvre and showed that he was in mourning by wearing red, while the queen dressed in white.

So the death of great persons was a spectacle, a public ceremonial, which influenced the arrangements for the more ordinary funerals. Funeral etiquette reflected the rigidity of court etiquette. Each famous person seemed, with his funeral, to play his finest role. The dying Louis XIII had funeral music of his own composition played. Chancellor Séguier asked that there be placed in the church of the Oratoire, around his coffin, four seated skeletons covered with great cloaks. Cardinal Richelieu was conveyed to his last resting place on a triumphal chariot on which were 2,000 lighted white candles. For the funeral of Henri IV the choir of the church of Notre-Dame was draped in black, as also were the great nave of the side aisles. Against each of the pillars stood a double row of lighted candles. All along the route to Saint-Denis the streets were draped in black.

The funeral spectacles were matched by the funeral oration. Bossuet, Massillon, and Fléchier made great assaults of eloquence, a sort of bel canto of an operatic grande finale, appreciated, even applauded as such. This is confirmed by the "reportage" of the marquise de Sévigné, who attended the funeral of the Chancellor Séguier as if it were a first night at the opera:

> Yesterday I attended a service for Monsieur le Chancelier at the Oratoire: it was paid for by the painters, sculptors, musicians, and orators, in a word, by the other liberal arts. It was the finest piece of decoration one could imagine: Le Brun designed it; the mausoleum reached to the ceiling, decorated with a thousand lights, and several figures suitable to the person to be praised. Four skeletons below carried the insignia of his offices, as if they had taken his honors from him with his life: one carried his cap, another his duke's crown, another his order, another the chancellor's mace. The four arts—Painting, Music, Eloquence, and Sculpture—were in tears at losing their protector. Four virtues—Strength, Justice, Temperance, and Religion—supported the first representation. Below, four Angels, or genii, were receiving this fine soul. The mausoleum was further adorned with several Angels, supporting a *chapelle ardente*, which reached the ceiling. Never has anything

so splendid, or so well conceived, been seen; it is Le Brun's masterpiece. The entire church was adorned with pictures, devices, and emblems relating to arms or to the chancellor's life: several of his principal actions were depicted. Mme de Verneuil [his daughter] wanted to buy all this decoration, at enormous cost. They have all, as a body, decided to decorate a gallery with it and to leave this mark of their gratitude and magnificence to posterity. . . A young father of the Oratoire came to make the funeral oration; I told M. de Tulle to get him to come down, and to take his place, that nothing could sustain the beauty of the spectacle, and the perfection of the music than the force of his eloquence. My daughter, at first the young man was all a-tremble. Everyone was in a like state, too. . . But as he overcame his nervousness, he embarked on so luminous a path; he had prepared his speech so well; he paid such measured praise to the deceased; he touched on everything with such skill; he had managed so successfully to mention everything which was worthy of admiration; he employed touches of eloquence and masterstrokes so pertinent and with such good grace that everybody, I say everybody, without exception, cried out at them, and everyone was charmed by so perfect and so successful an action. . . As for the music, it was beyond description. Baptiste [Lully] had taken the utmost pains with all the king's music; his fine *Miserere* was still more augmented; and there was a *Libera* during which all eyes were filled with tears; I cannot believe that there is any other music in heaven.[7]

That "opera," attended by all the great names of France, could draw on the most famous painter and the most famous composer of the seventeenth century.

Father Claude-François Ménestrier, the Jesuit appointed by Louis XIV as director of public entertainments, published a treatise on funeral decoration in which we learn that catafalques must be built in the form of round, oval, hexagonal, octagonal temples, and the like, and that a mausoleum must be built in the form of a temple, or columned portico, or pyramid, since the mausoleum was called thus after the superb tomb which Queen Artemis had built in memory of her husband, Mausolus, king of Caria. Pliny has described the thirty-six columns which formed its peristyle. At each of the wings rose a pyramid. "Pyramids," Father Ménestrier adds, "are closer to tombs than obelisks, which were originally circus ornaments." Nevertheless at the service which the Jesuits held in Rome for all their benefactors, in 1640, there were four great

[7] Mme de Sévigné, *Lettre à Madame de Grignan*, Friday 6 May 1672. The young preacher making such a remarkable début was Bossuet.

obelisks, representing the four corners of the world to which their society had extended its hold.

Father Ménestrier loved great machines. Indeed he describes the mausoleum as "a machine which one erects in the middle of churches for funerals." He certainly found his inspiration in antiquity, but he was very consciously baroque. The comparison which I have made with the opera was also made by Louis XIV's contemporaries. In Mme de Sévigné's description, quoted above, we are certainly at the opera. The church took part in these entertainments, even going so far as to carry them out, yet not without a touch of remorse. Hence Bossuet's grandiloquent exhortations to humility, which became in turn a spectacle. Hence, too, Father Ménestrier's reservations as he transformed churches into theaters for the funerals of the great, while at the same time criticizing the fact.

When the place in which the funeral is to take place is of a regular architecture, there are those who are content to drape the body of the columns and pilasters in black, to gild or silver the capitals, to place in the space between the arches tableaux of emblems, or devices, or actions from the life of the deceased, attached by black streamers, gauzes, or butterlies made out of black material. . .

The Italians, who are so correct in these decorations and who have a taste for fine things, entrust the execution of these works only to the most skillfull architects. For there is much to be said of the difference between church decoration for serious functions and theatrical decoration, and it is to be feared that such holy places and such ceremonies might come to resemble a ball, a comedy, or an opera, if left in the hands of those who are used only to working for such things.[8]

"It is from night and darkness that we have learnt to hang with black houses of mourning," Father Ménestrier tells us. And he quotes a number of funerals where the decorations struck him as being particularly successful: those of Francis I, of the duke of Modena in 1659, with its representations of 124 faces of the princes of the house of Este in statues, busts, and medals. Then there was the funeral of Philip III of Spain on August 4, 1621: "A very large machine in the church of Saint James in the Plaza Navone; it had four great sides with open porticoes, and re-

<hr/>

[8] Ménestrier, *Des décorations funèbres où il est amplement traité des tentures, des lumières, des mausolées, catafalques, inscriptions et autres ornements funèbres; avec tout ce qui s'est fait de plus considérable depuis plus d'un siècle, pour les papes, empereurs, rois, reines, cardinaux, princes, prélats, sçavans, et personnes illustres en naissance, vertu et dignité.*

entrent corners between the returns of the Corinthian columns, sixteen statues on as many pedestals, set forward, had these columns behind them, and represented the virtues. . . The summit of this edifice was a six-sided pyramid, with fourteen steps bearing candlesticks, at the top six corbels supported a crown under which was a bust of Philip III, and at the foot of the pyramid was a balustrade, on the pedestals of which were ten children, holding flags."[9]

Father Ménestrier also cites Turenne's catafalque, "which represented the tower of David between four palm trees," and the decoration of Saint-Denis for the funeral of Queen Maria Theresa: "Between the two canopies which crown the altars and the *chapelle ardente* rises a superb pavillion dotted with tears and fleur-de-lys, bordered with ermine, whose long, broad sides, attached to the four pillars of the great transept of the church, covered the place where the funeral ceremonies are to take place. Four pyramids, each with two sides, flank this area intended for the funeral ceremonies. They are girt with marble, dotted with tears, and adorned with antique camaieus, one of which, borrowed from a medal of Plautillus, shows the king and queen holding hands, and bears these words: *concordio Felix.*"[10]

Bossuet may stigmatize those "columns which seem to wish to carry to heaven the magnificent evidence of our nothingness," but his words were no less a contribution to the magnificence of the funerals of his time than were the works of Le Brun or Lully, or, indeed, than were the riot of trophies, hangings, oriflammes, allegorical tableaux, banners, coats of arms, mitres, helmets, symbolic animals, torches, unrolled carpets, and so on that decorated the churches for funerals.

And one was certainly attending a performance since, as Mme de Sévigné says, "the Court and city were summoned, roles were cast in the houses, and huge posters in large letters stuck to the walls. When the great day arrived the best company was to be found at the church; one admired the mausoleum which rose to the ceiling, decorated with great figures, adorned with a thousand lamps."[11]

The spectacle could also be in images, like that series of tableaux representing the actions of Philip II, king of Spain, which was the centerpiece of the decoration at the funeral of that king in Florence in 1598.

Spectacle it certainly was, though the mourning at court had a certain meanness about it, and, if Saint-Simon is to be believed, the tragedy

[9] Ibid.
[10] Ibid.
[11] Mme de Sévigné, *Lettre à Madame de Grignan.*

soon declined into comedy: "The oddest thing of all was that the king, who, at Monseigneur's death, had wanted those persons who wear mourning when he wears mourning to do so, although he himself did not wear mourning, did not want anyone to do so for Monsieur le Dauphin and Mme la Dauphine, except Monsieur le Duc and Madame la Duchesse de Berry."[12]

The last king of France to be given a funeral in the tradition of the Ancien Régime was Louis XVIII, on October 25, 1824.

Although it was formally never the custom at Notre-Dame to conceal the Gothic architecture beneath a decoration of draperies, Saint-Denis was draped in black, with draperies covering the arches and keeping out the light. "The church of Saint-Denis has disappeared; and it is in the midst of a veritable royal basilica, gleaming with several thousand lights, that the cenotaph of Louis XVIII has been erected."[13]

All around Suger's church were Ionic columns: ten marble columns surmounted by turrets, surmounted in turn by crosses between the black-draped columns. A number of galleries had been erected in the side aisles, and huge scaffolding for the galleries in the nave and choir. The entire vault was dotted with golden lillies. It was Hittorf, the future architect of the Gare du Nord, who designed the constructions and the hearse. The requiem mass was composed by Cherubini.

In the middle of the choir stood the cenotaph.

Its principal form is a rectangle, resting at the four corners on as many pilasters, in front of which rise, on each exterior face, two quite separate columns, resting on common pedestals; these pedestals are adorned with rich moldings. . . supported by angels holding in their hands upturned torches, all gold on a lapis ground. The columns and pilasters, covered for a third of their height with oak leaves, are decorated over the rest of their height by arabesques formed of poppy leaves, palm leaves, and fleur-de-lys. . . The capitals, of a composite Corinthian order with volutes and two rows of acanthus and palm leaves, are embellished with heads of angels and stars. . . A rich lacework, also carved and designed with palms and poppies, completes the cornice. Eight worshipping angels rise above the columns. . . At the top of the cupola which surmounts the monument is placed an azure globe dotted with golden stars.[14]

[12] Duc de Saint-Simon, *Mémoires* (abridged ed. 1788; complete ed. 1829–31).
[13] Legrand d'Aussy, *Des sépultures nationales.*
[14] Ibid.

This was certainly an anachronistic resurgence of the funeral splendors of the Ancien Régime after the storms of the revolution and empire. But the revolution itself, so indifferent to the remains of ordinary citizens, created a "Republican funeral" for its heroes and martyrs. One has only to think of the extraordinary ceremonies at Marat's death. After inaugurating his bust in a chapel erected at the Carrousel, it was paraded from street to street like a holy relic. Triumphal arches, mausoleums, and cenotaphs were erected to his memory. David's painting *Marat's Death*, placed on a pedestal in the courtyard of the Louvre, surrounded by the chorus from the Opéra singing hymns, attracted huge crowds.

In the seventeenth and eighteenth centuries, funerals gave rise not only to an ephemeral funerary architecture for the religious ceremonies but also to a more durable composition: tombs that were also conceived as scenes of dramatic action. Unlike the four-sided sarcophagi, these tombs were unusual in backing on to a wall. One no longer walked around the monument, but looked at it. It was a theater in the Italian style, with stone actors, of which we were the passive spectators.

The baroque influence of Bernini is evident here. For the mausoleums of Alexander VII, in Saint Peter's, Bernini represented the pope kneeling on a pedestal, at the summit of the monument. On each side, in the folds of bronze drapery, appear four virtues. Bernini's innovation lay in conceiving of a tomb as an animated scene in which all the figures take part in the same action. The pope is praying, death shows him the clepsydra, and the virtues weep over the death of the Holy Father.

This formula was to be used for later funerary monuments, whether in Père-Lachaise or in the memorials erected after World War I.

During his stay in Paris between June and October 1665 Bernini was to exert an influence, which, in the funerary domain, was to last until our own day. Before his arrival in Paris, French funerary art knew little more than praying and recumbent figures. Bernini's projects for the Bourbons' chapel in Saint-Denis and for Richelieu's monument at the Sorbonne put these praying figures into movement. The recumbent figures now rise from their half-opened tombs, and gesture toward the living. Funerary art, which had hitherto expressed repose or sleep, now began to speak, to declaim. Again, what Bernini was introducing was theater.

We have touched on the work of Charles Le Brun as organizer of funerals. We now find him designing tombs, introducing picturesque or dramatic subjects. The most astonishing was no doubt the tomb he built

Antoine Coysevox (1640–1720), tomb of Lebrun, church of Saint
Nicolas du Chardonnet, Paris. *(Photo Giraudon)*

Giovanni Lorenzo Bernini (1598–1680), tomb of Pope Alexander VII,
Saint Peter's Church, Rome. *(Photo Alinari-Giraudon)*

for his mother, who died in 1668, in the church of Saint-Nicolas-du-Chardonnet. It is a "sarcophagus of black marble whose raised gravestone offers a glimpse of the dead woman half emerging from the tomb, her hands joined in prayer, her eyes raised to heaven. Above an angel is sounding the trumpet of the resurrection."[15]

Le Brun also designed tombs for Turenne, who died in 1675, and for Colbert, who died in 1683. Turenne is represented semirecumbent and dying. Victory supports his right arm. At the back, in front of a pyramid, are two women: Value, who is weeping, and Abundance, who is looking at the soldier. Colbert's tomb, carved by Coysevox and Tuby, in the church of Saint-Eustache, shows the dead man perched on a sarcophagus, wearing his Court dress, kneeling in prayer. Two women, Fidelity and Abundance, are sitting on the plinth. Richelieu's tomb in the Sorbonne, carved by Girardon, was probably also designed by Le Brun. Richelieu is shown semirecumbent. Behind him, Religion, veiled, supports him. To the right two small genii bear the cardinal's coat of arms. At the foot, Science, draped, weeps.

One of Coustou's pupils, Louis de Roubillac (1695–1762) introduced the "picturesque" type of monumental funerary sculpture into England. Twelve of his tombs are known, the most famous being the mausoleum of Lord and Lady Nightingale in Westminster Abbey. The center of this monument is pierced by a double bronze door from which a skeletal Death, in white marble, is emerging. With his right hand he is throwing his dart at a dying Lady Nightingale, seated on a bench, while Lord Nightingale holds up his hand to stop the dart.

The most spectacular of the eighteenth-century tombs is no doubt that carved by Jean-Baptiste Pigalle for the maréchal de Saxe, in the church of Saint Thomas in Strasbourg. Inaugurated in 1777, this monument shows, in its lower part, a sarcophagus covered with white drapery, flanked by statues of Hercules and Death. On its upper part, the marshal, standing, is descending proudly into the tomb. Behind him is a pyramid. To his right, a lion, a leopard, and an eagle, that is to say, the nations which he conquered: England, Holland, and Austria. Between the marshal and Death, France is represented as a seated woman, wearing a cloak covered with fleur-de-lys. She is trying, with her right hand, to hold back the marshal, while with her left hand she is pushing away Death. Behind her, a small Cupid weeps.

About 1760 a new conception appeared, more sentimental than heroic

---

[15] Florence Ingersoll-Smouse, *La Sculpture funéraire en France au XVIIIe siècle*, Ph.D. diss., University of Paris, 1912.

Antoine Coysevox (1640–1720), tomb of Colbert (1685–87), church of
Saint Eustache, Paris. *(Photo Giraudon)*

Jean Baptiste Pigalle (1714–85), tomb of the maréchal de Saxe, church of
Saint Thomas, Strasbourg. *(Photo Lauros-Giraudon)*

in style. The century of Corneille and Racine gave way to that of Rousseau and Diderot. Stress was laid above all on conjugal love. When the dauphin, the son of Louis XV, died, Cochin consulted Diderot on the arrangements to be made for the tomb. Diderot immediately imagined a scene in the style of Greuze:

> I would have a funeral couch. On that funeral couch are two pillows. One of these pillows is unoccupied. On the other rests the husband's head. . . Beside the bed I would place Religion. Her arm is resting on her large cross. The hand of this arm points up to heaven. The wife is beside her, one arm resting on the thigh of Religion, to whom she is saying: "Look, he is making room for me, he is calling me." Conjugal Love, on the other side of the bed, invites her to lie next to her husband, but Religion interposes her hand and says: "I approve your happiness, but it must await the order from above." However, France, her back turned away from the scene, contemplates the loss that she has just sustained. . . I open a funeral vault. Illness is emerging from this vault, raising the stone on her shoulder. She orders the prince to descend. The prince, standing on the edge of the vault, neither looks at her nor listens to her. He is consoling his wife, who wishes to follow him. He shows her his children whom a crouching Wisdom is presenting to him. . . Behind this group, France raises her arms towards the altars. She implores, she is still filled with hope.

We have moved from the opera of Gluck to the bourgeois theater.

Emile Mâle writes of Philippe Pot's tomb at the Louvre: "Those great figures veiled in black terrify like nocturnal apparitions." Those characters, which are added to the effigy of the dead man, always intensify the gloominess of the scene. Michel Guiomar has observed that, like any strange object, those funerary statues bear a message, that they have a particularly ambiguous gaze. "Placed half way, these statues at least have a silent voice, and are turned towards us. . . Even though its eyes may be closed. . . the funerary statue always sees."[16]

The plastic gloom is increased by the drapery, since all drapery, in a funerary context, inevitably recalls the winding sheet, if not the ghost, which scarcely has any other form than its shroud. And Guiomar, who has made a special study of the principles of an aesthetics of death in music and literature, has also tried to discern in architecture suggestions of gloom achieved solely through abstract ornamentation, such as those

[16] Michel Guiomar, *Principes d'une esthétique de la mort: Les modes de présences, les présences immédiates, le seuil de l'au-delà*, Ph.D. diss., 1967.

[163

contrasts of black and white materials which, in tombs, do give a sinister impression. Of the painted decoration of the moldings and ornamentation in Michelangelo's Medici chapel in Florence, he says: "The dark green emphasis produced by the framing moldings introduces an element of gloom."[17]

Quite apart from any funerary reference, a gloomy space may appear, therefore, in architecture by a mere reading of the elements of a structure. Guiomar makes such a reading in Louis's theater at Bordeaux, an eighteenth-century creation. He draws particular attention to the staircase in the theater, which is funereal in suggestion. "It is a gloom, not of intention, but of fact: a gaping doorway opening on to corridors flanking the stalls occupies by its mass of dark absence the meeting point of the three staircases, those which descend from the second floor, and that which rises straight towards it. This arrangement is gloomy, for the door attracts and reverses the vanishing traces of the staircases."[18]

Those cemeteries of mummies, so beloved of the eighteenth century, are, again, theatrical productions, imbued with a taste for tragic gloom. Since the Middle Ages there had been mummies of saints, dressed, and exhibited under glass in churches. But such mummies were exceptional and were always presented as recumbent figures. They were "at rest." In the eighteenth century, quite ordinary mortals were, after being dried in the air, usually in church towers, placed in a row, standing or sitting and presented to visitors in their everyday clothes. In the Franciscan church in Toulouse these mummies are visited and presented as in a spectacle. In Rome where in a vault of the Capuchin church one can see the standing mummies of the monks and the lay brothers of Saint Francis, there existed a confraternity of gravediggers who organized an annual festival in which purgatory was represented using real corpses.

There were also private mummies. Necker, one of Louis XVI's ministers, kept at home, in brandy, the body of his dead wife. Then, on Necker's death, husband and wife were embalmed and placed in their estate at Coppet, on the shore of Lake Geneva.

But the most astonishing use of mummies in a spectacle, and one which in any case can still be visited today, is to be found in the Capuchin monastery at Palermo. From the mid-seventeenth century to 1881 the rich families of Palermo sent their dead to this monastery. There are at present 8,000 in the Capuchin catacombs, standing in rows, labeled, with the date of their death, bearing on their faces expressions that relate

[17] Ibid.
[18] Ibid.

not so much to the cause of death, as to the hazards of their drying and preservation.

> Vaulted galleries spread out and intersect like the streets of a city. The dead stand there, lining our route, a sinister company, a hideous mob. . . Two rows of niches rise on either side; the corpses are their statues. . . They have been cooked, arranged, dressed, some wearing only a shroud, others the clothes of which they were perhaps most proud when alive. Death is turned into a masquerade. But on their own these dead would have fallen, for they stagger and lean to one side; they have been tied up with string, secured with belts, nailed, fixed to the wall. . . Some have broken their bonds, torn their powdery dresses or shrouds; their disheveled heads drop to one side, and their fleshless arms hang pitifully loose. . . Here is a magistrate who still wears on his hollow chest a lace jabot; there is a child, yellowed and shriveled, and a little further on a girl lying in her wedding dress. On her black, desiccated head, she wears a white crown—gloomy irony. . . Light penetrates freely, through broad air vents in these funereal retreats; however, one meets passages where the darkness half closes them. The mystery deepens and terror increases. Cats and rats haunt these sad places, and, rolling skulls across the floor, stirring the tattered garments into motion, they pursue their mad chases through the galleries.[19]

A century after Lucien Augé's description, Jean Baudrillard went in turn to visit the corridors of the Capuchin monastery at Palermo, and still found the corpses

> carefully fossilized, with the skin, the hair and the nails, lying, or suspended from the shoulders, in serried ranks, through long corridors. . . Still dressed in a rough shroud or, on the contrary, in their best clothes, complete with gloves, and powdery muslin veils: 8,000 corpses in the pale early light from the airvents, in an incredible multiplicity of attitudes, grinning, languid, nodding, fierce or timid—a dance of death, which, before becoming a waxworks for tourists, had for a long time been a place for Sunday walks for the nearest and dearest of the deceased, who came to see them, recognize them, show them to their children, in living familiarity, a "dominicality" of death like that of going to mass or going to the theater.[20]

We always come back to the opera, whether it is a high mass requiring the services of a fashionable composer; a requiem; the theatrical production of the funerary monument; dead extras from a theater of death.

[19] Augé, *Les Tombeaux*.
[20] Baudrillard, *L'Echange symbolique*.

FUNERALS

The theatricalization of death in the seventeenth and eighteenth centuries extended, as we have seen, from representation in the death chamber to the spectacular tomb, with all the pomp and circumstance of the funeral procession. The theatricalization of death affected, in varying degrees, every class of society. Everyone feared sudden death, which would rob one of putting on a good performance in one's last scene. In our own time, on the other hand, sudden death is desired. For there is no longer a scene to be acted. Death is secret. At a time when the dying are practically abandoned to the care of the specialists of death, this last scene is too sinister to be wished.

12

The Funeral as Spectacle

Yet it should be said: where Christianity has not cast its divine light, funeral ceremonies contain many bizarre practices.

Edouard Hornstein
directeur du Grand Séminaire de Soleure, author of *Sépultures devant l'Histoire, l'archéologie, la liturgie, le droit ecclésiastique et la législation civile*, Paris 1868

The funeral procession is the last journey; perhaps a modernization of the immemorial journeys of the dead to the underworld.

There was the terrible last journey of the young captive who, for the Aztecs, embodied Tezcatlipoca, mounting alone the great steps of the temple, breaking with every step one of his flutes. After slowly climbing the steps, the pseudo-Tezcatlipoca would meet at the top the sacrificer, who laid him out on a stone slab and tore out his heart.

Dancing, eating, and drinking, in non-European primitive societies, and funeral meals in our own countries, transform mourning into festivity. The day of the death of a dear one must remain unforgettable. In ancient China, it was not unusual for families to ruin themselves to give their deceased a magnificent burial. In present-day India a man may have to work all his life to repay a usurer the debt contracted by his father for the burial of his grandfather. In ancient Annam a funeral procession cost a fortune. It required forty porters plus twenty monks, not to mention musicians, professional mourners, and standard bearers. A succession of floats formed an urban spectacle, which, it was hoped, would be incomparable. First there was the "house of the spirit," burned at the burial, then the "boat which carries the soul," then "the chariot of the soul." Last, there was the coffin with the funeral tablet on which was placed a large decorated paper house which was then burned so that it might become the house of the deceased in the other world.

Bizarre practices, perhaps, but, contrary to what the director of the seminary at Soleure naively believed, the funeral rites of the Christian West are no less surprising.

From the thirteenth to the eighteenth centuries the funeral procession was the object of a practically unchanging ceremonial; quite simply, the deceased was accompanied by a greater or lesser number of people. In urban funerals the four orders of mendicant friars—Carmelites, Capuchins, Dominicans, Augustinians—were an obligatory part of the processions and derived substantial sums of money from them. The order and composition of the procession—like the size of the "funeral hangings" in the home and church, the number and weight of the candles—were always fixed by the deceased in his will. The funeral, which often took place at dusk, was first of all a spectacle of light. The poorest had only thirteen candles; the rich at least a hundred. Between 1730 and 1770 these candles of the rich became enormous, weighing between two and four pounds.

Wills also stipulated the participation of the friars and poor in the procession. Usually thirteen poor were requested, for the figure thirteen represented the apostles, including Judas. Orphans, too, were often requested: "Thirteen charity children, each holding a candle in one hand, and, on the other arm, there was very often a piece of caddis cloth which they owed to the generosity of the deceased to clothe themselves."[1]

In the funeral processions the parish clergy sometimes carried a reliquary containing saints' relics. In this way the deceased was accompanied by the most illustrious dead person of the parish.

In Provence the custom of proceeding round the town consisted in taking the deceased, his face uncovered, along a route that was sometimes laid down in the will. This procession was accompanied by musi-

[1] Vovelle, *Piété baroque*.

cians, and the bells of all the churches rang out at the approach of the procession. Apart from the uncovered face, "the shroud which covered the bier made it known who the individual was who was being taken to the earth: it was emblazoned, and the arms, or, if there were none, the initials, of the deceased were copied out and carried in the procession by the poor who accompanied him."[2]

In the late eighteenth century certain testators prohibited this custom, and asked to be carried to the cemetery by the shortest route. Most of them were nobles or rich bourgeois like J. B. Dadaoust, of Aix, first advocate general, who ordered in his will that the poor of the hospitals should say a De Profundis at his death, though "expressly forbidden to accompany the body, for that merely dissipates and disturbs the household."

This humility, like ostentation, is also a way of playing a role before death. Certain notables asked that information about themselves be placed across the church entrance so that it might be trodden over by the faithful. But, before them, Richard Lion-Heart in the twelfth century had asked to be buried in the small church at Fécamp, so that Christians might walk over him. Richard II (*d.* 1399) asked to be buried under the eaves. In the thirteenth century, on the other hand, the seigneur du Châtelet wanted to be buried standing, in the hollow of a church column, so that villeins would not walk over his belly.

Pepin the Short also asked to be buried in front of the main doors of the church, lying on his belly, out of humility and to expiate the sins of his father, Charles Martel, who, to raise money for the war against the Saracens, had confiscated church property. In 1776 a canon of Reims wanted to be buried under the porch of the cathedral between two poor men, whose relations were rewarded by his heirs.

This list of such scenes of ostentatious humility could go on forever. But more surprising is the poverty in death of the three great European dynasties, the Bourbons of France, the kings of Spain, and the Habsburgs of Austria. Indeed, all the French Bourbons seem to have shown a marked lack of interest in their burials—even Louis XIV. Their coffins were simply lined up, without monuments, in the vaults of Saint-Denis. Similarly, in Vienna, in a vault of the Capuchin church, the Habsburgs lie in rows of tomb-shaped monuments. In the Escorial the praying figures of Charles V and Philip II alone flank the high altar. Their successors are below, on the left the kings, on the right the queens, in the vault

[2] Ibid.

which the monk who accompanied Saint-Simon in 1721 called the "muck heap."

Charles V, who retired after his abdication to a monastery at Yuste, asked that a funeral service be organized for himself, even though he was still in good health. Before the catafalque erected by the monks, Charles V, wearing mourning, a candle in his hand, prayed for the repose of his own soul. He died three weeks later.

Is there not a certain arrogance in such apparent humility? The anti-spectacle is also a spectacle.

But though certain great persons make a conscious effort to avoid the theatricalization of the funerary monument, none of them can dispense with the ritual of the funeral. From that of Lothaire, in 986, to that of Napoleon I, under Louis-Philippe, royal funerals have provided an urban spectacle that has something of the religious procession, the carnival, the military march past, the torchlight procession, the royal entry, the "triumph of death," the parade, and a theatricalization to be found in both classical tragedy and the medieval mysteries.

Robert Sabatier quotes from a document of the fifteenth century describing the funeral of Charles VI:

> At this time there were few people who remembered how such things had been done, in times gone by, how the kings of France had been taken to their burial, and in what order one should proceed. . . First a great litter was made with shafts fore and aft. In this litter were placed the coffer and body of the king, and on the said body were placed two linen sheets, and on these, by way of a covering, a large pall of cloth of gold, on a vermillion ground, with a border of azure velvet, and if the bier was being carried at a man's height, one could not see the coffer, for it was hidden beneath the said pall. But on all these things was placed the image of the king wearing the royal tunic and cloak.

Sabatier continues:

> This chronicle goes on to describe how the bier was followed by the king's officers dressed in brown, the cupbearers, the pantlers, and menservants, with the coat of arms of France, and carrying a torch weighing four pounds. The body and litter were borne by fifty menservants. The order of the procession was as follows: the mendicant orders; nine prelates, bishops, and abbots, wearing black copes and white mitres; the provost of Paris, staff in hand; the king's chamberlains, carvers, equerries and stewards; the four presidents of the *Parlement*, wearing vermillion cloaks lined with squirrel fur, holding the cords of the pall; the lords and clerks of the *Parlement*, the ushers,

the provost of merchants, and the magistrates. . . The people were in great mourning. The king was carried into Notre-Dame, which was brightly lighted and hung with chintz decorated with fleur-de-lys.[3]

The ceremonial hardly changed up to the funeral of Louis XVIII. For three centuries the order of the procession was to consist of:
1. The first equerry on foot, carrying the pennon of France, a banner of sky-blue velvet dotted with fleur-de-lys
2. The musicians, holding their instruments downwards
3. The hearse drawn by six horses harnessed in pairs, with covers of black velvet; armorers and arms-bearers surround the hearse
4. The friars of the mendicant orders bearing candles
5. Twelve pages dressed in black velvet, bare-headed, mounted on horses also covered with black velvet; footmen wearing mourning hold the bridles of the pages' horses
6. A show horse, entirely covered with crimson velvet, led by two equerries
7. The first chamberlain bearing the banner of France
8. The princes mounted on small mules, wearing deep mourning
9. The ambassadors in mourning
10. The knights of the Order
11. The lords and gentlemen of the Chamber
12. The captains of the guard[4]

When the body had been brought to Notre-Dame, a solemn service took place in the evening and the following morning. In the afternoon the procession, in the same order, set off for Saint-Denis. The monks of Saint-Denis came out to receive the body, held a solemn service in the evening and spent the night in prayer. The next morning the funeral itself took place, with the descent into the vault. The coffin of the last dead king remained on the steps of the vault until the arrival of his successor's coffin. All those who took part in the procession stayed and dined at the abbey of Saint-Denis.

More or less the same ceremonial took place for the queens.

At the funeral of Henri IV, the procession was enormous. It consisted of at least two thousand people; 172 archers, harquebuses and halberds pointing downwards; 500 poor, wearing great robes of black cloth, each carrying a burning torch; 24 criers of the City of Paris, ringing their bells; 33 poor scholars of a college; 83 Capuchins, 68 Minims, 224 Franciscans, 190 Dominicans, 100 Augustinians, 50 Carmelites, 35

[3] Robert Sabatier, *Dictionnaire de la Mort* (Paris: Albin Michel, 1967).
[4] Legrand d'Aussy, *Des sépultures nationales*.

Bernardins; 30 sergeants of the Châtelet wearing black robes and square caps, each holding a black stick in his hand; 200 gentlemen in waiting; 160 officers of the king's household; the notaries, procurators, barristers, clerks, burghers of the city, all in mourning; the religious of all the monasteries and convents of Paris; the messengers and postmasters, all in black robes and hoods; the king's preachers, confessors, and almoners; 17 archbishops and bishops in white mitres; the cardinals; the princes, dukes, and counts. From the Louvre to Notre-Dame, all the streets were hung in black, and each house had a lighted torch in front of it.[5]

It was certainly a performance laid on for the people, with all its spectacle, the special costumes, and the famous to be seen once in a lifetime. These funeral "exits" corresponded to the princely "entries," and drew the same crowds. Only two royal funerals failed to draw popular support: those of Henry III and Louis XIV. At the death of Henry III the people of Paris showed its joy by wearing green by way of mourning—green was then regarded as the color of madmen. By Louis XIV's death, the century was no doubt exhausted by such an exceptional royal longevity, since Louis XIV, with Charlemagne, was the only French sovereign to die in his seventies. The attitude of the people being what it was, the procession did not go through Paris, but traveled at night from Versailles to Saint-Denis, via Montmartre. On the way, people set up small tents for drinking, singing, and dancing.[6] The funeral of Louis XIV was no doubt the only royal funeral in France to arouse popular merriment. Far from regarding the nocturnal torch-lit procession as a sinister thing, the people considered the illumination as magnificent and "looked upon it as a festival."[7]

But it was not only royal funerals which were celebrated in the city. The entire aristocracy also ordered magnificent funerals, and, very soon, the upper bourgeoisie did not want to be left out.

In 1550, at the funeral of Claude de Lorraine, the first duc de Guise, there were 100 poor dressed in black and 100 poor dressed in white, each carrying a torch. In 1662, at the funeral of the Archduke Albert, in Brussels, 400 poor walked at the head of the procession with lighted torches, followed by 600 monks and nuns with lighted candles.

Even in small towns, such as Angers was in 1605, the funerals of great persons were no less magnificent than those in the capital. When Pierre de Donadieu de Puycharic, governor of the city and castle, died

[5] Ibid.

[6] Voltaire, *Le Siècle de Louis XIV* (Paris, 1751).

[7] Mathieu Marais, *Journal et mémoires sur la Régence et le siècle de Louis XV* (1715–1737), 4 vols. (Paris, 1868).

in that year, a procession began to form at 8 o'clock in the morning, consisting of four criers, followed by the captains and twelve civic companies "harquebuses under their arms and colors lowered" in sign of mourning, followed in turn by another row of criers, the four mendicant orders, and thirty-six poor dressed in new clothes and black hoods, each holding a large torch. Then came the pages, carrying on black pillows covered with mourning bands, which reached the ground, the "*pièces d'honneur*" of the deceased—spurs, gauntlets, helmet, sword, tunic, coat of arms—then his charger caparisoned with black serge, and two pages on horseback, one carrying the trumpet, the other the ensign of the governor of Angers. At the moment of the burial the civic companies, which had remained outside, performed a great "*escoupterie d' arquebusade*," as the castle cannons thundered, and the bells of all the churches of the city, which had been ringing without stopping since the morning, fell silent.[8]

Before banning these ostentatious ceremonies and striving to invent a secular practice, which was usually confined to throwing flowers into the common grave, the Revolution of 1789 gave in, nevertheless, to the attraction of a new splendor for the funerals of its own dignitaries.

The first Revolutionary funeral accompanied Mirabeau to the Panthéon, on April 4, 1791. The day before, the National Assembly had requested, and been granted, that the church of Sainte-Geneviève be consecrated to the burial of great men and that Mirabeau should be the first to be buried there. Michelet describes the scene:

> On April 4 there took place the largest, most popular funeral that there had ever been in the world before that of Napoleon on December 15, 1840. The people policed it themselves and did so admirably. There was no accident in that crowd of three or four thousand men. The streets, the boulevards, the windows, the roofs, the trees, were filled with spectators.
>
> At the head of the procession walked La Fayette, then, royally surrounded by twelve ushers forming a chain, followed Tronchet, the president of the National Assembly, then the entire Assembly, without distinction of parties. . . Immediately after the National Assembly, as a second assembly, before all the authorities, marched the serried ranks of the Jacobin Club. They had distinguished themselves by their display of sorrow, ordering a mourning of eight days, and an eternal mourning from anniversary to anniversary.
>
> This immense procession was unable to arrive at the church of Saint-Eustache before 8 o'clock. . . Twenty thousand national guards fired simul-

[8] Lebrun, *Les Hommes et la Mort en Anjou.*

[173

taneously, and all the windows shattered; for a moment it seemed that the church was collapsing on to the coffin.

Then the funeral proceeded, by torchlight. The ceremony was truly funereal at this hour. It was the first time that one heard two all-powerful instruments, the trombone and the drum. We arrived late into the night, at Sainte-Geneviève.[9]

First Mirabeau, then, later, Marat, those two heroes of the Revolution, were to have magnificent funerals, and both were to be taken to the Panthéon. By a strange reversal these two major figures were, as a result of two different political upheavals, to be expelled from the Panthéon and banished from history which, later, was to take them back (not into the Panthéon, but into history).

Let us turn to Michelet once again for a description of Mirabeau's expulsion from the Panthéon:

It was on a sad autumn day in that tragic year of 1794 when France had almost completed the task of exterminating herself, it was then that, having killed off the living, it set about killing the dead, tearing from its heart its most glorious son. It took savage delight in that supreme sorrow. The man of law entrusted with the task of carrying out this hideous act himself declares, in a crude, ignorant, barbaric report, which gives a strange idea of the time—I have the hand-written document: "When the procession *of the festival* had arrived at the Place du Panthéon, one of the citizens, an usher at the Convention, advanced toward the main doors of the said Panthéon, read out the decrees which excluded the said man, the remains of Honoré Riqueti Mirabeau, which were immediately carried in a wooden coffin outside the wall of the said temple, and, having been handed over to us, we took and laid the said coffin in the ordinary place of burial." This place was none other than Clamart, the cemetery for executed criminals. The body was carried there during the night, and buried, without any marking, somewhere near the middle of the area.[10]

The Revolution had tried to democratize funerals by means of funerary festivities, the arrangement of which had been entrusted to a painter who was less well known than David but who appears, according to Michelet, "to have been more powerfully inspired than David for the production of these popular representations." David, as we know, was Robespierre's artist. Sergent, for such was his name, was rather Dan-

[9] Jules Michelet, *Histoire de la Révolution française* (Paris, 1847).
[10] Ibid.

ton's. The funerary festivities arranged by Sergent led to such emotional scenes that Michelet attributes responsibility for the massacre of the Tuileries to that of August 10, 1792. On August 27 of the same year, Sergent organized a festival of the dead in memory of the victims:

> Through clouds of perfume the victims of August 10, the widows and orphans, in white dresses and black belts, carried in a chest the petition of July 17, 1791, which at the time had been presented in vain to the Republic. Then came huge black sarcophagi, which seemed to contain, to carry mountains of human flesh, then came the Law, a colossal figure, armed with his sword, and behind him, the judges, all the courts, with the court of August 17 at their head. Behind this court marched the formidable Commune, which had created it, with the statue of Liberty. Last, the National Assembly, bearing the civic crowns to honor and console the dead. Chénier's solemn chants, the bitter, terrible music of Gossec, the approaching night, which was bringing its mourning, the incense rising, as if to carry to heaven the voice of vengeance, everything filled all hearts with an intoxication of death.[11]

With the Consulate the splendors of the Ancien Régime reappeared. On February 9, 1802, the former duc de Bouillon went to his last resting place in a hearse drawn by six horses and followed by ten draped carriages and twenty ordinary ones. Fifty poor, dressed in black, escorted him, torches in hand. For the funeral of his mother-in-law, General Junot included in the procession fifty servants and three hundred poor.

So the dear poor, who were indissociable from funeral processions and who usually came in order to earn a new suit or even a piece of cloth, were back a mere ten years after the storming of the Bastille.

With the nineteenth century, the number of carriages and coaches in the funeral procession became a sign of wealth and power greater than this traditional mobilization of the poor. At the funeral of the poet Jacques Delille, in May 1813, there were 200 carriages. After lying in state for six days at the Collège de France, on a ceremonial bed, his face painted and his head crowned with laurel, Delille was carried in a coffin to the church of Saint-Étienne-du-Mont, then on to Père-Lachaise. The procession included the four Academies, in their entirety, the university in robes, and a crowd of torch bearers.

Finally, on September 23, 1824, for the funeral of Louis XVIII, everything was carried out as if there had never been the interval of the Revolution and empire. The body, embalmed with mercuric chloride, lay in state for six days as an uninterrupted flow of people, high and low,

[11] Ibid.

filed past it. The departure of the procession for Saint-Denis was announced by a salvo of a hundred and one bursts of cannon, the great bell of Notre-Dame, and all the church bells of the city. The journey took three and a half hours. The procession was led by a detachment of the gendarmerie of Paris, followed by the high command of the city, the first military division, the royal guard, the national guard, a semisquadron of the *gendarmerie d'élite*, three batallions of line infantry, two squadrons of light cavalry, sixty mounted artillerymen, two battalions of infantry, a deputation from the military academy of Saint-Cyr and from the Ecole Polytechnique. Four hundred poor carried the torches of the procession. Fourteen funeral carriages, each drawn by eight caparisoned horses, conveyed the royal princes, the great officers and senior functionaries of state. In a coach an archbishop carried the king's heart. On the hearse, the royal insignia decorated the coffin. Forty lifeguards and twelve pages flanked the hearse.

If one compares this procession with that of Henry IV one notices that, although the number of poor is almost the same, soldiers have largely replaced the clergy. Could it be that the extreme militarization of France by the First Empire had left such a strong mark that it was to survive throughout the nineteenth century, and even into the twentieth, when it was even felt necessary to employ troops to bury in great pomp a painter like Braque or an architect like Le Corbusier, who had never shown the slightest interest in things military?

On December 15, 1840, the transfer of Napoleon I to the Invalides, the body having arrived back from Saint Helena, was the occasion of an incredible disguising of Parisian architecture. The city bristled with flagpoles, pedestals, equestrian statues, obelisks, columns; the entire city was studded with eagles and colored with hangings. In order to receive the funeral boat, which had come from Le Havre, a "Greek Temple" had been built at Courbevoie. Sixteen horses caparisoned with gold drew a hearse with gilded wheels. Because the procession had to pass beneath the Arc de Triomphe, the Champs-Elysées had been transformed into an opera set. It was very cold. The elderly survivors of the *Grande Armée*, who had been asked to take part in the ceremony, were shivering with cold. Thirty thousand spectators in mourning watched the Ogre pass. Among them, standing on an official rostrum, was Victor Hugo, who related the events for us. At the Invalides, which had been opened for eight days to allow the public to come and visit the tomb of Napoleon I, two hundred thousand people had lined up for several hours despite the extreme cold.

In 1865 the duc de Morny, adulterine half brother of Napoleon III, president of the Chamber of Deputies, was placed in a coffin, and lay in state under the peristyle of the Palais-Bourbon. The funeral was attended by the entire parliament, all the official bodies, a division of infantry, and four squadrons of cavalry. Buried in Père-Lachaise, as was only right and proper, the duc de Morny was given 430 square feet and a chapel built by Viollet-le-Duc, the favorite architect of the Imperial family.

Napoleon III's successor, Adolphe Thiers, the executioner of the Communards, so unpopular with later generations, was, nevertheless, in 1877 given a funeral that must count among the great spectacles of the genre. There was an abundance of flowers in the procession, transported on dozens of litters. Thousands of spectators came to watch the procession from the Place Saint-Georges to the church of Notre-Dame-de-Lorette, then on to Père-Lachaise. The streets, the balconies, and even the roofs were filled with a crowd that was more curious than hostile. Buried in a green porphyry sarcophagus, in the Invalides, imitating that of Napoleon I, Adolphe Thiers seems haunted by the ghosts of the Communards, since his tomb is still subjected to insulting graffiti and even to damage.

Eight years later the nineteenth century died with Victor Hugo, who was "Panthéonized" in June 1885. "The Anthem of the Girondins alternated with Méhul's hymn. The white and red plumes of the Paris guard nodded out there like fields of daisies and poppies. . . At the end of the Rue Soufflot, reached by a triumphal ascent, is the Panthéon draped in black, with two giant braziers, their green flames moving in the wind. And we turned round and saw the black hearse appear, simple and striking."[12]

This was the hearse of the poor that Victor Hugo had asked to "carry him to the cemetery." The Panthéon suited him well, but he does not seem to have wanted it—any more than Jaurès, who was also buried there, though he had confided to Briand: "That temple is dark and empty. I'd prefer one of our small country graveyards, with its sun and flowers."[13]

Nevertheless, Jaurès was taken to the Panthéon in 1924 in an immense catafalque supporting an oak coffin, followed by twenty thousand people along the Boulevard Saint-Germain and the Boulevard Saint-Michel. Trumpets played passages from *Aïda*, the Eroica Symphony, and the "Internationale" in alternation. An anthem composed and di-

[12] Le Clère, *Cimetières et Sépultures de Paris*.
[13] Ibid.

[177

Edouard Detaille
(1848–1912), *Funeral
of Pasteur. (Versailles.
Courtesy S.P.A.D.E.M.
Photo Giraudon)*

rected by Gustave Charpentier was to being the spectacle to a close.

Another great national funeral was that of Pasteur in 1895. Just as, more recently, the *Institut* and the architectural bodies, which were the nightmare of Le Corbusier's life, were to be found in the front row to accompany his coffin, so the Academy of Medicine, which had fought so bitterly against Pasteur, insisted on playing the role of vulture. Two divisions of soldiers, now indissociable from the funeral processions of the great, also followed Pasteur. The cortège was so dense that it took two hours to reach Notre-Dame, where the president of the Republic awaited it. The body was buried in a temporary vault in the cathedral, until September 16, 1896, when it was taken to the Institut Pasteur and placed in a crypt of Byzantine style.

Apart from national funerals, which are the occasion, even in our own day, of funerary spectacles (one thinks of the transfer of Jean Moulin to the Panthéon in 1964 or of the requiem for Charles de Gaulle, with most of the heads of state gathered in Notre-Dame), private funerals have become more and more discreet, if not entirely avoided. One of the last funeral processions stipulated in a will, in which a naive bourgeois wanted to reconstitute aristocratic pomp for his own use, was that of Alfred Chauchard in 1909, founder of the Grands Magasins du Louvre, the Paris store. Chauchard had requested in his will that all his employees should follow his funeral procession from the Madeleine to Père-Lachaise and that the undertakers should wear the traditional dress of French lackeys. The hearse was decorated with orchids and followed by five wreath-laden floats. But the employees of the Grands Magasins du Louvre followed their boss grousing and grumbling, while at the cemetery the crowd jeered at the burial.

13

The Public Execution as Spectacle

As the unhappy wretches (they were being broken on the wheel) suffered, I examined the spectators. They were talking and laughing, as if they were attending some parade. But what revolted me the most was a pretty girl who seemed to me to be with her lover. She burst out laughing and made fun of the appearance and cries of the wretches.

Rétif de la Bretonne
Les Nuits de Paris, 1788–94

Public executions were for a long time one of the most popular forms of the spectacle of death.[1] The places of these executions are still marked in our urban surveys: we have the Place du Pilori (where thieves and other petty criminals were merely exposed to the insults and mockery of passersby), the Place de la Contrescarpe (a machine of torture), and the Place du Martroi. The word *martroi* no longer means anything. Yet it is to be found in a number of

[1] The gibbet, the rope, the hanged themselves were the objects of jokes that are to be found throughout medieval literature. "That hideous, atrocious execution, which made pain an object of laughter, was the ordinary text of the merriest of tales, the entertainment of ordinary folk, the inspiration of the legal fraternity" (Michelet, *Histoire de la Révolution française*).

[181

cities, townships, and even villages. It is often the name of the most important square. This square has kept the name of its long-since abolished punitive functions: the name comes from the Latin *martyrium*.

It was on the Place du Martroi that, for at least a thousand years, the spectacle of execution took place, whether by wheel, torture of various kinds, or guillotine. Every public execution attracted the crowds. People wanted to see whether the criminal would repent and whether the executioner would make a good job of it. The public execution was a spectacle with specific rites, as specific as those of the death of the bull in the corrida. And the executioner, who played the role of matador, was the object of critical scrutiny. He had to deliver the death blow according to the rules, otherwise the crowd might turn against him. And it was not uncommon for an executioner, failing several times to decapitate his man, to be stoned by the crowd. On July 23, 1625, the executioner failed to cut off the head of a Breton gentleman after twenty attempts, cutting into the condemned man's head and shoulder several times. The spectators began to jeer at the executioner, then threw stones at him, and finally rushed on to the scaffold, killing the executioner with the axe which he had used so badly.[2]

There was no sympathy for the executioner, then, but there was no indulgence toward the condemned man either. The crowd came to watch a drama played out by two characters, and it expected that these two protagonists would carry out their roles according to the rules. A criminal who showed fear was also insulted; a courageous victim was applauded; sometimes, the executioner himself was applauded.[3] "Some years ago, a son, having had his father murdered, was broken on the Place Dauphine, together with his accomplice, who carried out the deed. The parricide, who, using the bait of some trivial gain, had dragged a weak man down with him, appeared on the scaffold so hard, so haughty, so unrepentant (while his companion prayed and resigned himself to his fate) that at the first cry he uttered, under the first blow from the bar, a general burst of clapping broke out."[4]

[2] Lebrun, *Les Hommes et la Mort en Anjou*.

[3] Public execution is "a spectacle which is also sacrifice and exorcism . . . The participation of the people is essential to it. They help in the erection of the stake, and in the ritual of punishment. They are associated with the vindication of order, and with the triumph of the religious and civil judges. They assist in the exorcism of Evil. Those who try to avoid attending are severely punished" (Jacques Attali, *L'Ordre cannibale* [Paris: Grasset, 1979]).

[4] Mercier, *Tableau de Paris*.

No indulgence and no pity were shown. In medieval public opinion anyone condemned to execution could not be other than diabolical. The church had to struggle against its flock to insist that a confessor accompany the executioner. The bodies of the hanged were left suspended from their ropes, exposed for months—sometimes even for years—to the gaze of passersby.

"Gabriel Prudhomme, known as Massacre . . . hanged at Guéret on January 5, Twelfth Night's Eve, 1778 . . . was left hanging for eighteen months and twenty-six days and fell from the gibbet only on July 26, 1779, a Tuesday."[5]

When they were finally brought down, the bodies were left to rot at the foot of the gibbet. Indeed, the enclosure around the gibbet was used as a rubbish dump, and the bodies of the executed criminals were gradually covered up.

Judges, executioner, and sometimes monks carried the taste for macabre drama very far: there was, for example, the confraternity of Catalan penitents, who, wearing long black robes, their faces covered with mourning bands, accompanied the criminal to the execution, then carried off the body and buried it.

But the body of the condemned man was usually not only ill-treated to help it on its way, but it was not allowed to rest in peace after death. After the execution, the executioner carried the body of the condemned man to the gibbet.[6] This gibbet consisted of stone pillars connected by wooden crosspieces and was used to hang criminals outside the city, near the highways, where they were exposed until they rotted and fell. If the crime was committed in a town other than the criminal's own, the body was taken to the town of the crime and exhibited there.

In Paris, between the Faubourg Saint-Martin and the Temple, was erected the famous gibbet of Montfaucon, which consisted of sixteen pillars and crosspieces, thus making it possible to hang forty-five criminals at once.[7] This highly popular place was surrounded by taverns and pleasure gardens. It was not abolished until the mid-nineteenth century,

[5] Louis Guibert, *Livres de raison, registres de famille et journaux individuels limousins et marchois* (Limoges-Paris, 1888).

[6] In Rome those condemned to death were *exposed on the gemonies*, that is to say, on the double staircase on the facade of the prison, opposite the Forum. Then they were thrown into the Tiber.

[7] Up to the eighteenth century animals found guilty of causing the death of a man were also tried and hanged. But it was quite common to hang horses and pigs. As late as 1906 a dog was tried and executed in Switzerland for taking part in a robbery and murder.

[183

when it was turned into a knacker's yard. A place that for so long had seen men put to death was now used to sacrifice horses.

Familiarity between living and dead, which we still find in nonindustrial civilizations, was to be found in the Place du Martroi from the Middle Ages to the end of the eighteenth century. In no sense did the public execution terrify, or deter from crime. On the contrary, a criminal who "died well," that is to say, proudly, was more likely to arouse the latent violence of the crowd. After the beheading of the duc de Montmorency, the public rushed on to the scaffold and gathered up the blood that had been shed in handkerchiefs. Some even lapped it up off the boards.

Never had punishment been so horrible as in the period from the Middle Ages to the French Revolution—and never had the murder rate been so high. The condemned were hanged, burned, quartered, decapitated, drowned, and boiled, and the judges had to deal with an unceasing flow of highway robberies, murders, armed robbery, brawls between members of all classes, rapes, battered wives, maltreated children, and even manhandled priests. We deplore the violence of modern society, but though we should not underestimate it, it is nevertheless insignificant when compared with the normal brutality of earlier societies. If a violent argument broke out among the burghers of the Hôtel de Ville, it would almost certainly end in blows, and mutual hate would be handed down in the families from generation to generation. Nobles fought duels on the slightest pretext. Every village festival ended in brawls, often involving death. If a brawl broke out in a crowd, a veritable massacre could follow, like the one that followed the fireworks display in honor of the marriage of the dauphin, the future Louis XVI, to Marie Antoinette on May 30, 1770, and which accounted for 1,200 dead.

"These men turned an anxious face to the outside world, to an impenetrable nature still impossible to interpret. They were, at any moment, aggressive . . . Any argument, any dispute could get out of hand, and violence ensue. At Laon, in 1611, the inhabitants of the townships and villages had to be forbidden to carry the harquebus before sunrise and after sunset, in order to stop the inhabitants killing one another over the slightest thing."[8]

Diderot estimated that three hundred people were executed in France per year, around 1700. This figure is considerably lower than those given by Saint-Just, who declared that, under the monarchy, fifteen thousand smugglers were hanged every year. It is true that smugglers, like poach-

[8] Mandrou, *Introduction à la France moderne*.

ers, who, since an edict of Henry IV, had also been hanged, had not always been given a fair trial, and no records survived of such all too "summary" executions.

Between 1560 and 1640 an epidemic of trials for witchcraft took practically whole villages to the stake. Thousands of witches were burned, especially in eastern France.

The stake, reserved above all for witches and heretics, was the most shameful penalty, since a body reduced to ashes, and the ashes, cast to the wind, might not be reconstituted and rise in its entirety on the Last Day. Burnings at the stake were practiced until 1789, though there were far fewer of them after 1775. Poisoners, the sacrilegious, parricides, sodomites, and incendiaries were burned at the stake.

The stake consisted at first of a pole eight feet high, placed in the middle of the Place du Martroi. Faggots were arranged around it, and these covered with logs and straw. At the center, around the post, a space the size of a man was left. The condemned person was tied to the post at the neck, the waist, and the feet. The feet rested on the lower logs. The executioner led the condemned person to the post through a gap, which was then closed up with logs and faggots. The condemned person did not, therefore, climb the stake, but was enclosed within it: only his head and shoulders visible. The usual representation of someone being burned at the stake is therefore inaccurate. On a fifteenth-century miniature one can clearly see heretics buried in faggots up to the chest.[9]

In the Middle Ages, a refinement of the stake was sometimes used, namely, the use of green wood which took longer to burn. Under Louis XV, the condemned were burned in iron cages. But sometimes the executioner was kind enough to strangle the victim before setting light to the faggots. The ashes were then taken off in a dust cart and cast to the wind.

Suicides, which were frequent in antiquity and regarded as honorable, became with Christianity the object of particular opprobrium. Though very rare, courts were known to carry out a trial of a suicide's corpse, and the property of his family was confiscated and handed over to the king. It goes without saying that any religious burial, still less any burial in a cemetery, was refused them.[10]

[9] Robert Anchel, *Crimes et Châtiments au XVIIIᵉ siècle* (Paris: Librairie académique Perrin, 1933).

[10] Even in the Middle Ages suicides were an object of terror. A stake was driven into their bodies so that they would not "come back" as vampires, the corpse was hanged by the feet, its right hand cut off, then burned, or thrown on a rubbish dump. Suicide was

In 1718, at Château-Gontier, Marie Jaguelin, pregnant for six months, poisoned herself. After a due trial, the corpse was "tied to a hurdle and dragged upside down, the face touching the ground, through the streets and crossroads of the town, to the public square; there the executioner ripped out the body of the child, which was carried to the nearby church of Saint John the Evangelist, where unbaptized newborn infants are buried, then what was left of the unfortunate Marie Jaguelin was hanged by the feet to a post for an hour, with an ignominious sign stuck to the post, then burned at the stake, and the ashes thrown to the wind."[11]

But the choicest, rarest spectacle was the wheel. Execution on the wheel was introduced into France from Germany about 1534. In fact it was a double punishment, since the condemned man was first "broken," then exposed, bleeding, on a wheel until his death.

The man condemned to the wheel mounted the steps of the scaffold as the great bell of the church rang out its gloomy notes. Some prisoners undressed themselves. Others fought with the executioner's assistants, who tore off their clothes, and stretched them out on the cross. The condemned man was in fact stretched on a Saint Andrew's cross, consisting of two beams. Grooves were cut into the wood corresponding to the middle of the thighs, legs, upper and lower arms. The criminal, naked except for a shirt, his face turned upwards, was tied to the cross with ropes. The executioner struck the limbs with a square iron bar, on each notch, then gave two or three blows to the stomach. The first torture consisted, then, of breaking the criminal's limbs with twelve blows from a bar. Dislocated and bleeding, the criminal was then carried to a small coachwheel placed horizontally on a pivot. Tied to this wheel he was then exposed to the public who came and watched him die. The death agony might last all night.

For the execution of Damiens, the failed regicide of Louis XV, in 1757, an attempt was made to copy as closely as possible the execution of Ravaillac in 1610. An enormous crowd attended the execution, filling the square, blocking all the windows, and covering the roofs.

---

rare in the Middle Ages and has constantly increased since the nineteenth century. At the present time, there is an average of 20 suicides a day in France. Death by homicide is twenty times fewer than by suicide. Although murder is less common in prison, there is an increase in prison suicides. During World War II, 4,615 Japanese Kamikazes committed suicide in their target-planes in order to sink American ships. As they got into their planes, the Kamikazes, dressed in white, the color of mourning, were given a white urn for their ashes.

[11] Lebrun, *Les Hommes et la Mort en Anjou.*

Damiens was executed on the Place de Grève, traditionally the square of the great Parisian execution-spectacle.

Louis-Sébastien Mercier describes it as narrow, though it had just been widened. Peddlers and hawkers moved among the crowd awaiting the execution, shouting their wares, selling refreshments and ballads about the condemned man. Householders around the square rented out their windows on the day of an execution.

> One reproaches the populace for rushing to see these odious spectacles; but when there is an unusual execution, of a famous criminal, perhaps, Society rushes to see it, just like the lowest of the low . . . Our women, so tender-hearted, of such nervous disposition, who faint at the sight of a spider, attended Damiens' execution, I repeat, and were the last to take their eyes off the most horrible, most disgusting spectacle that justice has ever thought up to avenge kings . . . One reproaches the populace that on that very day people played cards in the Place de Grève; that they gambled while awaiting the boiling oil, the molten lead, the red-hot pincers, and the four horses, who were in the end to quarter the assassin.[12]

Famous as the execution of Damiens was, horrible as it was, it was not exceptional in the eighteenth century. In Paris, apart from the Place de Grève, people were hanged, put to the wheel, or burned on the Croix-Rouge, the Croix-des-Petits-Champs, the Place Saint-Michel, the Place Maubert, the Quai d'Orléans at the foot of the Pont de la Tournelle, the Place Dauphine, the Carrefour de Buci, the Porte Saint-Antoine, the Porte Saint-Martin, the square of the Porte Saint-Denis, the Barrière du Trône, the Place de la Bastille, and the Place du Tertre at Montmartre. Executions took place, therefore, all over the city and, if one moved from one place to another, more or less continuously. There was only one pillory in Paris, at Les Halles, and it was used only for bankrupts. In the eighteenth century people no longer had their hair cut off, or were put away in convents, or were castrated; the wheel was not used for women, nor was hanging, and nobles were not whipped. But bawds were always paraded stripped to the waist, on a donkey, wearing a straw hat; suicides were always dragged on a hurdle, and children hanged from under the armpits. In addition to the death penalty, torture, the galleys, flogging with branding, the cutting off of a hand, the piercing or cutting out of the tongue were also in use.

Those condemned to death were executed the same day or the day

[12] Mercier, *Tableau de Paris*.

after sentence was passed. In Paris, it was a short walk along the Seine from the Châtelet or the Conciergerie to the Place de Grève. In the executioner's cart, the condemned man sat on a plank of wood, his hands tied, his back to the horse, with his confessor beside him and the executioner behind him. Executions often took place at night, by torchlight, which increased their theatrical character.[13]

We are now in a better position to understand why the crowds of the Revolutionary period were able to see the spectacle of the guillotine as a new kind of performance; and why, for the men of the Convention, the guillotine appeared to be a preferable mode of execution compared with the stake, the wheel, or boiling oil.[14]

"Only one man has been beheaded in Paris for about forty years. And the executioner is inexperienced in this task," wrote Louis-Sébastien Mercier, eight years before 1789.[15] But under the Ancien Régime beheadings were unusual since they were reserved as the death penalty for nobles. It was this measure of favor that the *Conventionels* wanted to extend to all citizens.

In his *Memoirs* the executioner Sanson calculated that, between July 14, 1789, and August 27, 1795, the number of victims amounted to 700,705. Of this number the spectacular guillotine did not account for 2 percent. In fact, this machine, designed to effect a rapid and speedy end, was slow. Almost half the number of victims, that is to say, 290,000, fell at the frontiers in the armies of the Republic. Under the Revolution, foreign wars were still the greatest single cause of death. This was followed by civil war, which accounted for more or less the same number of deaths as the wars against the European coalition, that is to say, 299,000 Frenchmen died in this way: 180,000 Vendéens, 87,000 Republicans killed by the Chouans, 32,000 other victims of civil wars in other regions of the West. To this should be added the uncontrolled massacres, like those of September in Paris which account for 3,400 deaths, others in the provinces 18,500, and 400 killed in invaded castles. With its 13,800 victims, including 2,649 in Paris, the guillotine was, then, the least deadly

[13] "It is the fashion, at present, to hang thieves by torchlight" (*Journal* of E. J. F. Barbier, January 1722).

[14] "At Metz, in 1500, 3,000 people gathered on a frozen lake to watch the drowning, in midwinter, of two girls who had beaten a boy to death with sticks. Philippe de Vigneulle describes how, in 1510, all his fellow citizens gathered to watch the execution of a coiner condemned to be boiled in oil. The entire population was there, and, on the square, one could not 'turn one's feet.' The wretch was thrown, head first, into the great cauldron full of boiling oil" (Mandrou, *Introduction à la France moderne*).

[15] Mercier, *Tableau de Paris.*

instrument of the French Revolution. But it was a new spectacle, and it attracted the crowds. It might even be said that it was the great gadget of the Revolution. Carrier had its image engraved on his seal. Miniature guillotines were sold as children's toys. They were worn on watch chains, as trinkets. At the Punch and Judy theater, in the Champs-Elysées, the guillotine replaced the traditional scaffold.

The present Place de la Concorde, the then Place Louis XV, became the Place de la Révolution. The guillotine which beheaded Louis XVI, in addition to 1,119 aristocrats and Revolutionary deviationists, stood permanently on the site of the obelisk.

At the entrance to the Tuileries gardens, and therefore quite close to the guillotine, a restaurant, which still existed in 1852, included on its menu the names of those to be guillotined that day. This restaurant with its macabre menu was always full—tables even had to be booked well in advance. Robespierre and his friends dined there the day that Danton and Camille Desmoulins were executed. Later, Robespierre himself appeared on the menu.

Camille Desmoulins once wrote in his journal, on a day apparently like any other: "Today, a miracle happened in Paris: a man died in his bed."

In eastern Paris, in the Place du Trône—thus named in 1660 in memory of the throne erected in honor of Louis XIV and Maria Theresa on their return from their coronation at Reims, de-baptized in 1793 and called Place du Trône-renversé—a guillotine was also set up between June 14 and July 27, 1794, and executed 1,306 individuals, that is to say, an average of 30 a day.

The carts filled with those condemned to death crossing the city, the recognition of the stars of the Revolution or of the Ancien Régime, the rolling of drums, the last cry from the crowd, these were all new factors in the urban spectacle of death. Simply by virtue of the fact that so many of the condemned were intent on playing their last roles as self-conscious men of the theater, the scaffold and the guillotine became a stage from which the audience expected to hear speeches from great actors. When Danton, on the scaffold, said to the executioner: "Show my head to the people, it's worth the trouble," tragedy ended in apotheosis. And there was the scene when a carpenter, the executioner's assistant, seized the decapitated head of Charlotte Corday, showed it to the people, and slapped it.

When Hébert, who had so praised the guillotine, appeared himself in person to be guillotined, it was a real festival. "From early morning, speculation grew; carts, benches, scaffolding, everything was prepared to facilitate this pleasant spectacle. The square became a theater; one paid dear to stand all day waiting. 'Everything booked,' people cried, with a strange touch of humor. All around, it was like a fair, the Champs-Elysées filled with smiling, laughing people, with peddlers and store-holders; a bright, strong March sun shone overhead."[16]

An even more terrible spectacle was that of the so-called "murderers of Robespierre" (who was still alive) in June 1794. The fifty-four con-demned were all wearing the red shirt of parricides, until then worn only by Charlotte Corday. From the Conciergerie to the Place de la Rév-olution (the present Place de la Concorde) the procession took three hours, and the execution one hour. Troops and cannon followed the carts. Nothing so splendid had been seen since the death of Louis XVI.

This taste for the execution-spectacle was to last a long time, the last public execution taking place in France in June 1939, in the presence of ladies and gentlemen in evening dress.

The nineteenth century, in particular, brought up with the great kill-ings of the Revolution and empire, was to feel sadistic pleasure in the public executions so vigorously denounced by such romantic writers as Hugo, Lamartine, and Lamennais.[17] To Joseph de Maistre's remark, "The scaffold is an altar," Lamartine was to reply, "The scaffold, among us, is no more than the altar of fear on which a trembling Law orders the sacrifice of human victims."

Let us note in passing that although it is strange to find Jean Jacques Rousseau among the supporters of the death penalty, it is no less strange to read Marat's and Robespierre's opposition to capital punishment.

Now that executions are no longer public, they are no less sordid. Alone in his cell, handcuffed, the condemned person awaiting pardon from on high, forces himself to read, to eat, to put on weight. He must be in good condition for the day of the execution. Great care is taken that he does not commit suicide, since his death must be carried out by a properly qualified specialist. Only a priest and a lawyer may visit him. Awakened at dawn on the day of the execution, most of the condemned behave like automata. Almost all show courage and dignity. But some

[16] Michelet, *Histoire de la Révolution française.*

[17] "These public executions were above all choice spectacles, which hoarse criers announced in the morning at all the Paris crossroads, and which, before being trans-ferred in the first years of the July monarchy to the Barrière Saint-Jacques, where they were to take place at first light, . . . took place in the very heart of Paris, in the Place de Grève, in one of the most illustrious of urban settings, in the bright light of the after-noon, arousing abominable scenes of collective hysteria" (Louis Chevalier, *Classes labo-rieuses et Classes dangereuses* [Paris: Plon, 1958; paperback, 1978]).

are so overcome with panic or anger that they struggle, shout, vomit, roll around on the ground, and even (though this is curiously rare) throw themselves at the procurator.[18]

The most recent common-law criminals to be condemned to death in France have been guillotined within the walls of their prison, and the last political prisoners to be condemned to death were shot in the fortress of Vincennes. Executions are attended by the lawyer, or lawyers, of the condemned man, the presiding judge or his stand-in, the advocate-general or his stand-in, the examining magistrate, and a clerk of the court. Political prisoners condemned to death are buried at Ivry, and guillotined common-law prisoners in the common grave at Thiais. In the coffin the decapitated head is placed between the legs of the body. The families are now allowed to recover the body for reburial in the family vault.[19]

Execution is no longer an urban spectacle.

[18] Thomas, *Anthropologie*.
[19] Heuse, *Guide de la mort*.

III

THANATOS

and the

Goddess of Reason

or Rational Death

14

Functionalism and Death

The dead are men who have ceased to function . . . They no longer produce or consume.

Jean Ziegler
Les Vivants et la Mort, 1975

The men of the Renaissance and the classical age saw the human body as architecture; the men of our industrial civilization tend rather to compare it to a machine; a machine which wears out, parts of which may be replaced, and which one day will become unusable. In 1969, in Great Britain, a bill was proposed intended to legalize social euthanasia on the grounds that no useful purpose was served by prolonging human life beyond a certain age. The legislators fixed the "useful age" at eighty. The bill was not passed. No doubt it fixed the useless age rather too late. From retirement at sixty-five to eighty, the burden on society must still have seemed too heavy. Do we not constantly hear that there will be too many of us wishing to benefit from retirement, since the proportion of active contributors is diminishing dangerously? The old, whom traditional societies turned into sages, are increasingly being rejected outside the bounds of normality. The third age is a sort of third world, Jean Baudrillard remarks, "a considerable burden on social administration . . . A third of society is thus placed in a state of social parasitism and segregation."[1]

To the reprobation attached to the old person, who is inactive and a low consumer in a society entirely directed toward production and consumption, is added the disqualification given to death. There is no longer a good or bad death. All death is bad in itself. Worse than that, it is absurd. It is a deplorable accident, a sabotage of our rationality. Just as natural catastrophes—earthquakes, storms, volcanic eruptions, flooding—appear as a sort of attack against our good social organization, natural death is a scandal. We may be able to accept violent death as a sort of defiance of nature. Death from road accidents fascinates in particular, because it is a sort of burned-out connecting rod. This accidental death is felt less as an accident than as a modern passion, a tribute paid to the sovereign machine.

But ordinary, uneventful, organic death is repugnant. As soon as a person is in danger of death, everyone hurries to send him off to the hospital, where he will be taken charge of by specialists. For no provision is made for the dying in the modern city except the hospital. "It is not normal to be dead today . . . To be dead is an unthinkable anomaly . . . Death is a delinquency, a deviance."[2]

Where are Greuze's fine patriarchs dying in the bosoms of their families? Late twentieth-century death is transformed into a machine bristling with pipes in a hospital ward, which itself resembles a factory for producing the sick. In this medical factory reign thanatocrats, who are able to extend or shorten the agony. They alone know, they alone are masters of life or death.

"The dying person is expelled from the drama which he is undergoing; his personal needs (or those of his relations and friends), his demands, his wishes will no longer be taken into account . . . A class of thanatocrats is being created, administering the death of others according to technological norms, which it alone defines and controls."[3]

Jean Zeigler adds that the nurse, contrary to the widespread assumption, is there to supervise not health, but the patient. The good patient is cooperative, conforms to the regulations. The bad patient is unstable, anxious, depressed. He isolates himself. He refuses to function as a hospitalized patient. He even goes so far as to seek individuality. Worse,

[1] Baudrillard, *L'Echange symbolique*.
[2] Ibid.
[3] Ziegler, *Les Vivants et la Mort*.

some even carry indecency so far as to express moods. When I myself was in a large Paris hospital and asked the specialist whether I might resume my work at least part-time in order to improve my morale, he replied, contemptuously: "Your moods are no concern of mine."

In American hospitals there are thanatologists whose task it is to remove, or conceal, the fears of the dying. And there are psychiatrists specializing in the suppression of mourning on the part of the living (the pathology of mourning is curable).

Just as the Church has abolished extreme unction, replacing it by a "sacrament of the sick," the mourner who persists in his sorrow is put into quarantine. If death is an "accident," mourning is an illness.

The old person is inconvenient, but premature death is a social scandal. We demand a "normal" lifespan, a sort of legitimate reward for our time as producers. Death, occurring just before retirement, always seems like a con. He went just before he retired! One feels that the dead man has been wronged, dispossessed of his right to rest. Not too long a rest, which would cost society too much, of course, but a "normal" period of rest. It remains to be seen what is implied by this "normal."

Molière's graybeard, the old man of comedy or tragedy, is forty or fifty years old. But, thanks to a rational regime, the notion of longevity is already to be found in Descartes. His methodical observation of man-the-machine must lead him logically, he thinks, to live for a hundred years. But he failed to take into account the demands of Christina of Sweden, who brought Descartes's life to an end at forty-four.

In the eighteenth century it no longer seemed impossible to reach the age of a hundred. Fontenelle almost achieved it. Saint-Germain, Cagliostro, and Mesmer even claimed to be immortal. So a new phenomenon appears in the eighteenth century, namely, the refusal to grow old, a prefiguration of our refusal to die.

The graybeards of the seventeenth century are often mocked, but they assume their age quite happily. In any case, they do not hide it, and are rather proud of it. In the next century Diderot wrote to Sophie Volland: "I am . . . I would not dare to tell you: my age is terrifying." He was fifty-six. In fact, like most of the famous men of the eighteenth century (Montesquieu, Rousseau, d'Alembert, Beaumarchais), Diderot was to die after the age of sixty-five.

In the *Memoirs* of the duc de Luynes, we see that many people lived to be eighty. Malebranche, the Abbé de Saint-Pierre, Fontenelle, Crébillon père, King Stanislas, Rameau, all approached or exceeded the age of eighty-five.

Louis-Sébastien Mercier says that a man can no longer be called old until he is seventy. There is, therefore, an astonishing leap in longevity, from the seventeenth to the eighteenth century, and in any case a considerable transformation in awareness of aging. One becomes old only twenty years later. But, for two hundred years, the awareness of aging and the age of death have not moved. All our extraordinary medical machinery has not been able to push back the age of death. Our optimistic statistics derive only from the increasing rareness of infantile morality, which used to be on such a frightful scale. Life expectancy at birth is still only sixty-five, as chance would have it legal age for the cessation of productivity.

In the eighteenth century, when philosophers were preparing for the advent of the goddess of Reason, there was a proliferation of books on the subject of hygiene. Men's health became a matter of great concern. Polluted air was held responsible for every disease. In this context the physician became a person of considerable importance. From being an object of ridicule in the farces of the seventeenth century, he became in the eighteenth century a man of skill, a man of science who was replacing the priest. "Tronchin is replacing Bossuet," says Vovelle, emphasizing the de-Christianization of the second half of the eighteenth century.[4] The period between 1720 and 1750 was "the high point of Catholic conquest."[5] From then on Catholicism continued to decline, right up to the de-Christianization of the revolutionary period.

The priest, once a necessary witness of death, had, therefore, in two centuries, been replaced by the physician. The priest, who was supposed to have the benefit of a dialogue with God, was called to the deathbed to help the dying person prepare his journey into the beyond. As in all traditional societies, he fulfilled the function of the ferryman. The thanatocratic physician, on the other hand, is merely an admirable mechanic, a sort of superior watchmaker who tries to get your machine to keep time. The rationality of our culture has inevitably included illness and death in its system, even if illness and death still seem irrational.

It is this irrational, unseemly element that one tries to eliminate. The men of industrial societies die alone. "Everything is done so that the living may be aware of nothing. In a few hours the presence of the dead is effaced, their bodies taken away, memory of them frozen. The noise of the city masks our terror. In the middle of the traffic, a procession crosses the city. A special space is ready to receive it."[6]

[4] Vovelle, *Mourir autrefois*.
[5] Vovelle, *Piété baroque*.
[6] Ziegler, *Les Vivants et la Mort*.

But since the society of production and consumption does not wish to lose anything, since the final putrefaction of any body offends it, it has invented a new form of anthropophagy: the recovery of healthy organs from a person who has just died, with a view to transplanting them into a sick body, and thus turning a sick person into a healthy, productive one. Man's essential organs—kidneys, heart, lungs—are today bought, stockpiled, and sold. In American hospitals illustrated catalogues of organs for sale are circulated. Banks and exchanges in organs are at the disposal of this "death control," which corresponds to "birth control."

In the United States, 80 percent of deaths now take place in hospitals, which have become air-conditioned "moritories."

Hospital doctors have at their disposal a power that may seem disturbing when one remembes the docility with which they responded in Germany to Nazi orders compelling them to hand over to the political authorities clinical information about any patient occupying a hospital bed for longer than five years. As a result of the reports of the German thanatocrats, 275,000 patients suffering from senility, epilepsy, Parkinson's disease, and multiple sclerosis were thus eliminated to make room. Again there is that obsession with room and profitability that, logically, leads to the elimination of the incurable and senile.

All our modernity, all our present, was played out in that second half of the eighteenth century when philosophy took over from religion, the scientific from the spiritual, the doctor from the priest. The Christian city, which had remained intact since the eleventh century, was to collapse, giving way to the industrial, mercantile city. When the men of science and reason attacked the church, they attacked the urban cemetery. These men of progress were keen classifiers. They wanted a space for everything. They paved the way for our segregation of spaces and men.

Voltaire writes: "You go into the Gothic cathedral of Paris. You step on ugly, ill-aligned, uneven stones. They have been lifted over and over again to throw boxes of corpses under them. Walk through the charnel-house known as the Saints-Innocents. It is a vast enclosure dedicated to the plague. The poor who die very often of contagious diseases are buried there pell-mell; sometimes dogs come and gnaw at their bones, and thick, cadaverous, infected vapor rises from them. It is pestilential in the heat of summer and after rain."[7]

This denunciation was taken up again some years before 1789 by

[7] Voltaire, *Dictionnaire philosophique* (Paris, 1764).

Louis-Sébastien Mercier: "The cadaverous smell is noticeable in almost all churches, which is why many people no longer want to set foot in them. The wishes of the citizens, the decrees of the *Parlement*, demands of all kinds have been of no avail. The sepulchral exhalations continue to poison the faithful. It is claimed nevertheless that the musty, or cellarlike smell, which reigns in these enormous piles of stone, is a smell of death."[8]

However, an edict from Louis XVI in 1776 forbade burials in churches and even in private chapels, except for the bodies of archbishops, bishops, priests, patrons of the churches, and founders of chapels.[9] An attempt was made to return to the origins of burial in churches, which had once been reserved for the religious. But in the late seventeenth century the nobility and haute bourgeoisie were no longer alone in having forced open the gates of the clergy. Practically half the population of the cities was buried in the churches. Craftsmen and tradesmen in turn managed to get in,[10] and, in the stampede, 10 percent of the lower classes: coachmen, carters, bakers, soldiers. Most testators described at length where precisely in the church they wished to be buried. The most sought-after site, was, of course, the choir, near the altar, followed by the lady chapel, or, again, under the pew which rich families possessed in the church.

But many churches, which had received bodies for several centuries, had become virtual charnelhouses. With each burial, the paving had to be partially removed. Sometimes the gravedigger had no alternative but to place the new corpse on top of an earlier one. This resulted in a raising of the ground level and, through the disjointed flagstones, foul smells rose. Some churches, after having had vaults dug, had subterranean cemeteries at their disposal. But many places of worship, absolutely saturated with corpses and skeletons, had no alternative but to send their dead to the Saints-Innocents.

The normal place of burial was the ground surrounding the church,

[8] Mercier, *Tableau de Paris*.

[9] Having oneself buried on one's own property implied the ownership of a consecrated place. Only the nobles, then, could be buried in their private chapels. But they usually preferred to be buried in the parish church, where lords and priests had reserved places at their disposal. Some nobles asked to be buried in the chapel of a hospital which they had helped to fund.

[10] There is nothing surprising in the fact that this rising social class, which had just acquired "noble" burials, should at first be opposed to the cemeteries being moved outside the city. When, in 1765, this question was discussed for the first time in the City Council, the provost of the merchants protested and the project was adjourned.

and the best place the wall of the church itself or the ground bordering it. But, in the eighteenth century, after being devoured by the graveyard surrounding it, the church in turn devoured this graveyard. There were new devotions: the Way of the Cross, Benediction, Souls in Purgatory led to extensions of the church. So side chapels, a more comfortable sacristy, a more spacious presbytery, a catechism hall, et cetera were built. The church grew to the detriment of the graveyard. So much so that in the end those corpses in the church and around the church became an embarrassment to the clergy themselves, who joined forces with the physicians to demand cemeteries outside the towns. Only the inhabitants of each parish insisted on keeping their dead near them. Despite protests and disputes with the king's men, the edict of Louis XVI, which laid it down that "cemeteries which, because placed near dwellings, might pollute the air, will be removed, as far as circumstances permit," was nevertheless to take only four years to be put into practice. The removal of the Saints-Innocents began in 1780, that of the graveyards of Saint-Roche and Saint-Eustache in 1781, that of the Île Saint-Louis in 1782, that of Saint-Sulpice in 1784. From the cemetery of the Saints-Innocents, raised nearly ten feet above the neighboring streets by the accumulation of skeletons, 20,000 corpses were exhumed. Over a thousand cartloads of bones were transported to the quarries of Tombe-Issoire, which were renamed catacombs.[11] Eight or nine centuries of dead were taken out at night, over seven winters, by torchlight. Two million Parisians, from the ninth to the eighteenth century had come to end their days in this space, which was to become a market, like most of the disaffected cemeteries, and which has now become a small public garden decorated by Jean Goujon's Innocents' Fountain.

But although there was a certain amount of grumbling, although the inhabitants of the parishes protested, saying that their graveyards were perfectly healthy, there was no revolt, as certain parish priests had warned there would be. The almost total indifference of the population to the removal of the urban cemeteries is surprising and foreshadows the abandonment of the dead during the forthcoming revolution.

It was only after the restoration that the church was to see that it had been tricked. In his *Génie du Christianisme*, Chateaubriand was to echo the somewhat passive resistance to the expulsion of the dead from the city: "Lycurgus did not fear to set up tombs in the middle of Lacedae-

---

[11] Michelet attributes the idea of moving the old parish churchyards to the catacombs to Lavoisier (*Histoire de la Révolution française*).

mon; he thought, as does our religion, that the ashes of fathers, far from shortening the days of the sons, rather prolong their existence, by teaching them moderation and virtue, which lead men to a happy old age; the human reasons which have been opposed to these divine reasons are far from convincing."

Anyway, the modern cemetery was no longer to be an urban space. The dead, relegated to the periphery, were affected by the segregation of the spaces of the city. And even the smallest villages, which had nothing to fear from contamination caused by the accumulation of corpses, or by lack of space, were to follow suit and destroy their churchyards, and expel their dead from a perfect setting to a space that might have preserved the charms of the countryside if it had not immediately been surrounded by walls and railings. Having become a specialized space, the cemetery is, by that fact, a neutralized space. A dead space intended for death.

The regulations relating to cemeteries and funerals of June 12, 1804 are, more or less, in force today. They definitively forbid burial in churches and towns, and at least 35 to 40 meters from the urban limits. Bodies must not be superimposed upon one another, but juxtaposed. The coffin is obligatory. No open ditch must be used again before five years have elapsed. The cemetery must be planted with trees (which were once proscribed from cemeteries because they were thought to hold the miasmas suspended in the air and which are now regarded as purifiers). Concessions are possible for the building of monuments, but the legislators regarded them as exceptional, just as they regarded authorized gravestones as exceptional. Indeed, the new cemeteries originally had the empty look of the mortuary spaces of earlier times. If one takes Père-Lachaise one realizes that in 1806 there were only nine gravestones, and only 130 by 1812. Then, from 1814, the fashion began to spread, and the personalization of the place of burial, which the legislators had seen as exceptional, became the rule. This led to a new conception of the enclosed cemetery, the cemetery-museum which we have discussed above.

The mechanical civilization was also to introduce other novelties bound up with technical inventions: the railway and electricity. In fact, the rationality of death converges with the rationality of the railway to produce mortuary stations. Similarly, the artisanal mechanization of the guillotine was followed by a new machine for capital punishment: the electric chair.

The first mortuary stations were built in England about 1850. One had already existed in London, near Waterloo Station, run by a private company, the London Necropolis Company. This station connected, by a special railway, the British capital to the necropolis of Woking, some twenty-five miles away.

In Wales, at Rookwood, a mortuary station, built in 1868, was demolished and rebuilt a hundred years later in Canberra, Australia. On the facade of this station, the "Angels of Renown" welcome the arrival of passengers after their last journey.

In France, under the supervision of Baron Haussmann, we were to see several plans for mortuary stations, all rejected by the municipal council because Parisians no longer wished to be separated from the dead of their surburban cemeteries, which had now become, with the growth of the city, urban. These funerary stations would have been the Parisian termini of the special railway transporting the dead to some distant necropolis, as in London. Like the railway carriages, they would have respected the class divisions of the railway services: waiting rooms and carriages for all three classes.

During World War II the extermination camps had sorting stations where the human flock was sorted out before being sent either to forced labor or to immediate death. The rails that led to the Auschwitz camp entered the outer wall beneath a hugh porch and came to a dead end. Some camps had on their facades trompe-l'oeil pictures suggesting village railway stations, intended "to improve the psychological efficiency" of the survivors of the "death trains."[12]

The great extermination center of Treblinka included railway facilities of this kind.

Kurt Franz . . . hit upon the idea of transforming the platform where the convoys arrived into a false station . . . Lalka carried his concern for detail so far as to have his men paint two doors leading to the waiting rooms, first and second class . . . Next to the ticket window a large timetable announced the departure times of trains for Warsaw, Bialystok, Wolkowysk, etc . . . Lalka also had some flower beds designed, which gave the whole area a neat and cheery look . . . The flowers, which were real, made the whole scene resemble a pretty station in a little provincial town. Everything was perfect, and yet something was still lacking: nothing much, a detail, a little touch that would give that stamp of authenticity which cannot be invented . . . "The clock!" he said suddenly, slapping his brow, "Of course, that's it! A station without a clock is not a station."[13]

---

[12] *Le Temps des gares*, Catalogue du C.C.I. (Paris: Centre Georges-Pompidou, 1978).

[13] Jean-François Steiner, *Treblinka* (Paris: Fayard, 1966); *Treblinka*, tr. Helen Weaver (New York: Simon and Schuster; London; Weidenfeld and Nicolson, 1967).

Electricity and gas central heating, two elements of modern home comfort were very soon transformed into means of a speedy and "clean" elimination of those condemned to death.

In 1899, one could read in the *Petit Journal illustré*:

> The Americans, avid for progress, are applying electricity once more to the death penalty. The last word in improvement has not yet been found, since death is not as instantaneous as one would wish. A certain woman, Place, who had murdered her daughter-in-law in Brooklyn, did not, in fact, succumb to the action of the first current, though it rose, for a few seconds, to 1,760 volts. In fact, one lives between the first and second charge, one's lips move to say a prayer. The spectacle was so terrifying that even the confessor could not bear it and turned away. The woman doctor and nurse showed more firmness. The condemned woman gave proof of great courage.[14]

In fact this electric death was still at an artisanal stage, if one compares it to the tailorized death practiced by the Nazis in the concentration camps. Everything there was expressed in the most rational terms. To the strains of the deportees' orchestra, preferably playing Wagner, the prisoners selected for death, but unaware of the fact, were marched out into pseudo shower rooms, where they undressed; then, instead of water, poison gas was pumped in through the shower hoses. The bodies were then put into crematorium ovens and reduced to ashes. Sometimes, German industry recovered the human fat for use in making soap. The Nazis also collected, of course, the clothes, jewelery, gold teeth, hair, and even sometimes skin, which was turned into parchment.

There is an identification of the city and the cemetery, the cemetery and prison in the eighteenth century: the cemetery and the housing estate in the twentieth. Now a mortiferous Italian architect has identified the cemetery with the office and factory. On May 6, 1971, the Italian city of Modena set up a national architectural competition with a view to extending the old cemetery of San Cataldo. The first prize was given to the architects Aldo Rossi and Gianni Braghieri for their project entitled "Sky Blue." Marked out at its perimeter and center by a rectilinear row of galleries with porticoes housing columbariums, with an ossuary at its central point, this cemetery aimed at being integrated in the modern city. "The cemetery must be regarded as a public building whose walks offer the necessary clarity and rationality . . . From the outside it is enclosed by a wall pierced with windows. In this way it does not con-

---

[14] *Le Petit Journal illustré*, April 9, 1899. Quoted by Sabatier in *Dictionnaire de la Mort*.

trast too obviously with other public spaces. Through its arrangement and situation it also reflects the bureaucratic aspect with which it is endowed . . . as a reminder of the modern city . . . The cube [of the sanctuary] is an abandoned or unfinished house . . . while the cone (which surmounts the common grave like a great chimney) looks like the chimney of a deserted factory."[15]

[15] Henri Bonnemazou, *Traverses*, (Paris, 1975).

15

The Ideal Cemetery of the Philosophers and Poets

My friends, think that I am asleep.

Epitaph of the chevalier de Boufflers
in the cemetery of Père-Lachaise

To the rational space of death, which corresponds to the functional spaces of the industrial and commercial city, is contrasted, in that same late eighteenth century, the funerary space of the philosophers and poets.

Whereas Catholic preachers wallow in a morbid literature, appearing to be interested only in sickness and deathbeds, the philosophers "denounce the Christian exploitation of death" and try to counter it, reviving ancient Stoicism, with the idea of death as sleep.[1]

In Greek mythology Hypnos, god of Sleep, is the twin brother of Thanatos, god of Death, and both are sons of Night. The word *cemetery* comes from the Greek *koimêtêrion* (place where one sleeps). Homer and, after him, Virgil describe death as a "deep rest," a "deathly sleep." Hyp-

[1] Favre, *La Mort au siècle lumières.*

nos is depicted clean shaven, whereas Thanatos is wild, bearded, hairy of body. The two brothers are often represented winged, and laying out a body for death. Saint Paul, who was so profoundly marked by Greek civilization, also gives death the image of sleep. For him the cemetery is "an immense dormitory" where the sleeping dead await resurrection.

In the sixteenth century, Protestantism revived the belief of the primitive church that death was merely a state of sleep prior to the resurrection of the body. Luther says that death is a "deep, untroubled sleep," that the grave is a "bed of repose." The expression "asleep in God" is a Huguenot one, but it was to become one of the great themes of popular belief. For once the philosophers and poets of the eighteenth century, though taking up an ancient idea, are at one with a certain popular memory that, despite the church and its infernal images, passively refused to allow itself to be dispossessed of that old pagan idea that the dead have an immobile, invisible, silent life, but one that is nonetheless as real as that of the living. In popular belief the dead body hears and remembers. One takes care, therefore, when speaking in the presence of a corpse. Silence is observed both in the death chamber and in the cemetery: one whispers there, one does not shout. One says that one is afraid of "waking the dead."

This ancient belief has passed into our modern culture. Believers pray quietly for their dead, and nonbelievers do not know what else to do but observe a minute's silence. Nor have close on two centuries of rationalism prevented the survival to our own time, when death is evacuated as much as possible, of a ritual that is a simulacrum of communication with the dead: visits to the cemetery, the bringing of flowers, a few moments of contemplation, the upkeep of the grave.

In our present-day cemeteries, funerary inscriptions that refer to sleep are in the majority. One sees porcelain pillows, ceramic poppies, beds like that of the Pigeons in Montmartre cemetery. In the nineteenth century, neo-Gothic baldachinos, which were common in cemeteries, were simply bed-testers, just as the wrought-iron structure which surrounds gravestones is an imitation of a bed frame. From the columned bed to the bed-cage, there is still the same idea of sleep. "Here, sleeping the last sleep . . ." is a common inscription.

Receiving the king of England on a pilgrimage to the war cemeteries of Flanders, General de Castelnau expressed an opinion that has become more or less part of our culture: "They sleep, but they will awake one day; and as they await the hour of the great awakening, the many monuments whose touching and symbolic forms your majesty has deigned to remark on, give life, as it were, to the immaterial substance of our beloved comrades . . . From the height of these commemorative stelae, they see us, watch us, and speak to us."[2]

No doubt we owe this unexpected return of the dead as ghosts to the resistance put up by the philosophers and poets of the late eighteenth century and the romantic period to the rationalization of death brought about by the Industrial Revolution.

A poetics of tombs and country churchyards grew up in the eighteenth century, just as the destruction of the old cemeteries was about to take place. Young's *Night Thoughts*, published in 1745, was translated into all the European languages, and its success continued for two generations.[3] Young speaks of night, and not of tombs, but he spread a sort of fashion for the lunar landscape which, inevitably, led to a taste for gloom. He opened the way to the poetry of cemeteries, which followed the poetry of *Night Thoughts*. In 1748 Harvey published his *Meditations among the Tombs*, in which he examines funerary inscriptions in a village church. In 1751 Thomas Gray published his *Elegy Written in a Country Churchyard*, which combines the poetry of country churchyards and melancholy, nocturnal reverie before tombs, and met with considerable success. Delille was to imitate it in France, in Chant 7 of his *L'Imagination*.

The eighteenth-century philosophers and poets were performing a worthy deed. They were trying to tame death. To the images of horrible death perpetrated by Bossuet and his successors, they opposed, like Greuze in painting, the image of a kindly death, of the return to the bosom of the earth amid a beloved and clement nature.

One cites as an example the death of Jean Jacques Rousseau, taken out, after drinking a cup of the coffee with cream of which he was so fond, for a final visit to the shady trees of Ermenonville. He returned home to die, a smile on his lips, and asked for the blinds to be left open so that he could see "that beautiful sun once more."

Stoicism and pantheism. This pantheism turns up again in the will of the marquis de Sade, who asked to be placed in the wood of Epernon: "in the first thick copse on the right . . . Once the ditch has been filled in, it will be sown with acorn so that . . . all trace of my grave will disappear from the surface of the earth."[4]

This new space of death is paralleled by a new landscaped space: the English garden. The progressive-minded aristocracy, of the type that

[2] René Puaux, *Le Pèlerinage du roi d'Angleterre aux cimetières du Front* (Paris: Association France-Grande-Bretagne, 1922).

[3] In the prison of the Luxembourg, on the night before his execution, Camille Desmoulins was reading Young's *Night Thoughts*.

[4] Gilbert Lély, *Sade* (Paris: Gallimard, 1966).

patronized Jean Jacques Rousseau, designed idyllic gardens on their estates, where grand ladies might come across happy shepherds. These gardens (one ought perhaps to say landscapes) were composed like the painted landscapes of Claude Lorrain. Implicitly, and under the influence of Rousseau's *Julie* and *Emile*, this ordered nature was to be the setting of a society of the future that would be opposed to the coming industrial society by making a success of a patriarchal society living happily in a rural paradise.

The marquis de Girardin, who accommodated Rousseau in his estate at Ermenonville, wrote a book on landscape.[5] In creating a new landscape, the marquis de Girardin wished to set up a model for a new economic order. His estate at Ermenonville had been transformed successfully into a Rousseauist garden. He had instituted festivals for his villagers, with prizes for virtue and good behavior among their children. All the men of the estate, masters and servants, wore the same clothes: jacket and trousers made of English blue linen. All the women wore the same linen apron and the same black hat.

In what better setting could Jean Jacques Rousseau, to whom the marquis de Girardin had given, on top of everything else, a rural tomb in the island of poplars, die?

There is nothing sinister about Rousseau's tomb, designed by Robert, with sculptures by Le Sueur.[6] But let us see what the marquis says about it:

> One cannot but feel a sense of veneration when one catches sight of Jean-Jacques's tomb in the midst of the poplars. This monument lends great character to the whole landscape . . . On the southward side, one sees a bas-relief representing a woman seated beneath a palm tree, the symbol of fecundity; she is holding with one hand her son, to whom she is giving suck, and with the other a copy of *Emile*. Behind her is a group of women making an offering of flowers and fruit on an altar erected before a statue of Nature. In a corner one catches sight of a child setting fire to a pile of swaddling clothes and various fetters for young children, while others jump around, playing with

[5] René-Louis de Girardin, *De la composition des paysages* (1777), Afterword by Michel H. Conan (Paris: Editions du Champ urbain, 1979).

[6] There is an obvious continuity between the landscaped gardens and the landscaped cemeteries that were to be set up in the United States and northern Europe in the twentieth century. The romantics dreamed of cemetery-museums, which were to appear in the nineteenth century. "In Switzerland the cemeteries are sometimes placed on rocks, where they overlook lakes, precipices and valleys. The chamois and the eagle take up residence there, and death grows on those precipitous sites, like those alpine plants whose roots are plunged into eternal ice" (Chateaubriand, *Le Génie du Christianisme*).

a cap, symbol of liberty. The two pilasters at the side of the bas-relief are decorated with two figures; one represents Love, the other Eloquence, with their appropriate attributes . . . On the corresponding pilasters are Nature, represented by a mother giving suck to her children and, Truth, a naked woman, holding a torch. Lacrymatory vases are carved on the two small front faces: on the pediment of this side two doves expire at the foot of an urn over flaming, upturned torches. Such is, in all its details, the monument which holds Rousseau's ashes.[7]

The fashion in architecture for ruins, urns, artificial tombs corresponds to the literature of tombs and cemeteries—and also, no doubt, to the fascination exerted over late eighteenth-century architects by prisons.

One remembers the words of Pierre Nicole: "The entire earth is the general prison of all men, and one escapes from it only by the sentence of death to which they have all been condemned by God's justice."[8]

Piranesi was not alone in designing prisons. The prison, like the monastery, is, of course, a utopian architecture, an architecture of isolation, and, in that period of transition at the end of the eighteenth century, when everything was about to change, architects in search of new forms expended their dreams on prisons. There were many architects contemporary with the Revolution who were to design model prisons, as if the prison was to become a model and archetype of an ideal, hierarchized society, a society regulated by the clock.

Indeed, the comparison between the prison and the cemetery is made by Morelly, who proposes to build prison and cemetery next to one another, with "cavities spacious and strongly barred enough to shut away their inmates for ever, and then to serve as tombs for citizens who have deserved to die without benefit of a religious ceremony."[9]

During this same period the contradictions are often quite blatant. The country churchyard celebrated by the English poets may be contrasted with the vault of the Gothic novel, so dear to Mrs. Radcliffe, or Rousseau's tomb among the poplars of a garden designed by a philosopher-marquis with Morelly's cemetery-prison.

[7] *Promenade ou Itinéraire des Jardins d'Ermenonville* (Paris, 1811). This work is attributed to Stanislas de Girardin, René-Louis's eldest son. He was brought up by his father according to the principles of Rousseau's *Emile*. Stanislas de Girardin picked out on the spinet musical scores written by Rousseau, in the latter's presence, and accompanied him when Rousseau sang his songs.

[8] Pierre Nicole, *Essais de morale* (Paris, 1678).

[9] Morelly, *Code de la Nature ou le Véritable Esprit de ses lois de tout temps négligé ou méconnu* (Paris, 1755).

Like those citizens of Athens and Rome who went out to sleep on tombs because the dead inspired them with prophetic dreams, the poets of nights and tombs are not morbid. They are trying to listen to the beyond.

Edgar Morin is wrong in supposing that archaic peoples are no more indifferent to death than the civilized.[10] On the contrary, all primitive civilizations show a fear of death, and a terror of the dead (as possible ghosts), which is less acute among highly civilized nations. Extreme civilization brings, on the contrary, a certain Stoicism, and even, one might say, a sort of contemptuous indifference to death. This Stoicism with a smile is to be found as much in Socrates as in Rousseau. Thucydides tells how the ancient Greeks, when struck by the plague or besieged in a city, did not abandon themselves to despair but on the contrary sought ways of enjoying to the maximum the last moments of life which still remained to them in an excess of pleasure. Nor is there any metaphysical fear among those Romans of the fifth century A.D. described by Salvianus during the final barbarian attacks: "The din of arms around the ramparts, and the noise of spectacles in the circuses, the cries of the dying and the clamor of the bacchanals merged together. The day before they were reduced to captivity, the most noble, most elderly citizens threw themselves into debauchery with the coldest indifference for the misfortunes and massacres which were to follow."[11]

In the late eighteenth century, with its revival of the antique and its contempt for religious beliefs, "a whole society seemed at last to live as if death no longer threatened it, as if the dead were no longer important to it."[12] Yet the *Danses macabres* were still being distributed by pedlars. In Christian literature disgust for life and yearning for death were being expressed more than ever. In their sermons, preachers offered a terrifying image of the human condition. But those sections of society influenced by free-thinking *philosophes* mocked such "superstitions." When they found themselves in the prisons of the Terror, they kept up their social graces, their gallantries, their battles of wit, as if the revolution had not seized their goods and threatened their heads.

"At the Conciergerie, the inmates played cards, sang, danced, seemed quite carefree and happy. Then, when the jailer called out names, it was often with bursts of sardonic laughter that the unfortunate climbed into the fatal cart."[13]

[10] Morin, *L'Homme et la Mort dans l'Histoire.*
[11] Salvianus, *On the Government of Providence* (fifth century A.D).
[12] Favre, *La Mort au siècle lumières.*
[13] Père L. Natavel, *La Peur de la mort et sa guérison infaillible* (Paris, 1934).

Whether aristocrats or members of the Convention, almost all were atheists. Right up to the scaffold, all showed an indifference to death very like defiance.

It is true that the period marked by Diderot, Robespierre, and Auguste Comte saw the appearance of a new belief: that of the eternity of the dead in the memory of the living. Our dead live in the sorrow of our memory. However, modern as this belief may seem, it is to be found in the mythologies of certain primitive peoples. For the Oceanic peoples, "true death, that is to say, nonexistence, appears only with the loss of the collective memory. The dead continue to live as long as the living know their names."[14]

This mythology of the people of the dead which exists only in the memory of the living contains the notion of the "great dead," who are less mortal than others. Glory is a secular immortality, similar indeed to that of the saints. And it is certainly true that Plato, Seneca, Ramses II, and Vercingetorix continue to live in our collective memories and are therefore not quite dead.

A certain immortality is also accorded such pairs of lovers as Abelard and Héloïse. Diderot wrote to Sophie Volland: "Those who have loved one another all their lives, and ask to be buried next to one another, are perhaps not as mad as people think. Perhaps their ashes come together, mingle, and are united . . . Oh my Sophie! All that would be left to me, then, would be the hope of touching you, of feeling you, of loving you, of seeking you, of being united with you, of merging with you, when we are no more . . . Leave me this chimera. It is a sweet consolation and will assure me of eternity in you and with you."[15]

This wish may be compared with that of Saint-Simon in the previous century: "I wish that, wherever I die, my body will be brought and buried in the vault of the parish church of the said place of La Ferté, next to that of my most dear wife, and that there be made and fixed in place rings, hooks, and chains binding our coffins so tightly together, and so well rivetted, that it will be impossible to separate them from one another without breaking both of them."[16]

Serenity before death is also to be found in Thomas More's *Utopia*. In the ideal world which he imagines, the Utopians

do mourn and lament every man's sickness, but no man's death, unless it be one whom they see depart from his life carefully and against his will. For

[14] Exhibition catalogue, *Rites de la mort*.
[15] Diderot, *Lettre à Sophie Volland*, October 6, 1759.
[16] Saint-Simon, *Mémoires*.

this they take for a very evil token . . . They, therefore, that see this kind of death, do abhor it, and them that so die they bury with sorrow and silence. And when they have prayed God to be merciful to the soul, and mercifully to pardon the infirmities thereof, they cover the dead corpse with earth. Contrariwise all that depart merely and full of good hope, for them no man mourneth but followeth the hearse with joyful singing, commending the souls to God with great affection. And at the last, not with mourning sorrow, but with a great reverence they burn the bodies. And in the same place they set up a pillar of stone with the dead man's titles there engraved.[17]

Thomas More himself, when faced with the executioner's axe, was able to die, if not gaily, at least, it would seem, with great serenity.

One thinks of that fresco of Nefertiti, opposite Luxor, of which André Malraux says: "At the entry of his tomb, Ramses's wife plays against an invisible god of the dead, whose appearance we are aware of only through his pawns on the chessboard. Before the void, she gambles her immortality."[18]

[17] More, *Utopia*.
[18] Malraux, *Lazare*.

16

The Revolution in Funerary Practice from 1789 to the Restoration

Begin at last the reign of pure philosophy, O Frenchmen, and destroy your tombs.

Lequinio
Préjugés détruits, 1792

One of the first initiatives of the Convention, as far as the space of death is concerned, was obviously the secularization of the cemetery, which was now placed under the local authority. The church was dispossessed both of the civil registers and of its monopoly of burial. Whereas once men were born and died within the bosom of the church, they now died under the authority of the state.

But as the new republican state was to pass from vehement anticlericalism to being anti-Christian, it was to try to establish a new liturgy, even a new spirituality. And, quite naturally, this new mortuary ideology was to seek its sources in the poetry and philosophy of the eighteenth century.

The *Conventionels* were violently divided into two parties, which we tend, despite their profound antagonism, to confuse: the cult of Reason and the cult of the Supreme Being. The cult of Reason, unlike that of the Supreme Being, was anti-Christian. It was represented principally by Hébert, who was inspired by Voltaire, and it could be said that his *Père Duchesne* was a "true but faithful echo of Voltaire's laughter."[1] On the other hand, the idea of the cult of the Supreme Being, associated principally with Robespierre, drew on Jean Jacques Rousseau's *Le Vicaire savoyard*. Robespierre, who hated Voltaire, also hated, and, one might even go so far as to say, felt a veritable repulsion for, Hébert's vulgarity. A third tendency, represented by Hérault de Séchelles, was inspired by Diderot's love of humanity.[2]

The ideology of the Revolution was really a mixture of these three tendencies, in which the religion of nation and of humanity predominated.

The antireligious movement began in the provinces. The cult of Reason, which was first to astonish, then terrify Europe, first erupted in southwestern France. Among the protagonists of the cult of Reason were often to be found former priests or monks, like Nevers or Fouché, a former Oratorian. When Fouché's wife gave birth, the former Oratorian himself baptized his son with the name of Nièvre. Then he ordered that every priest should marry.

On September 19, 1793, Fouché published at Nevers an edict on religious worship and the cemeteries:

> *Article 4.* In each municipality, all dead citizens of whatever sect will be taken twenty-four hours after death, and forty-eight hours in cases of sudden death, covered by a funeral veil on which will be painted the image of Sleep, to the place set apart for common burial, accompanied by a public functionary, their friends wearing mourning, and a detachment of their brothers in arms.
> *Article 5.* The common place where the ashes will lie will be set apart from any habitation, planted with trees under the shade of which a statue representing Sleep will be erected. All other signs will be destroyed.
> *Article 6.* On the gate of thie field consecrated by religious respect to the shades of the dead, the following inscription will be placed: "Death is an eternal sleep."

[1] F. A. Aulard, *Le Culte de la Raison et le Culte de l'Etre suprême, 1793–1794* (Paris: Alcan, 1892).

[2] Hérault de Séchelles, Discours à la fête du 10 août 1793.

Fouché, then, borrowed this symbolism of sleep from the philosophers and poets of Night, who, as we have seen in the previous chapter, had revived it from pagan antiquity. The inscription on cemetery gates, at the revolutionary period—"Death is an eternal sleep"—was due not to Robespierre's "Rousseauism," as Pierre Gascar believes, but to Fouché.[3] On the contrary, Robespierre was indignant about it, as his speech of 8 Thermidor, Year II, shows. What angered him, of course, was not the metaphor of sleep but the idea of eternity as sleep, which implies a negation of the soul. For Robespierre the immortality of the soul, as understood by the old religion, had to be transformed into an immortality of memory. That is why, in the new funerary liturgy advocated by Robespierre's supporters, the eighteenth-century funeral oration was replaced by hymns to the glory of heroes. Magnificent funeral ceremonies were celebrated to the memory of Rousseau, Voltaire, Marat, and Le Peletier de Saint-Fargeau.

On October 10 Fouché issued a new order, correcting the previous one and including a special homage to "great names," decidedly Robespierrist in tone: "All those who, after their deaths, are considered by the citizens of their commune to have served the nation well will have on their graves a stone decorated with a carved crown of oak leaves." But any other sign was to be destroyed in the cemeteries, with the exception of a single statue: that of Sleep.

On October 16 Chaumette presented Fouché's report on cemeteries to the Commune. He added that, in place of cypresses, odoriferous trees should now be planted in public cemeteries. "The brightness and scent of flowers should give rise to the sweetest of thoughts," said Chaumette. "I would like, where possible, to be able to breathe in my father's soul." Chaumette also had something to say about the funeral procession. Instead of the priest, he advocated that civic officers, wearing red caps, should walk in front of the procession bearing this inscription: "The just man never dies, he lives on in the memory of his fellow citizens." The funeral shroud would be replaced by a blue, white, and red drape.

Under Hébert's influence the Convention gave an enthusiastic welcome at first to such public acts of declericalization and to all kinds of anti-religious masquerade. At Nevers, Fouché organized a pagan festival on a large plain near the city. "The Sacred Fire of Vesta" was lighted, and a "Temple of Love" was built there in which weddings took place. On June 26, 1793, Lakanal proposed a plan of national festivals intended to replace all the previous religious feasts. In his republican calendar,

[3] Pierre Gascar, *L'Ombre de Robespierre* (Paris: Gallimard, 1979).

which was to be adopted, the poet Fabre d'Eglantine abolished Sundays by the simple expedient of imposing a ten-day week. All saints' names were replaced by "objects which make up the true national wealth." Another poet, Marie-Joseph Chénier, proposed to the Constituent Assembly that only one religion—that of the fatherland—should be adopted. The entire region of Corbeil declared that it had renounced Christianity and replaced in its churches the statues of Saint Peter and Saint Paul with busts of the two Republican "martyrs": Marat and Le Peletier de Saint-Fargeau.

On November 10, 1793, the first ceremony took place in the Temple of Reason, in Paris, formerly known as the cathedral of Notre-Dame. The goddess of Reason was played by an actress who, throughout the Revolutionary period, was to take her role very seriously. A hymn by Marie-Joseph Chénier, to music by Gossec, was sung to the goddess of Reason. In the provinces goddesses of Reason were not "professionals" but usually young ladies of the bourgeoisie chosen for their beauty. Indeed, the cult of Reason, despite Hébert's plebeian style, was profoundly bourgeois. So Robespierre had no difficulty in accusing the cult of Reason, which was ignored by the popular masses, of being elitist. Once he had managed to get Hébert and Chaumette guillotined, Robespierre set about transforming the cult of Reason into the cult of the Supreme Being, under the direction of the painter David—to music by the same Gossec.

The festival of the Supreme Being was a return to a pantheistic Christianity, and its liturgy was much more inspired by Catholic practice. Among the accusations against Robespierre, one of the most serious was to be his "religious despotism." When he, in turn, was arrested with a broken jaw, his enemies were to mock his Supreme Being who did nothing to save him. Nevertheless, after Robespierre's departure, temples to the Supreme Being continued to be opened in the provinces. The decree of 3 Brumaire, Year IV, which organized seven national festivals, did not abolish the cult of the Supreme Being but pretended to forget it, its seven festivals being: the festival of the Foundation of the Republic, the festival of Youth, the festival of Spouses, the festival of Gratitude, the festival of Agriculture, the festival of Liberty, and the festival of the Old.

At Lille a festival of Liberty was also a festival of the Dead, since it was observed that among the seven national festivals, none had been devoted to the memory of the dead. An Elysium had in fact been constructed, with lakes, shrubberies, woods, grottoes, hills, pyramids, and tombs. Inscriptions to the memory of the friends of Liberty could be read on the monuments. In the middle of the composition, at the summit of a rock, rose a statue of Liberty. But Rousseau's grave at Ermenonville, surrounded by its poplars, had also been reconstituted. Marat's funerary urn had been placed on a pedestal. Monuments to Le Peletier, Barat, and Viala had been erected.

The cult of tombs, of tombs reserved solely for exceptional individuals, was opposed by Hébertist leftism, which did not want any tombs at all, but a common grave for all. One Hébertist, Lequinio, a *Conventionel* from Brittany, even advocated the profanation of graves: "Begin at last the reign of pure philosophy, O Frenchmen, and destroy your tombs."

While the architects of the Revolutionary period continued to produce splendidly utopian funerary projects, following the lead set by Boullée and Ledoux, the Hébertist tendency to abandon burials altogether predominated among the population as a whole. It is symptomatic that this hiatus in the cult of the dead corresponds to a total cessation of religious practices.

"The abolition of the ceremonies of Catholic worship, the break in tradition where urban administration, and especially the burial of the dead, was concerned, the state of anxiety and anarchy in which France had lived since the Terror had led, by the end of the century, to the almost complete abolition of the honors accorded to the dead and to their proper burial."[4]

But we have seen how this disaffection had begun shortly before the Revolution with the great removal of the urban cemeteries. Indifference to death, so manifest during the Revolution, when people played with it as at poker, existed long before the Terror. Louis-Sébastien Mercier wrote in 1781: "Whoever wishes to be mourned after his death must not die in Paris. The passing of a funeral procession in the street is perceived with extreme indifference . . . No sooner has a man breathed his last than he is snatched, still warm, from his bed; the only concern of those left behind is to rid themselves of his body . . . One flees the place, one abandons the body to an old man. This old man is some poor, subordinate priest, who guards the corpse at night, and who is given twenty sous and a bottle of wine for his pains."[5]

However shocking Lequinio's words may be, they certainly stem, as he argues, from "pure philosophy," or, at least, from the so-called philosophy of the Enlightenment. And the rejection of the tomb represents a return, in the last analysis, to an unconscious primitive Christianity.

[4] Paul van Tieghem, *Le Préromantisme*, vol. 2 (Paris, 1930), previously published as *La Poésie de la nuit et des tombeaux du XVIIIᵉ siècle* (Paris: Alcan, 1921).

[5] Mercier, *Tableau de Paris*.

This rejection of the tomb is also to be found among two eminent Christians: Calvin, who asked to be buried quite simply in the earth, with no stone to mark the site of his burial, and Lamennais, who wrote in his will, "Nothing will be placed on my grave, not even a simple stone." And in the seventeenth century, Bossuet constantly inveighed against the vanity of tombs.

Volney, who visited Egypt in 1783–85, speaks of the pyramids in a pre-Revolutionary tone:

> It is pitiful to think that in order to construct a vain tomb, an entire nation had to be tormented for twenty years; one shudders at the thought of all the injustices and vexations it must have cost to transport, to cut, and to pile up so much material. One feels indignation against the extravagance of the despots who ordered such barbaric works . . . This labyrinth, these temples, these pyramids in their massive structure, reveal not so much the genius of a rich, art-loving people than the servitude of a nation tortured by the whims of its masters . . . While the art lover feels indignation in Alexandria at seeing the columns of palaces sawn off to make millwheels, the philosopher, after recovering from his initial feelings at the loss of any beautiful object, cannot but smile at the secret justice of fate, which gives back to the people what cost it so much pain, and which subjects to the humblest of its needs the pride of a useless luxury.[6]

At a time which saw a return to Greco-Roman Stoicism, Volney's words are reminiscent of the moralizing tone of Pliny the Naturalist, who said much the same about the pyramids, and, while admiring their achievement, attacked the folly and vain ostentation of royal wealth.

In view of this it is surprising that after thirteen centuries of Christian burial the ancient practice of cremation was not revived. A debate on cremation took place in 1789 but, although it was sometimes practiced, after over a thousand years of prohibition it was not to be advocated. The first cremation did not take place until 1794. The *Constitutionel* Fontaine, who died at Montpellier, was in fact solemnly burned in the Champ-de-Mars and his ashes sent to the Convention, which, not knowing what to do with them, ordered that they be placed in the National Archives! Before the cemetery-museum, the notion of a cemetery-archive made its appearance, but it was not to survive.

Under the Directory in 1797, following an academic competition, the grandiose project for a crematorium on the Butte Montmartre was considered for a time, but the plan was not implemented since the As-

---

[6] Volney, *Voyage en Syrie et en Egypte* (Paris, 1787).

sembly of the Five Hundred rejected the principle of cremation by a slender majority.

The equality of the dead achieved by the destruction of tombs was to lead to a posthumous massacre of kings, queens, princes, and princesses when they were dragged from their burial places in the royal abbey of Saint-Denis. In a report to the Convention, Barère demanded that August 10, 1792, the day when the monarchy had been overthrown, should be commemorated by destroying the mausoleums of Saint-Denis. "The powerful hand of the republic," he said, "should be ruthless in effacing those proud epitaphs and demolishing those mausoleums which recall the terrifying memory of our kings." The Convention approved the destruction, which was fixed for August 10, 1793.

On August 6, 1793, workmen armed with hammers and crowbars, escorted by soldiers and curious spectators, began to smash the tombs of the kings (in chronological order), beginning with the tomb of Dagobert, the first to have been buried in the royal abbey. Then they attacked the tombs of Pépin the Short, Charles Martel, Clovis II, and Charles the Bald. Of Charles Martel and Clovis II there remained in the sarcophagi only a few bones and a small pile of ashes; of Pépin the Short, a few ashes and gold threads. A former monk of the abbey, Dom Druon, attended the profanation of the tombs and carefully noted down what he saw.[7]

From Hugh Capet, all the kings except three (Philippe I, buried at Saint-Benoît-sur-Loire; Louis VII at Barbeau, near Melun; and Louis XI at Cléry) were buried at Saint-Denis.[8] But the oldest tombs dated only from the thirteenth century, the abbey having been looted several times.[9] The practice of erecting a tomb for each monarch was maintained only until Henry III, the Chapelle des Valois having been the last funerary monument of the monarchy. In the basilica, apart from the

[7] Dom Druon, *Journal historique de l'extraction des cercueils royaux, dans l'église de Saint-Denis, fait par le citoyen Druon, ci-devant bénédictin*, cahier 16 X 20 de dix feuillets, Archives nationales. I also consulted the book by Dr. Max Billard, *Les Tombeaux des rois sous la Terreur* (Paris, 1907).

[8] To these three kings who excluded themselves from Saint-Denis, we should add the two last kings of France who died in exile: Charles X and Louis-Philippe. Louis-Philippe was buried in the church of Saint-Louis de Dreux.

[9] The destruction wreaked first by the Normans, then by the Armagnacs, was such that in the twelfth century there no longer existed any of the original tombs at Saint-Denis. Suger substituted for them new mausoleums, some of which were in turn destroyed by the Huguenots, then by the armies of the Fronde. The Sans-Culottes were not the first, then, to profane them. It was just that their destruction was more rational and thoroughgoing.

princes and princesses, were also buried such famous churchmen or soldiers as Suger, the Cardinal de Retz, du Guesclin, and Turenne.

Between August 6 and 8, 1793, fifty-one monuments were destroyed. The remains of the monarchs were taken out of the open tombs and thrown into a common grave dug in ground to the north of the church. The skeleton of Charles V, who died in 1380, was well preserved. Near the cranium the vermeil crown was intact, as was a scepter surmounted by vermeil acanthus leaves to the right of the body, and, to its left, the silver hand of justice. Of Philippe Auguste, who was imprudent enough to have himself buried in a tomb of chiseled silver, nothing remained, the carving having been stolen several centuries before. Of Marguerite de Provence, only two small bones and a kneecap remained. The empty grave of Saint Louis caused some degree of astonishment, because the vandals were unaware that in 1297 the king's bones had been taken out of the tomb for his canonization. Only Louis IX's chin remained at Saint-Denis, the cranium going to the Palais de Justice, a rib to the abbey of Pontoise, one hand bone to the medical faculty in Paris, a piece of shoulder to the abbey of Royaumont, et cetera. On the other hand, in his lead coffin the skeleton of du Guesclin was intact. Henry II and Catherine de Médicis were also rediscovered in their state robes lying on a bed of gilded copper tinsel. Only one tomb escaped destruction, that of Gondi, Mazarin's adversary, whom, out of antipathy, Louis XIV had had buried secretly at night. During Viollet-le-Duc's work of restoration, under the Second Empire, the famous architect found Gondi's tomb next to the site of that of Francis I.

The only body saved from the common grave and preserved as a historical curiosity was that of Turenne. On October 11, 1793, the opening of Turenne's tomb revealed a body in a total state of preservation, a sort of dry mummy, of which the facial features had hardly altered. This phenomenon led him to being placed at first in an oak box and exhibited to the gaze of the curious. The guard placed to protect this relic, which was neither religious nor aristocratic, but military, made a little money on the side by removing all the teeth, and selling them to visitors. No doubt Turenne's body would have been gradually depleted at the request of collectors of relics if, in June 1794, a professor of botany at the Jardin des Plantes, had not requested the "historical object" for his natural history collection. The Convention acceded to the request, and, for four years, Turenne's body, exhibited among fossils and antediluvian animals, was to be one of the great attractions of the museum. People lined up to look at it, very much as they do today to see Lenin's mummy in Moscow.

As we know, all the Bourbons, from Henry IV onwards, were buried at Saint-Denis, without any funerary monument, the lead coffins, enclosed in oak coffins, being simply placed in the crypt on iron tressels, forming two long lines with a narrow passage between them. This vault, fifty-two feet long and twenty feet wide, contained therefore fifty-four coffins, the last being that of the dauphin, the eldest son of Louis XVI, who died on June 4, 1789.

It was only on October 12, 1793, the day after the discovery of Turenne's body, that it was decided to open the vault of the Bourbons. Ever respectful of chronological order the first coffin to be opened was that of Henry IV. After removing the white shroud, the king's body appeared even more intact than that of Turenne's. It was set up against a pillar, where it remained for two days, an object of public curiosity and amusement. A soldier cut off a lock from the white beard and used it as a false moustache. A woman struck the dead man, and knocked him to the ground. Another citizen pulled out two of his teeth, a third pulled off one of his sleeves. However, a sculptor managed to make a cast of the head after a hundred and eighty-three years of burial. Then the body of Henry IV, like that of all the Bourbons, was thrown into a great ditch, and covered with quicklime to accelerate decomposition.

On November 12, 1793, a convoy of six carts brought the treasures found in the tombs of Saint-Denis, or in the church, to the Convention: there were gold and silver statues, weapons, goblets, crowns, jewelry, chalices, ciboria, and relics. Indeed Saint-Denis had been in possession of relics which, to say the least, were of dubious authenticity and which Philippe Auguste and Saint Louis had bought from the emperor of Constantinople, believing them to be, for example, one of the wine jugs from the marriage at Cana, a bone of the prophet Isaiah, some of Jesus Christ's blood, milk from the Virgin Mary, one of the nails from the crucifixion, one of Saint John the Baptist's shoulders, studded with silver and gold, King Solomon's goblet, decorated with gold and set with precious stones.

To these might be added more recent objects: Joan of Arc's sword, Saint Louis's chin studded with gilt silver and precious stones, one of Saint Eustache's arms, and a finger from the body of Saint Bartholomew.

These precious objects and "curiosities" were placed in wooden chests decorated with flags. The carts were driven by men wearing chasubles, surplices, and other ecclesiastical costumes found in the abbey, and singing revolutionary songs. At the head of the procession, astride a donkey, was Citizen Pollart, formerly a Benedictine monk, in religious dress.

On arrival at the Convention, Pollart walked up to speaker's tribune brandishing the skull of Saint Louis, which he had taken out of its golden reliquary: "We were not tempted to kiss this stinking relic; this skull and the sacred rags found with it will no longer be the ridiculous objects of the veneration of the people, and nourish superstition, lies, and fanaticism. We bring you, citizen legislators, all the gilded filth to be found in the Franciade."

For Saint-Denis had been rebaptized and was now known as the Franciade.

An enthusiastic Convention cheered, drank out of the chalices and ciboria, and were delighted by the dances of the false ecclesiastics. All the objects bought by Pollart were broken up or taken off to the Hôtel des Monnaies to be converted into gold and silver coins. The crown of thorns, which Louis had bought believing it to be Christ's, was kept in the Bibliothèque Nationale until 1804, then transferred in 1806 to Notre-Dame, where it still is. The "holy nail," which was taken off by the Inspection des Mines to be analyzed, was kept there until 1824, when it was handed back to the Archbishop of Paris. Most of the stone and marble statues were saved from destruction at the last moment by the archaeologist Alexander Lenoir, who claimed them, on behalf of the Commission for Arts, for the Musée des Monuments Français, which the National Assembly had voted to set up in the former convent of the Petits-Augustins, today the Ecole Nationale Supérieure des Beaux-Arts. In those sarcophagi that had been saved at Saint-Denis, Lenoir kept the remains of Héloïse and Abelard, Molière, and La Fontaine, whom he had also managed to save from destruction.[10] He was also to inherit Turenne's mummy.

Indeed, on August 2, 1796, a deputy from the Isère pointed out to the Conseil des Cinq-Cents the scandal of seeing "the remains of the Great Turenne placed between those of an elephant and a rhinoceros." On 24 Germinal, Year VII, Turenne's body was taken to Alexander Lenoir's Musée des Monuments Français, where it was to remain on exhibition for two years. On September 22, 1800, the First Consul had it solemnly transported to the Invalides.

At two o'clock in the afternoon, to the sound of cannon, Turenne's body, placed on a triumphal chariot drawn by four white horses, crossed Paris in the midst of an immense crowd. A piebald horse, like the one ridden by Turenne, harnessed in the manner of the seventeenth century,

---

[10]On July 6, 1792, the presumed bones of Molière were exhumed from the cemetery of the church of Saint-Eustache and placed in a sarcophagus designed by Alexandre Lenoir. From the museum-cemetery of which Lenoir was both the inventor and the guardian, Molière's remains were transferred on May 6, 1817, to the cemetery-museum of Père-Lachaise.

headed the procession, led by a Negro. Turenne was welcomed at the Invalides by the former *Conventionnel* Carnot, who had escaped the guillotine and was now minister of war: "Here is the body of that warrior, so dear to every Frenchman . . . Henceforth, O Turenne, your Manes will inhabit this place; they will remain naturalized among the founders of the Republic."

From the destruction of the tombs, so dear to Hébert, we pass to the rehabilitation of the tombs that accompanied the resurrection of hierarchy, order, and pomp so dear to the First Empire. The lead from the roof of the basilica of Saint-Denis was removed in 1795. The former abbey was reroofed with tiles and slates the following year, when it became a public market; it was later used to house hand mills, then, for ten years or so, it became a military hospital for the armies of the republic.

The Corinthian columns that had decorated the outside of the Chapelle des Valois were used to construct an artificial ruin in the Parc Monceau. With the debris from the tombs that Lenoir had been unable to save, a symbolic hill was made at the top of which was placed a statue of Liberty. When, on October 10, 1794, the remains of Jean Jacques Rousseau were transported to the Panthéon, the procession halted before this "symbolic mountain," opposite the church porch.

The same acts of vandalism were repeated in most of the churches, in Paris and in the provinces.[11] At the Champs-Elysées of Arles a large number of the Roman and Gallo-Roman sarcophagi, for example, were carried off by carters, who broke them up and used them to repair roads in the Rhone valley, which had been damaged by flooding.

Many illustrious bones had been buried in the church of Saint-Gervais. The Convention, having melted down the lead from the tombs, had the bones buried in the churchyard; they were later transported in bulk to the catacombs. In this way the remains of Scarron, Philippe de Champaigne, and Couperin disappeared. The tombs to be seen today in the church are empty. The remains of Rameau and Colbert, removed from

[11] Michelet justifies the profanation of these tombs by a nation in danger, since the army needed the lead and copper from the coffins: "How could people so cruelly abuse the men of '92 for disturbing those tombs? Did not the France of the living, so close to perishing, have the right to ask the help of the France of the dead, and to obtain weapons from them? Ah! If the best of those dead had been asked, if one had been able to know the opinion of a Vauban, a Colbert, a Catinat, on this matter, all that ancient heroic France would have replied: 'Do not hesitate, open up, look around, take our coffins, nay, take our bones. Do not hesitate to take all that remains of us and use it against the enemy'" (*Histoire de la Révolution française*).

the church of Saint-Eustache, were thrown into common graves. After the restoration excavations were carried out to locate Colbert. It was thought that his pelvic bone and legs were identified, and these were replaced in his mausoleum.

The hearts of the kings of France, buried in urns, were sold in 1793 to make mummy; a painter, Martin Drolling, was to use the powder of these crushed hearts for his paintings. The portrait of a bourgeois, L. C. Maigret, which is in the Louvre and which dates from the same year, may have been painted with powder from the kings' hearts.[12]

It is impossible to speak of the space of death during the Revolution without mentioning once again the guillotine and Dr. Guillotin, who is supposed to have invented it.

In fact, the system of decapitation of the guillotine type existed well before the Revolution of 1789 and Dr. Guillotin. Lucas Cranach, who died in 1553, designed a guillotine. It had been known, therefore, from the Renaissance. In Scotland it was used for the execution of nobles. In 1632, at Toulouse, the maréchal Henry II de Montmorency was decapitated by an "ax blade placed between two wooden posts, held by a rope. One lets go of the rope, it drops, and separates the head from the body."[13]

So Dr. Guillotin did not invent the guillotine, but he advocated the adoption of this machine, which had been very little used under the Ancien Régime for all those condemned to death, whatever the nature of their offense and social class.

In 1792 commoners were still hanged or put to the wheel. Equality before death was not always applied in the case of capital punishment. Questioned as to the possibility or not of executing all condemned prisoners by the sword, whether they were nobles or commoners, the executioner Sanson replied: "After each execution, the sword is no longer in any state to perform another. Being subject to blunting, it is absolutely necessary that it be sharpened again . . . It should also be noted that very often swords are broken in such executions."

It was not unknown, as we have seen, for an executioner to have to take three or four strokes before managing to cut off a head. But it was above all the barbarity of hanging, the wheel, the stake, boiling oil, and

[12] The *Saint Paul* in the church of Saint-Sulpice is not by the same Drolling, as has sometimes been said. This Drolling, a pupil of David's, was in fact born in 1786 and died in 1857. The Drolling who concerns us here was an Alsatian, whose first name was Martin. He was a genre painter in the Flemish manner and also a decorator at the Manufactory of Sèvres (1752–1817).

[13] Jacques Chastenet de Puysegur, *Mémoires* (Paris, 1632).

other cruel forms of execution practiced under the Ancien Régime that met the disapproval of Dr. Ignace-Joseph Guillotin, the most expensive and most sought-after physician in Paris, a friend of Marat and a notorious freemason, elected a deputy for Paris in 1789.

Guillotin was not the only one to advocate equality of execution for all criminals condemned to death, but he was a very well known and very influential individual. He was one of the founders of the Grand Orient of France, a freemasonic society whose organizer was Choderlos de Laclos, author of *Les Liaisons dangereuses* and whose grand master was Philippe d'Orléans, the future Philippe Egalité. In the Lodge of the Nine Sisters, which was Guillotin's, the worshipful masters were in turn to be the astronomer Lalande and Benjamin Franklin. In the lodge Guillotin was to meet Houdon, Greuze, Chamfort, Hubert Robert, Parny, Florian, Louis-Sébastien Mercier, Prince Charles Rohan, the duc de La Rochefoucauld, and the marquis de Condorcet. Among the apprentices were to be found Danton, Brissot, Pétion, and Sieyès.

On October 10, 1789, Guillotin got a law passed which laid it down that "offences of the same kind will be punished by the same kinds of penalty, whatever the rank or condition of the offenders." It was a penal revolution so far-reaching that, as we saw above, it had still not been implemented in 1792. On December 1, 1789, Guillotin proposed to the Assembly to adopt, for purposes of equality in capital punishment, what was still called the "simple mechanism": "The mechanism falls like thunder," he declared, "the head flies off, the blood spurts, the man is no more."

So the guillotine was not an instrument for the multiple decapitation of the nobility but, on the contrary a machine intended to deprive the nobility of the privilege of decapitation.

It was a German pianomaker, Tobias Schmidt, who was to be given the task of constructing the "simple mechanism," under the supervision of Dr. Louis. As a result the first popular nickname given to the instrument was the "Louison" or "Louisette." Dr. Louis first tried his "Louisette" on living sheep. When satisfied with the performance of his mechanism, he had the "Louisette" taken to the almshouses of Bicêtre, where it was used to decapitate human corpses in the presence of Dr. Louis and Dr. Guillotin. The latter noticed that the curved blade might leave the severance of the head incomplete, and suggested that an oblique blade, which was to become one of the characteristics of the instrument, be substituted for it.

The *Conventionnels* were philanthropists. They believed that by using the guillotine they were annihilating evil and that after a final cartload the golden age of the republic might begin. For these judges, barristers, and magistrates of the Ancien Régime, used to ordering criminals to be burned, hanged, quartered, put to the wheel, the guillotine seemed, Michelet tells us, "an indifferent thing; it was, in their opinion, as if one died in one's bed—a little earlier it is true—but, in any case, one must die."

The first criminals to be guillotined, in 1792, were common-law criminals. Nicolas-Jacques Pelletier, executed on the Place de Grève on April 15, had stabbed to death a private citizen for stealing his wallet. A huge crowd attended this inauguration of a new spectacle of public death.

Some days later, three soldiers who had attacked a lemonade seller in the Palais Royal with their sabers were decapitated in turn. On August 21, 1792, the first political victim, an aristocrat, Louis-David de Collenon d'Anglemont, accused of having "acted against the people," on August 10 was "guillotined."[14]

After being variously called "Louison," "Louisette," and "Mirabelle," the mechanism was soon to be baptized by journalists "guillotine." Hébert called it the "national razor."

The term *guillotine* was launched. It was to stick, much to the chagrin of good Dr. Guillotin, who lost all his rich clientele and who was terrified by the Terror. In turn, an army doctor under the republic, a professor at the new Ecole de Médecine under the empire, a proponent of vaccination, he died in 1814, and was buried at Père-Lachaise.

On October 21, 1790, the National Assembly passed measures allowing executed criminals to be buried in public cemeteries and not to be thrown on the rubbish dump, as under the Ancien Régime. The first cemetery at Clamart, opened in 1783, where the two hundred unknown persons found drowned in the Seine or dead on the public highway each year had been buried. It was also in this cemetery that Rétif de la Bretonne was buried in 1806.

But as the number of criminals guillotined increased each year, three special cemeteries had to be set up. One in the former kitchen garden of the Benedictines of Ville-Lévêque, better known as the cemetery of the Madeleine; the other, known as the cemetery of the Mousseaux or Errancis, between the Rue de Monceau and the Rue du Rocher; the third, at Picpus, for those guillotined in the Place de Trône.

---

[14]"The execution by torchlight, before the dark facade of the palace still stained with the massacre, had a most sinister effect. The executioner himself, quite accustomed as he was to such spectacles, could not resist adding his own contribution. Just as he was holding up the head of the executed man, and showing it to the people from the top of the scaffold, he fell and landed on his back. People ran up to him: he was dead" (Michelet, *Histoire de la Révolution française*).

The first two cemeteries have been destroyed; the third, closed to further burials, has become a private cemetery.

The first of these cemeteries for the guillotined, that of the Madeleine, had been chosen for its closeness to the Place de la Concorde, a place of execution.

Soon saturated, the cemetery of the Madeleine was closed on March 25, 1794, and replaced by the Cimetière des Mousseaux. One thousand one hundred and nineteen guillotined were buried there, including Danton, Camille Desmoulins, Fabre d'Eglantine, Chaumette, Malesherbes, Lavoisier, Robespierre, Saint-Just, and Fouquier-Tinville. Closed in turn in 1797, the anonymous bones of the executed were to be transferred in bulk to the catacombs between 1844 and 1879.

For the guillotine set up in the Place de la Nation, a new cemetery was opened in the garden of a convent of canonesses, the present number 35 Rue du Picpus. Two ditches twenty-six feet by twenty, and twenty feet deep, were dug, and a hole opened up in the convent wall to allow access for the cart containing the decapitated bodies. The corpses tipped on to the ground had been completely stripped of their clothes by the executioner's assistants. Bleeding, decapitated, and naked, the victims were then dragged by their feet into the common grave, where they were piled up. Between June 14 and July 28, 1794, the bodies of 1,356 guillotined were buried there, including those of André Chénier, General de Beauharnais (Josephine's husband), sixteen Carmelites from Compiègne, executed on July 17, 1794 (they are the subject of Bernanos's play *Dialogues des Carmélites*), and 108 high-ranking aristocrats: princes, princesses, dukes, and marquises.

But if one examines the social background of the victims, one is rather surprised to see that members of the nobility were in a small minority (159), only one more than one-sixth of the total. There was also a small minority of ecclesiastics and religious (131). Most of the victims were workers, clerks, housekeepers, or servants (702), that is, over half, followed by soldiers (178) and lawyers (136).[15]

In 1803 the Princesse de Hohenzollern-Sigmaringen and a few other relations of executed aristocrats bought the site, which became "the private cemetery of Picpus," reserved solely for the descendants of the victims of 1794. So, *qua* son-in-law of the duchesse d'Ayen, La Fayette was buried in this cemetery in 1834.

During the revolution a new phobia arose concerning the urban cemeteries. Though the figure of the guillotined was tiny compared with

[15] Le Clère, *Cimetières et Sépultures de Paris*.

that of the ordinary burials in Paris, the daily repetition of the passing of carts filled with the executed could not fail to affect people's thinking. The king and the Girondins rotting in the cemetery of the Madeleine were making their neighbors ill. The Commune, after closing the Madeleine, buried the new guillotined in a corner of the Parc Monceau. The residents of the new commune of Les Batignolles immediately declared that they were inconvenienced by the smell from the corpses. Furthermore, those of the Rue Saint-Honoré complained of the incessant passing of carts. At the time this quarter was the most commercial—and smartest—in Paris. The population, tired of the spectacle of the guillotine, fled the arrival of the carts, which were all the more horrible in that on their return from the present Place de la Concorde they were streaming with blood and left behind them red traces in the street. Since the guillotine was affecting trade, the guillotine had to move to the other end of the district—to the Barrière du Trône. From now on the carts would travel only through a popular district. But before long the workers of the district were also to complain of the spectacle and the smell. So much so that Michelet suspected that this popular disgust for the guillotine was the cause of the strange indifference shown by the inhabitants of the Faubourg Saint-Antoine to the arrest and execution of Robespierre, whom they had previously regarded as a god.

"The discontent of the Faubourg was extreme, and not without reason. Blood flooded the square, and no other remedy had been found than to dig a hole a yard in every direction from where it fell . . . The hard, clayey soil absorbed nothing: everything decomposed where it lay. The smells were frightful even at a distance. The hole was covered with planks; but this did not prevent anyone, when the wind was in the wrong direction, from smelling the odor of decomposition, and being sickened by it."[16]

Poyet, the city architect, suggested "that the blood be caught in a wheelbarrow lined with lead which, each day after the execution, would be taken away."

The situation of the district was not very reassuring. It was placed between three cemeteries, all three alarming. When Sainte-Marguerite was full to overflowing, they had to open Saint-Antoine, and there each grave had only a few inches of ground to itself. While at Picpus, to which the guillotined were taken, the sight was unbearable. The clay rejected everything, refused to hide anything. Everything remained on the surface. Liquid putrefaction spread and bubbled under the July sun. The highways department, which

[16] Michelet, *Histoire de la Révolution française.*

230]

made its report, dared not answer that the chalk should absorb this terrible smell. The ditches were covered with planks, and the bodies were dropped through trap doors. Chalk was thrown down in large quantities, but so much water was clumsily poured in at the same time that things became still worse . . . The Commune, warned on 8 Thermidor, thought that they could wait a day or two more, and simply suggested "burning thyme, sage, and juniper over the ditches during burials."[17]

This popular aversion for the guillotine, after some years of infatuation, this disgust for the cemeteries where executed criminals were buried, did, no doubt, have some influence on Robespierre's fall. Collot d'Herbois sensed this when he replied to those who were beginning to have doubts as to the effectiveness of the Terror: "What will remain to us, then, when you have demoralized the public execution?"

The abandonment of funerary rites and individual tombs gave rise to some reaction under the Directory and an attempt to reinvent secularized funerals under the Consulate.

On October 5, 1793, Legouvé read to the Institut de France his "Sépulture," a poem imbued with the ideology of the "progressive" philosophers and poets of the years preceding the Revolution. Nevertheless what Legouvé was advocating was so opposed to the practice of his time that his poem was not published until 1801.

He protested against the profanation being perpetrated on graves, against neglecting traditions, against the absence of processions and solemn rituals. It was one thing for the Law to forbid a priest to accompany the body, but why were relations and friends similarly debarred? Why turn the common grave into a universal rule? It may be right to forbid the erection of magnificent mausoleums on the grounds that they are an indecent exhibition of personal pride, but why prohibit modest tombs, placed in the country, preferably in woods, or among grass and trees? They would become places of pilgrimage. The tomb, said Legouvé, should be a lesson in civic virtue. This is a new notion, but it is not unconnected with more ancient ones. Instead of drowning the memory of good citizens in anonymity, added Legouvé, the State ought to encourage the living to seek inspiration from their example. This is obviously the same idea which inspired the Panthéon. But Legouvé asked that the national territory be a pantheon for all.

Eight years later, the same year that Legouvé was able to publish his poem, the Institut put the question of burial up for competition, at the request of the minister of the interior, Lucien Bonaparte.

[17] Ibid.

[231]

The question, What ceremonies should be used in funerals, and how should the places of burial be administered? produced forty projects by way of an answer. All adopted the principle of burial outside cities for reasons of hygiene, the replacement of priests by "funeral magistrates," and secular ceremonies. Some recommended embalming.

A very clean break is noticeable with the monumentality of pre-Revolutionary projects. The authors are more in favor of large, open, green spaces, without monuments. No stone tombs, but at most a small inscription over the grave. Grass, trees, streams. In other words, an English-style garden, of the kind so dear to the philosophers and poets of the late eighteenth century. There also appears the idea of dispersing graves, encouraging burial in land owned by families. For J. Girard, "Private burials would have the double advantage of strengthening our attachment to the family, to property, to the nation."[18]

The idea of a pantheon for great men was rejected by some who also preferred dispersal to places associated with the dead. By having himself buried at the tip of the Grand Bé, in Brittany, Chateaubriand was to follow this tendency fifteen years later.

The first prize was given *ex aequo* to Amaury Duval and the Abbé Mulot.

The idea of vegetal metempsychosis, which is implied in most of the reports, is also to be found in Mulot's project. But Mulot was original in proposing new funeral ceremonies. A decree of 21 Ventôse, Year X, had already prohibited carrying the bier on foot, which was common during the Revolution. Now bodies had to be taken individually to cemeteries in hearses, drawn by two horses keeping in step. For the poor the city was to provide the shroud and coffin. Mulot added that the procession should be headed by a crier dressed in black, wearing a black crepe hat, waving a bell, shouting: "Respect to the dead!" Behind him musicians playing mournful tunes "would remind us of the Lydian mode and tones of the funeral flutes of Greece and Rome."[19] Those taking part in the procession would carry flowers and branches of trees. After suggesting that a poet should be entrusted with the task of composing a "Funeral Song," Mulot goes on to describe the costume of the funeral officer: "A hat darkened by black feathers, a medal visibly hanging around his neck, surrounded by a serpent swallowing its own tail, the symbol of immortality; a rod two meters high, bearing the true inscription: *Our Days Are*

[18] Joseph Girard, *Des tombeaux et de l'influence des institutions funèbres sur les moeurs* (Paris, 1801).

[19] Abbé François-Valentin Mulot, *Discours sur les funérailles et le respect dû aux morts* (Paris, n.d.).

Numbered; last, a butterfly, emblem of the soul which survives; black clothes and a full cloak of the same color."[20]

In another memorandum Mulot proposes the vitrification of bodies: "Since bones produce a fairly large quantity of glass, it would be possible to distribute to those left behind medallions that would be much more highly prized than a fragile painting."[21]

This unexpected proposal to vitrify human bones with a view to turning them into medallions and busts in the image of the dead person turns up again in another memorandum, this time from Pierre Giraud, architect of the Palais de Justice in Paris. But Giraud, like Mulot, was merely taking up an idea suggested by a certain Becker, who, in 1669, published at Frankfurt a *Physica Subterranea*, a method of vitrifying the substances of the human corpse.

Giraud, as an architect, proposed a monumental cemetery in the style of Ledoux and Boullée, consisting of a portico around a central pyramid. In the basement of the pyramid was placed the crematorium oven required for the vitrification of bodies. The columns of the portico were made of glass deriving from human bone, as also were all the monuments under the gallery. The crematorium oven enclosed four boilers capable of containing one, two, three, and four corpses immersed in a caustic solution, which transformed the human substances into glass, a new incorruptible form of the human body. With this glass could be made commemorative medallions and plaques.

"How many children would be naturally deflected, from their earliest youth, away from crime and even from dissipation simply at the sight of the medallions of their virtuous ancestors . . . I would even like it to be possible for that child who was most deserving of his parents, of his peers, and of his nation, to be the natural heir of the bones, ashes, or medallions of his ancestors; that he should be able to carry them about with him like furniture, the cost being borne by the rest of the family."[22]

This brings us back to the practices of the Australian aborigines, who carry the bones of their parents in a small bag around their necks.

Among the other projects submitted to the competition, one proposed the hanging of a black flag at the door of the house of the deceased and the proclaiming of the names of the dead every ten years in public

---

[20] Ibid.

[21] Abbé Mulot, *Vue d'un citoyen sur les sépultures* (Paris, n.d.).

[22] Pierre Giraud, *Les Tombeaux ou Essai sur les sépultures, ouvrage dans lequel l'auteur rappelle les coutumes des anciens peuples, cite sommairement celles observées par les modernes, donne les procédés pour dissoudre les chairs, calciner les ossements humains, les convertir en une substance indestructible et en composer le médaillon de chaque individu* (Paris, 1801).

sessions for each arrondissement, with a brief speech of praise "of those whose virtues and talents deserve that honor."

On his return from exile, the poet Jacques Delille also asked that monuments to great men be erected in gardens, among flowers and trees; that the tomb of the humblest person should adorn the family garden. He describes with horror the profanations of the tombs of Saint-Denis.

On 23 Prairial, Year XII (1803), the Consulate reiterated the prohibition of all burial "in churches, Protestant meetinghouses, synagogues, hospitals, public chapels, and generally in any closed building in which citizens meet for worship, or within the boundaries of towns and townships." Furthermore, each commune had to make provision for a distinct burial for each religion or, failing that, to divide the cemetery into as many distinct parts as there were different religions, with a separate entrance for each religion. This article did not fall into abeyance until 1881.

On February 20, 1806, Napoleon decided that the abbey of Saint-Denis would once again be a place for funerals and that his dynasty would be buried there. But it was only after the restoration, on the occasion of the transfer of the remains of Louis XVI and Marie Antoinette, that Saint-Denis became once again the royal necropolis.

The royalist Desclozeaux had watched from the window of his apartment, which looked out over the new cemetery of the Madeleine, the secret burials of the king and queen. After buying the disaffected cemetery in 1794, he had the site where the monarchs had been buried surrounded by a hedge and trees. Excavations, carried out on January 18, 1815, uncovered the intact head of Marie Antoinette, her gartars, and a few pieces of her stockings. The next day Louis XVI was found.

On January 21, at seven in the morning, all the regiments of Paris, wearing black armbands, lined the route from the Rue d'Anjou to Saint-Denis. The cortege with the princes, the hearse, and a hundred Swiss guards reached Saint-Denis at 12:30.[23]

A decree from Louis XVIII then closed Lenoir's Musée des Monuments Nationaux and transported the tombs and statues preserved by

[23] "On beholding the catafalque leaving the Cimetière de Desclozeaux, laden with the remains of the Queen and King, I felt a strong emotion; I followed it with my eyes with a fatal presentiment. At last Louis XVI resumed his couch at Saint-Denis; Louis XVIII, on his side, slept at the Louvre. The two brothers were together commencing a new era of legitimate kings and spectres: vain restoration of the throne and the tomb, of which time has already swept away the dual dust" (Chateaubriand, *Mémoires d'outre-tombe*, vol. 3 [Paris, 1849]; *The Mémoires of Francois René Vicomte de Chateaubriand, Sometime Ambassador to England*, tr. [London, 1902]).

the archeologist to Saint-Denis. Tombs and statues were reconstructed piece by piece, though a certain amount of confusion ensued, some individuals acquiring new heads.

A fine example of this reconstruction is the tomb of Héloïse and Abelard at Père-Lachaise, composed of pieces of an arch taken from the church of Saint-Denis, bas-reliefs from the monuments of Saint Louis's brother and son, rose windows inherited from a demolished chapel at Saint-Germain-des-Prés, and two statues of unknown persons dating from the fourteenth century.

In January 1817 the charnelhouse of the Valois was excavated, but the masses of bones, mixed with earth, made no identification of the bodies possible. By torchlight, these bones were nevertheless taken back to Saint-Denis, where they were placed in Turenne's empty vault.

Under the restoration a number of memoranda were written protesting against the secularization of the cemeteries and their exclusion from the cities, and demanding a return to graveyards around churches. Some even proposed buying back collectively the new cemeteries so that they might be an inviolable property. This was because the new industrial and commercial world, which was to dictate such matters in the nineteenth century, was greedy for profitable space, and the cemeteries impeded the expansion of the city. Sometimes a cemetery was destroyed to enlarge a public square or a fairground, to straighten a street or a road, to build a school, or the like. And with the building of the railways, which extended their straight lines over the countryside, even the country churchyards were not exempt from such public expropriation. "Is it not repugnant to feel the earth, where so many sleep their last sleep, shaken to their foundations by these rolling houses which pass like thunder?"[24]

In 1824 L. F. de Robiano de Borsbeek painted a somber picture of the violations of cemeteries which, at a time that saw the restoration of funerals, had taken the place of the violations of tombs perpetrated during the Revolutionary period. But such violation was no longer motivated by a desire to profane. It was all done in the name of profit, with utter disregard for the consequences:

They arrive on the site armed with picks; the walls collapse on to the open tombs; the carts come in and load the rubble, the soil and the bones altogether; horses' feet crush bones on rubble from walls which were intended to protect them forever . . . And where are these degraded remains going? To the highways department, a torture hitherto reserved to malefactors and

[24]L. F. de Robiano de Borsbeek, *De la violation des cimetières* (Paris, 1824).

[235

great criminals! Sometimes they are used to backfill the building of a theater
. . . We have even seen workmen and bands of men and women fighting over
the bones, and selling them to sugar refineries . . . Where has your heart
found the courage to traffic the ashes of your fathers and of our fathers, your
wives and our wives, your sons and our sons, your friends and our friends?
And when you have sold or let your burial plots, and turned them into vegetable plots, do you not sometimes worry that the produce grown there might
one day turn up on your table?[25]

Against this vandalism of the cemeteries, appears, in the nineteenth
century, as we have seen, the new ideology of the cemetery museum. It
was in one such cemetery-museum, the new cemetery at Montmartre,
that the goddess of Reason was to be buried in 1829, in a simple tomb
marked by two low, truncated columns.[26]

[25] Ibid.
[26] I am referring, of course, to Thérèse Aubry, a professional dancer and actress who,
in 1793, played the role of the Goddess of Reason in the Republican ceremonies.

17

The Mortiferous Architects

It is right to remark here, in view of the useful but overexclusive preoc-cupations of modern rationalism, that the engineer, as builder and sci-entist, may compete with the architect, as builder and poet, where a factory or any other purely utilitarian building is concerned, but never for a tomb.

César Daly
Architecture funéraire contemporaine, Paris 1871

In moving away from the utopia toward reality, the rational ceme-teries of the architects are going to become more concrete—and this despite two contrary utopias, the cemetery-museum and the cemetery-park, both expressions of romanticism.

In the twenty years before the Revolution of 1789, years that saw the beginning of the great removal of the urban cemeteries and, ultimately, their secularization, appeared several architectural projects tending toward a rationalization of places of burial. Curiously enough, they were called *catacombs*, a term used to denote the great subterranean ossuary into which the "remains" of the parish churchyards of Paris were to be packed.[1]

In earlier times, though architects built tombs, they played no role, in Western Christendom, in the more general design of the space of death.

[1] The word is a probable alteration of the Greek *kata*, "below," and *tumba*, "tomb." In Low Latin, *katatumba* became *catacumba*. By extension, ossuaries were later to be called catacombs.

[237

Indeed, the Christian graveyards were unique in being gardens attached to churches or cloisters. The idea of building new cemeteries, as one designs new cities, cemeteries which, unlike those being superseded, would be hygienic and practical, could only come about at a time when functional prisons and the first "industrial estate," Claude Nicolas Ledoux's Salines d'Arch-et-Senans, were being designed.[2]

One of these "catacombs" has a circular plan, with a central obelisk. Five concentric galleries divide up the space into six zones, each assigned to a particular category of burial. In the basement of the obelisk eight vaults were reserved for "persons of distinction." A colonnade, backing on to the inside of the outer wall, "would serve as burial for those whose memory one may like to perpetuate in epitaphs or other remarkable monuments."[3]

Another "catacomb," designed by Renou, consists of two galleries, one circular, the other square, the circle being inscribed within the square. In place of the obelisk of the previous project, a chapel is placed in the center. Between the circular gallery and the chapel is a burial area for ecclesiastics. The nobility and upper bougeoisie occupy the mausoleums of the circular, porticoed gallery, the middle classes the square gallery, against the outer wall. Last, the lower classes are accorded a large space, landscaped with trees and flowers, in which the common graves are hidden.

A third "catacomb," planned for the plain of Aubervilliers, would have been a sort of large garden with, at the center, a huge temple for the royal family. Around this temple would be placed, naturally enough, the graves of nobles. A third circle, with statues, would house the great men of the nation, as in Westminster Abbey. Two thousand chapels would be reserved for private, freehold family vaults and tombs.

It is in this third project, then, that we see the emergence both of the idea of the pantheon and of the idea of freehold family vaults. But for the time being the idea of the pantheon, which was "in the air," developed in two different directions: the museum of great men in some magnificent building, as is the case with Westminster Abbey and the Panthéon in Paris, and the dispersal of famous men to natural settings. These two ideas meet in the fact that the nature referred to at the time was a very landscaped one, a nature of parks, albeit parks in the English style. The museum and the botanical garden are two themes dear to the eighteenth

---

[2] Pierre Giraud, who presented a project for a "functional" cemetery, also designed prisons. And Chateaubriand points out that in the early nineteenth century prisons were built on the sites of disaffected cemeteries.

[3] Ariès, *L'Homme devant la mort*.

century, as also were those of the gallery of great men and eternity through memory. The cemeteries being proposed by architects at this time were, then, monuments to be visited, containing other, smaller monuments which, themselves, ought to be remarkable, or parks dotted with artificial ruins and real graves.

It was in such a spirit that Bernardin de Saint-Pierre suggested that a place should be chosen near Paris where the bodies of those who had served their country well might be buried: "In the midst of trees and verdure there would be monuments of every kind, distributed according to the different merits of those commemorated: obelisks, columns, pyramids, urns, bas-reliefs, medallions, statues, plinths."

The marquis de Girardin, a great lover of English-style parks, gave Jean Jacques Rousseau a tomb under poplars at Ermenonville. The comtesse d'Houdetot, one of Rousseau's less fortunate female acquaintances, had a monument to Voltaire built in her park at Sannois near which were placed busts of Fénelon, Saint-Lambert, and Rousseau. Buffon's grave, too, in the chapel at Montbard, soon became a place of secular pilgrimage.

This concern for posterity, for "memory," is not unconnected with the quite new taste for "memoirs" and "confessions," and the quite new practice of naming a street after some individual who, it was thought, deserved to be perpetuated.

Joseph Girard, who was given an honorable mention in the competition for the regulations to be adopted in funeral ceremonies, in the Year IX (1800), went back to the Rousseau-inspired cemetery-park. In his project, the cemetery is like a sort of rediscovered earthly paradise:

We shall mark the location of those fields of repose, far from inhabited spots . . . sheltered by hills, watered by streams, which will encourage and maintain a vegetation capable of absorbing the vapors which will be given off into the atmosphere.

This field of repose will be enclosed by walls or ditches, which will protect it from any insult. The wall will be covered by hedges and climbing plants which will hide it from all view. It will be laid out with paths, where melancholy may indulge its daydreams: these will be shaded by cypresses, aspens, and weeping willows, whose trailing hair depicts for us the abandonment and disorder of sorrow. Streams will murmur beneath this sacred shade: guardians will keep watch lest any profanation sully its purity. These places will thus become an earthly Elysium, where men, tired of the pains of life, will rest, protected from their blows.[4]

[4]J. Girard, *Des tombeaux*.

[239

Pierre-Léonard Fontaine (1762–1853), cenotaph in the form of a
pyramid, 1785. *(Photo Bibl. nat. Paris)*

Taking up one of Bernardin de Saint-Pierre's ideas, Girard goes further. He proposes to enliven public places, in town and country, not by
statues or obelisks recalling the memory of great men, but by the actual
tombs of these great men. "If we had encountered, for instance, La Fontaine in the middle of a wood, the usual residence of the animals to
whom he gave speech, we would have imagined that we had seen him
. . . Going into the theater, the young artist would have paid homage to
the shade of Corneille . . . Boileau, placed along one of our most frequented walks, would have continued to threaten our vices with his
mordant wit and his satirical pen . . . On the edge of some meadow Jean
Jacques, presiding over children's games, would have shown his *Emile* to
their masters."[5]

[5] Ibid.

Finally, Girard advocates private burial places which, as we know, were banned during the revolution. These would have "the double advantage of tying us to the family, property, and the nation, by the gentlest and most useful of bonds . . . Ah! Why should the gentle farmer not enjoy the prospect of resting in the midst of the field he has cultivated . . . At the foot of some ancient oak, escaping from the storms of the noontide heat, he would eat his modest meal."[6]

The First Republic hesitated between the two tendencies of the monument-museum to great men and the park-promenade dotted with tombs. On April 4, 1791, the Constituent Assembly abolished Catholic worship in the church of Sainte-Geneviève, baptizing it the Panthéon, and in 1798 the Directory thought of replacing the Panthéon by the Jardin de l'Elysée.[7] The most deserving citizens would be buried there, among statues representing Héloïse, du Guesclin, Molière, Turenne, and so on.

Unlike the Pantheon in Rome, the church in the Rue Soufflot has the disadvantage of its great dome, which was intended to be a great architectural achievement but which owes its continued existence only to reinforcements carried out in the nineteenth century by the architect Rondelet. Indeed, this dome gave rise to a great deal of discussion when it was decided to turn the church into a pantheon. The architect Charles de Wailly (1730–98) proposed giving this pantheon a more solemn character by removing the dome which, though it may be suitable to a church, seemed to him to be incongruous with a "national monument" and replacing it by an open circular colonnade through which one could see the sky between the columns.

How many columns there were in these pre-Revolutionary buildings! And how many pyramids! Contrary to popular belief, the fashion for pyramids in French architecture existed, therefore, long before Napoleon's expedition to Egypt.

[6] Ibid.

[7] The new church of Sainte-Geneviève, begun in 1764 by the architect Germain Soufflot (1713–80), was designed in imitation of the Pantheon in Rome, an ancient temple consecrated to the worship of all the gods. There is nothing surprising in the fact that the Constituent Assembly should, therefore, have thought of making its own pantheon. In 1806 Napoleon handed back this church to Christian worship, on condition that it would also be used as a burial place for the dignitaries of the empire. In 1830 Louis-Philippe again secularized the church, which became not the Panthéon, but the Temple de gloire. In 1851 Napoleon III returned it to Christian worship. In 1885, on the death of Victor Hugo, the Third Republic secularized Sainte-Geneviève for a third time, when it became once more, as it has remained to our day, the Panthéon. Sainte-Geneviève is nevertheless still present there, since Puvis de Chavannes was commissioned to depict her life in a series of large murals.

Etienne Louis Boullée (1728–99), cenotaph in the Egyptian manner.
(Photo Bibl. nat. Paris)

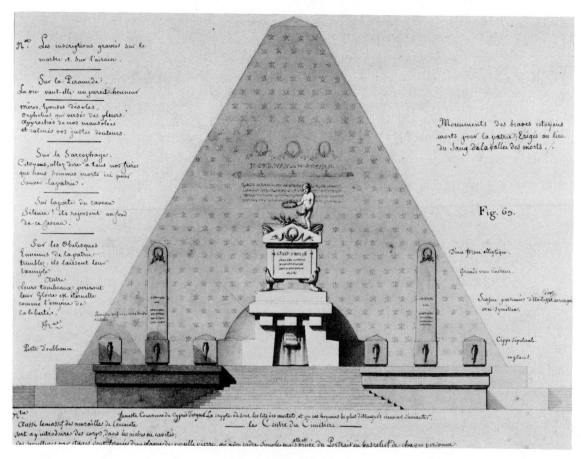

Jean-Jacques Lequeu (1757–1825), "Monument to brave citizens who
have died for the nation." *(Photo Bibl. nat. Paris)*

Jean-Jacques Lequeu (1757–1825), tomb of Lars Porsena. *(Photo Bibl. nat. Paris)*

In 1774 Michel-Ange Challe built a gigantic pyramid for the funeral of Louis XV in Notre-Dame-de-Paris. In 1785 Fontaine was awarded the Grand Prix for a cenotaph in the form of a pyramid surrounded by a circle of sixteen small pyramids. This idea was also used by Boullée when he proposed surrounding a great cenotaph in the form of a truncated cone by eight pyramidal cenotaphs. Indeed, Boullée had described

[243

ÉLÉVATION DU CIMETIÈRE DE LA VILLE DE CHAUX.

Claude Nicolas Ledoux (1736–1806), view of the cemetery of the city of Chaux. *(Photo Bibl. nat. Paris)*

a tomb in the form of a pyramid as a "cenotaph in the Egyptian manner."[8] Lequeu also gave the form of a pyramid to his "Monument to brave citizens who have died for the nation" and to his 1791 project for Porsena's Tomb. Three truncated pyramids support an enormous globe surmounted by a lid on which is bizarrely placed a baldachin of slender columns.

But Egyptomania also affected England, for in 1779 John Soane

[8] But Boullée, who was sixty-one in 1789, knew of the pre-Columbian pyramids through Robertson's *History of America*. In Boullée's library was also to be found Athanasius Kircher's work on the Tower of Babel, with illustrations reconstructing Nineveh and Babylon. It was these "reconstructions" which inspired his two projects for "cenotaphs with their walls" (J. M. Pérouse de Montclos, *E. L. Boullée* [Paris, 1969]).

244]

Coupe

Claude Nicolas Ledoux (1736–1806), plan of the cemetery of the city of Chaux.
(Photo Bibl. nat. Paris)

planned a national mausoleum to the memory of the earl of Chatham, flanked by two small pyramids.[9]

Apart from pyramids, the pre-Revolutionary and Revolutionary architects were very drawn to obelisks and globes. The sphere seemed to them to be the symbol both of eternity and equality. Ledoux said that it was the form best suited to expressing the sublime.

In his strange engraving *View of the Cemetery*, Ledoux shows planets moving across the sky. No doubt he was referring to a cemetery of spirits, where souls reside in the heavenly bodies.

But he returns to the form of the sphere for the great subterranean necropolis with which he endowed his ideal city of Arc-et-Senans. In fact it is a spherical pit, 245 feet in diameter, with three stories of galleries. At the level of each gallery light filters down through small arched windows. There was no decoration and no opening at the summit of the sphere. At the zenith of the vault a skylight allowed a little light to filter through. Even in bright sunlight the immense dome remained in shade. It was designed to impress as much from the outside as from the inside; it was surrounded by a desolate landscape, without trees, without grass, without water.

Claude Nicolas Ledoux wrote of his cemetery: "The ground opens up to reveal the retreats of death; as long as we are, death is not yet, when it is, we are no more; evils crowd in upon us and fall into its depths; man springs up after crossing the perilous deserts of life. Two staircases, which art has cut out of this imperishable mound, descend to the antipodes of the world."

Ledoux's Rousseau-inspired cemetery is far removed from the romanticism of the park-cemetery. It is closer to the prison, itself an enclosed space (the ideal functional space!), of which Ledoux was to supply a version in 1786 with his prison at Aix-en-Provence. This fascination with the sphere, with the spheres of the cosmos, is given architectural expression in the proliferation of cenotaphs to Newton, who died in 1727. The first, and most astonishing, of those projects is that of Boullée, which dates from 1784. But Labadie was also to design a "cenotaph" to Newton in 1800, and Delépine a "hemispherical tomb" in honor of Newton, in 1818.[10]

---

[9] We have seen how, in the seventeenth century, Father Ménestrier wrote in his treatise *Des décorations funèbres* that pyramids were more appropriate to tombs than obelisks.

[10] Pierre-Jules Delespine (1756–1825) exhibited in 1814, at the Salon, the project for a monument to be erected at the entrance to the Paris catacombs.

Pierre-Jules Delépine (1756–1835), tomb in honor of Newton. *(Photo Bibl. nat. Paris)*

The cenotaph to Newton designed by Etienne Louis Boullée (1728–99) was in the form of a sphere emerging from a circular base in the midst of a garden of flowers and cypresses.

The interior of this memorial contains only the sarcophagus, nothing else is allowed to distract from it. Everything is dominated by the gentle curve of the vault. Light enters through tiny, star-shaped openings grouped like constellations in the sky . . .

The sarcophagus seems so small in relation to the vault that no real contrast results. The skillful arrangement of the whole produces an effect of inexorable tension. From every point of the huge vault the gaze is captured by the tiny sarcophagus, the only object visible in the chamber. This cham-

[247

Etienne Louis Boullée (1728–99), cenotaph for Newton. *(Photo Bibl. nat. Paris)*

ber itself becomes a vast magnetic field traversed by innumerable lines of force. Thanks to an extraordinarily simple procedure, the void is filled with life.[11]

This superb project may nevertheless be compared, at least as far as the contrast between the tiny sarcophagus and the immensity of the vault is concerned, with what Soufflot imagined for his church of Sainte-Geneviève: the saint's modest tomb isolated in the middle of the church.

Boullée's globe for the Newton cenotaph may again be compared with the project for a temple of immortality by Jean-Nicolas Sobre, one of Ledoux's pupils. In fact this temple would have been hemispherical, but, by being reflected in a lake, it gave the illusion of a complete globe.

Boullée's magnificent design enlarged the projects for funerary architecture: a conical cenotaph surrounded by trees, a great funerary monument on a mountainside; a cenotaph surrounded by a colonnade. Jean-Jacques Lequeu (1757–1825), the third of the great architects of the

[11] Emile Kaufmann, *Trois Architectes révolutionnaires* (Paris: S.A.D.G., 1978).

248]

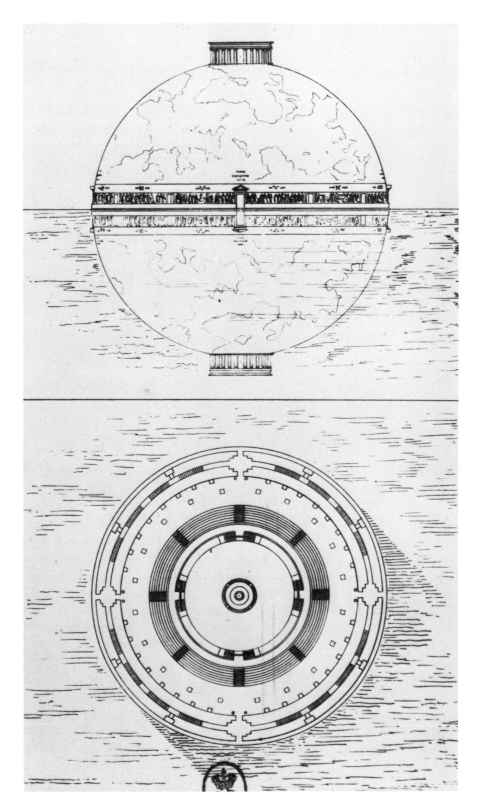

Jean-Nicolas Sobre, plan for a temple of immortality. *(Photo Bibl. nat. Paris)*

Jean-Jacques Lequeu (1757–1825), "Sepulture for the Most Illustrious and Most Learned Men of Voorhaut." *(Photo Bibl. nat. Paris)*

pre-Revolutionary and Revolutionary period (the other two being, of course, Ledoux and Boullée) also produced a number of architectural propositions intended not for the living but for the dead. His "Sepulture for the Most Illustrious and Most Learned Men of Voorhout" is a huge pillar made up of decreasing cylinders, ending in a conical dome surmounted by a temple. His "Monument to the Glory of a Number of Illustrious Men of the City" is a column surmounted by two wings; his "Mausoleum for Voltaire," a polygon with arcades, a sort of kiosk containing urns. His "Pluto's Palace" is an infernal gateway guarded by two chimeras. Under the restoration he designed his own tomb, which bore the following legend: "Sepulchre of the author, brother of Jesus; he bore his cross all his life."

Compared with Boullée and Ledoux, and Boullée especially, Lequeu is an altogether more extravagant artist. But, beside pure forms, there also appear other very composite projects, which seem to hesitate between neoclassicism and an eclecticism seeking new combinations, like the society which produced them, and which, as we know, was tearing itself apart while undergoing profound changes. The final resort, as with

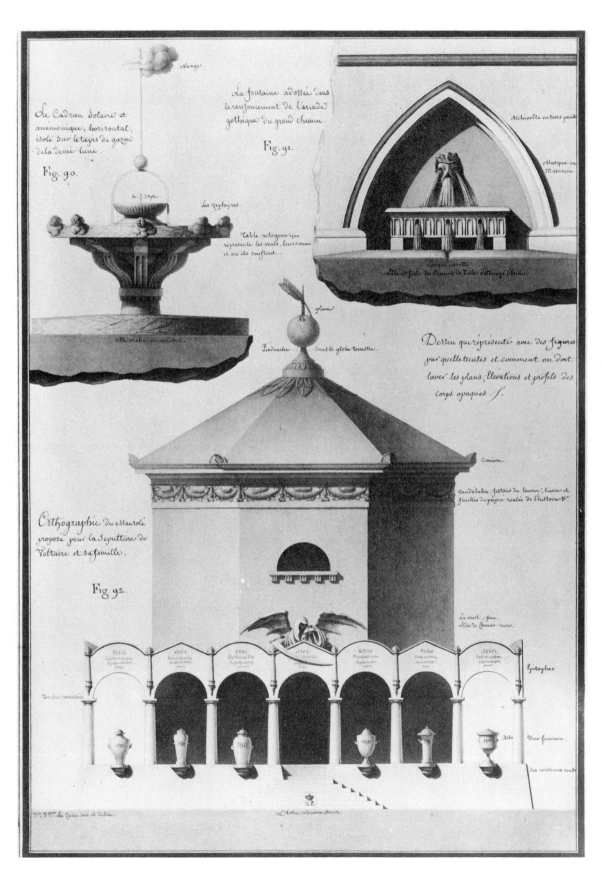

Jean-Jacques Lequeu (1757–1825), mausoleum for Voltaire. *(Photo Bibl. nat. Paris)*

Jean-Jacques Lequeu (1757–1825), Pluto's palace. *(Photo Bibl. nat. Paris)*

the painter David, is to draw on the repertoire of a Roman republican utopia, to which the symbolic forms of freemasonry were added. Neuf-forge designed a cemetery portal surmounted by an obelisk in which niches were decorated alternately with sarcophagi and medallions. Le Canu, in his projects for tombs, brought together several discordant elements: truncated pyramids, urns, garlands. Jean-Charles Delafosse (1734–89), one of the best designers of ornaments and furniture in the reign of Louis XVI, in his *Plan général des cimetières pour être construits aux deux extrémités de Paris* (1776–80) brings together prisms, cylindrical bodies, statues of weepers, and surmounts the cupola of his sepulchre with a column.

Others, continuing the tradition of parks in the style of Hubert Robert designed tombs among ruins (the designs of J. L. Legeay).[12] This ruinomania was to continue throughout the romantic period, and, in England, from 1812 to his death in 1837, John Soane incorporated in his own house the ruins of a monastery, an Egyptian crypt, and a monk's cell.

Although, as we have seen, funeral ceremonies for ordinary citizens had practically disappeared during the Revolution, collective funerals provided an opportunity for ephemeral architecture. One of the designers of these funerals in a new style was the architect Jacques-Joseph Ramée (1764–1825), who was responsible for the "Autel de la Patrie" on the Champs-de-Mars in Paris, set up for the festival of the Federation on July 14, 1790. The whole piece formed a round platform in the middle of which was placed the altar. It was reached from the bank of the Seine through a triumphal arch consisting of three equal gates. In front of the Ecole Militaire a rostrum had been constructed for the king and the National Assembly. The cylindrical altar was placed on a truncated pyramid. The same year, in September Ramée designed the funeral ceremonies organized at Nancy in honor of those who had fallen in battle. The engravings that depict this event show a profusion of staircases, smoke, and flags.

The desire for equality is expressed either in the notion of tombs for all or in that of the common grave for all. We have seen how the Convention advocated and imposed the common grave for all—or almost all, for it soon made an exception to its rule of the egalitarian ditch by creating the Panthéon. The individualistic nineteenth and twentieth cen-

---

[12] Just as, during the Revolution, the revolutionary musicians were aesthetically Mozartian, the architects, despite all their efforts, found great difficulty in divorcing themselves from the Louis Seize style.

turies were to adopt the individual tomb for all. By the same token the collective monumental cemetery in the manner of Ledoux and Boullée was to be abandoned in favor of the cemetery-museum: not a single great monument but a mass of small monuments. Exceptional in this regard were the great military ossuaries like Douaumont, built in 1932, which contains the remains of 300,000 French soldiers killed at Verdun—the equivalent of the population of a city like Bordeaux or Nantes.

The cemeteries were expelled from the cities in the late eighteenth century because they were thought to be unhealthy. In the nineteenth century, engineers demonstrated (with the same conviction as the doctors who, a century earlier, had declared the contrary), that the cemetery was not unhealthy. It is true that the dead were buried at a greater depth, or enclosed in sealed vaults. Similarly, trees, forbidden in cemeteries because they were thought to prevent the ventilation of miasmas, were recommended for their purificatory properties. In each case "specialists" merely "proved" what a particular society wanted to hear at a particular moment.

In the new cemetery-museum the architects designed tombs for private individuals, as they designed separate houses for the same individuals when alive. César Daly, architect and director of the influential *Revue générale de l'Architecture et des Travaux publics*, published in 1877 an album of 119 plates of specimens of tombs designed by architects under the Second Empire.[13]

In his preface, while regretting that his period is lacking in an architectural style, he expresses satisfaction that architects have a monopoly of funerary monuments, engineers competing with architects only for utilitarian buildings. César Daly fails to realize that the true architectural style of his time was precisely the result of the structural experiments of engineers and of a few architects using metal. The tombs built at Père-Lachaise, Montparnasse, or Montmartre by architects such as Viollet-le-Duc, Davioud, Duc, and Vaudoyer reveal nothing but reminiscences of the past. With their sarcophagi in the Roman style on even taller pediments, obelisks, towers, chapels, and Greek temples, we seem to be in a cemetery alternately Egyptian, Roman, and Gothic (while, in reality, we are in that nineteenth century of the ironmasters, steam, iron, and steel).

"The public," writes César Daly, "far from being shocked by this

[13] César Daly, *Architecture funéraire contemporaine: Spécimens de tombeaux, chapelles funéraires, mausolées, sarcophages, stèles, pierres tombales, croix, etc.; choisis principalement dans les cimetières de Paris et exprimant les trois idées radicales de l'architecture funéraire: La Mort, l'Hommage rendu au Mort, l'Invocation religieuse à propos du mort* (Paris, 1871).

servility to the past, praises it, even demands it: when alive, one wants to live in a Gothic house or a villa in the style of Louis XIII with a Louis XIV drawing room and a Pompadour boudoir; when dead, one rests in the shadow of a Greek stelae, with or without a Christian cross, or, like the great painter Delacroix, one decides, after mature reflection, that one will lie in a classical tomb like that of Scipio."[14]

Some wills, like that of Delacroix, lay down in meticulous detail the form of tomb desired. Sometimes it is the living who express themselves through the choice of burial which they make for their dead. As César Daly rightly remarks: "Each tomb is the residence of a dead person, and, consequently, the expression of an individual; but it is also a word of farewell addressed to the deceased by those left behind, that is to say, an expression of their feelings; and, to that degree, the living also express in it something of themselves."[15]

The only architect to be a precursor and pioneer of metal construction, and to concern himself with the space of death, was the astonishing Hector Horeau. At some unspecified date, which must be before 1868, Horeau designed a "Monument for the Cremation of Dead Bodies," in which we find the inevitable pyramid, but, this time, it is a high transparent pyramid made up of metal trellis work, ending in a turret in which the cremation would be carried out.[16]

In his project for a cemetery, Hector Horeau combines hygienic, economic, circulatory, and egalitarian preoccupations:

At the entrance to the cemeteries will be chapels, with funeral rooms, where corpses may be laid out, once death has been declared, after being brought from the house during the night or morning; *salles ardentes* with candles, lanterns, or braziers constantly lit, for ventilation and disinfection, where the corpses would lie until the onset of putrefaction; in this way it will be possible to place the same facilities at the service of several bodies, which would be at once prompt, economic, and in the spirit of the religion which proclaims that we are all of the same flesh and blood.

We should encourage the tendency to cremation, many people already preferring to have the envelope of their being reduced to ashes, instead of leaving it to be fed on by worms; by encouraging cremation, one would remedy the serious inconvenience of cemeteries, in which funerary monuments would be erected, in the form of pyramids, on which would be placed the ashes of the dead, previously burned some distance away, or even at the

[14] Ibid.
[15] Ibid.
[16] *Catalogue Hector Horeau* (Paris: Musée des Arts decoratifs, 1979).

summit of the monuments proposed, by methods avoiding any smell. With cremation, instead of being a danger to public health, cemeteries would become parks, healthy walks, and instead of paralyzing the circulation and the lives of the living, one might walk through new cemeteries in every direction according to the needs of viability above and below ground.[17]

This concern for circulation, which was to assume such importance in urbanism that the traditional city was to emerge from it utterly crushed, is taken up by Horeau as an argument against public executions: "Until capital punishment is abolished, let us annihilate the dangerous victims of ignorance by electricity, or by a pneumatic machine, so as not to have any longer the bloody spectacle of the scaffold, which attracts the population, prevents circulation of traffic, and which, far from reducing crime, on the contrary, stimulates the braggadocio of many criminals."[18]

In 1876 the Swiss architect and military engineer Schaeck-Jaquet proposed the first cemetery to be built of concrete. On a square, checkered plan, 10,000 graves would be distributed over a site of 65,000 square feet. The vaults arranged in three or five stories, with a "sanitary void" under the construction, would form therefore a sort of mortuary housing complex. After choosing a raised, well-drained site, Schaeck-Jaquet excavated to a depth of nearly twelve feet, and covered the surface with a layer of concrete. On this concrete bed were to rest the foundations of the tombs. The superimposed stories of tombs would be separated by cemented stoneslabs. After thirty years, the bones of the various vaults would be collected together in an empty space under each corridor. The corpses, hermetically sealed in their mortuary cells, would nevertheless be visible for two weeks through windows. This would prevent people being buried alive.[19] As an additional precaution, an electric wire, con-

---

[17] Hector Horeau, "Assainissement, Embellissements de Paris, ou Edilité Urbaine mise à la portée de tout le monde," *Gazette des Architectes et du Bâtiment* (Paris, 1868).

[18] Ibid.

[19] The fear of being buried alive was so common in the eighteenth century that many wills demanded that the coffins be closed only thirty-six or forty-eight hours after death. Diderot's *Encyclopédie* echoes this sentiment: "In fact one often sees on exhuming bodies after several months that they have changed position, posture, situation; some appear with the arms and hands gnawed with fury. Dom Calmet recounts, on the word of an eye witness, how, after a man had been buried in the cemetery at Bar-le-Duc, noises were heard emanating from the grave; it was opened the next day, and it was found that the wretch had eaten his own arm. At Alais (Alès) one saw the coffin of a woman whose right-hand fingers were caught under the lid of her coffin, which had been slightly raised."

nected to the hands of each corpse, would ring a special bell in the guardian's quarters, if such an individual who had been buried alive awoke. This wire would break of its own accord after a certain number of days. In this way, Schaeck-Jaquet believed, a solution had been found to "all the questions of health, safety, economy, arrangement, and sobriety."[20]

In 1881 the architect J. Courtois-Suffit proposed a funerary system much more economic still in plan. Fifty acres seemed to him to be enough to fulfill the burial requirements of a city like Paris forever.

Courtois-Suffit's concern that one day Paris would be surrounded by necropolises was unfounded; Paris certainly did become surrounded, but by boxes for the living. The Courtois-Suffit system was original in that it rejected both burial and cremation, while providing a cemetery which could be used permanently without ever getting full. How was this to be done? Apparently by the slow burning of the gases, given off by the corpses. In view of the fact that a human body of 100 pounds is made up of water, accounting for over two-thirds of its weight (that is, 70 pounds), bones (one-tenth of the weight, that is 10 pounds, and various gases weighing 18 pounds, Courtois-Suffit advised against deep graves, where the decomposition was too slow (between 14 and 18 months before the body was reduced to a skeleton, according to Orfila), and advocated placing it in permanent contact with the atmosphere.

> Set up a current of air which constantly crosses it, and direct this air, mixed with products from the fermentation, on to a fire, where the miasmas will be burned. Such is the proposition the apparatus for which we are about to develop . . . Without oxidation, there is no fermentation; without fermentation, there is no decomposition. Now the condition *sine qua non* of oxidation is the presence of oxygen in the vault . . . Allow the decomposition to occur naturally in the vaults, facilitating by free access of air the phenomena of fermentation and oxidation . . . Then capture the gases as they are given off, collect them, and conduct them to a fire where they will be purged of all infectious germs before returning to the atmosphere . . . The human remains are respected, the nonvolatilized residues are preserved intact . . . Nothing is changed from the present practice of burial.[21]

In the Courtois-Suffit system, then, it is not the human body which is burned, but only the gases. "Vapors and gases, such is the ultimate

[20]Schaeck-Jaquet, *La Sépulture, particulièrement les cimetières et nécropoles* (Geneva, 1876).

[21]J. Courtois-Suffit, "Projet de cimetière perpetuel par la crémation lente des gaz," *Moniteur des Architectes*, no. 3 (1881).

stage of the human body," cries the architect, launched enthusiastically on his demonstration: "We propose to drain the gases as one drains water in the fields, to collect these gases as they are formed, and lead them to a fire, where they will be purified."[22]

In fact, the ultimate stage of the human body is still, in this system, the good old skeleton so dear to the Middle Ages. If five vaults, placed one on top of another, may be used indefinitely, if the cemetery would never become full, it is because every five years the bones, with their water and gases removed, would be handed back to the families, who would be liable to pay the costs of placing them in a collective ossuary.

The pollution of water by nonfunctional cemeteries surfaces again in 1887, in the memorandum of an architect from Nantes.

"No site is naturally good for the creation of a cemetery," writes Paul Coupry, "and all may become so." In modern cemeteries, he continues, water seeps into the graves. "We do not understand how, to this day, river water or spring water has been allowed to bathe or simply wash the corpses, so that all the putrefaction of those corpses, diluted and carried off by those waters, outside the cemetery, later come and poison our food and infect the air."[23]

The cemetery proposed by Paul Coupry must, therefore, overlook the city so that the miasmas and gases would be carried off by the wind. All parts reserved for burial would be at a high level in order to be outside the reach of water. A broad ditch around the cemetery, forming a square 360 feet on each side, would prevent any water outside from seeping in. The coffins would be placed on battens, which would themselves be placed over drains. No contact with stagnant water would therefore be possible. "We would like to see the cemeteries of the future," writes Paul Coupry, "become, in their general arrangements, veritable monuments. So we have imagined transforming the principal ditches into catacombs, whose construction might be more or less monumental, according to the resources of the inhabitants of the city. There the rich families would find burial vaults awaiting them when required."[24]

Confronted by the desacralization and depoeticization of the cemeteries of the twentieth century, a few, very few, architects have reacted not by proposing rational cemeteries, as in the late eighteenth century, but by trying to create a secular funerary space that is neither gloomy nor ridiculous.

[22] Ibid.

[23] Paul Coupry, Fils, *Les Cimetières barbares du XIXᵉ siècle remplacés par les cimetières de l'avenir* (Nantes: June 1887).

[24] Ibid.

Such architects have conceived of this space not so much as architects but as town planners.

The first examples of this modern funerary architecture have come from the Protestant countries of northern Europe. In 1912 the city of Stockholm bought, for the creation of a new cemetery, a site of nearly 240 acres of sandy ground planted with pine trees. As a result of a public competition in 1914, the prize winners, the architects D. Asplund and S. Lewerentz, began their work in 1917. The Chapel of the Forest was completed in 1920, Lewerentz's Chapel of the Resurrection in 1922, and Asplund's crematorium in 1937–40. This cemetery, which is still held up as an example, is very simple, even severe, in conception, perfectly suited to the very striking landscape. It deliberately breaks with the monumental cemetery, as it does also with the ostentatious individual funerary monument, and is closer to the romantic (and preromantic) view of the cemetery-landscape.

The same tendency is to be found in the work of the Finnish architect Alvar Aalto, who published two unexecuted projects of funerary architecture.[25] The first, the chapel of Malm Cemetery, in Helsinki, submitted for a competition in 1950, has three chapels grouped in such a way that ceremonies could take place in one without interfering with those taking place in another; the second, for Lyngby Cemetery in Denmark, submitted for a competition in 1952, also made provision for several chapels in order to allow services to take place at the same time. Access to the chapels was also arranged in such a way that no procession could meet another. All these chapels are connected to the crematorium, to which the dead would be carried by people, and not by a mechanical conduit. Grass, water, and paths were arranged to produce a peaceful environment.

In France, the architect Robert Auzelle also advocates the cemetery-park. From his thesis at the Institut d'Urbanisme de Paris of 1942—*Les Problèmes de sépulture en urbanisme*—to his incomparable book, *Dernières Demeures*, of 1965, Robert Auzelle has continued, side by side with his work as a town planner, to concern himself with the space of death. His intercommunal cemetery of Le Parc, at Clamart, forms part of a wooded area. The buildings, which are all single story, spread horizontally in an oblique line. But the stress is laid on the setting of lawns and flowerbeds that punctuate the drainage ditches and to the landscaped routes provided by the paths. With the park split up into small cemeteries, isolated

[25] *Alvar Aalto* (Zurich: Girsberger, 1963).

among wooded areas, we could not be further away from the spirit of the Cimetière de Thiais.

Robert Auzelle is against freehold vaults and advocates a return to ossuaries. Although a law of 1924, still in force, makes it obligatory for a cemetery to possess an ossuary, ossuaries have fallen into disuse. Robert Auzelle has included ossuaries in his intercommunal cemeteries of Fontaine-Saint-Martin at Valenton and of Les Joncherolles at Pierrefitte-Villetaneuse. The ossuaries at Les Joncherolles are covered with concrete shells—funerary architecture, as Auzelle shows, is not necessarily backward-looking.

Not only has Auzelle concened himself with designing an environment of vegetation for his cemeteries, but he has insisted on using sculptures to give a certain counterpoint or punctuation to the overall design. Since in our secularized cemeteries there are no longer any great central crosses, or calvaries, or lanterns, is it not desirable to find other ways of articulating space? At Valenton Cemetery the sculptor Pierre Sabatier has marked off the areas used for services by metal screens, and in the axis of the esplanade the sculptor Pierre Szekely has punctuated with blocks of granite, symbolizing the ages of life, a series of pools and huge flowerbeds. At the cemetery of Le Parc at Clamart the sculptor Maurice Calka has cast in concrete a monumental cippus composed of the signs of the zodiac placed in the large oval lawn. Certain tombs designed by Robert Auzelle are in themselves remarkable funerary sculptures of a new type.

But whether it is a question of a few Scandinavian examples or of the sole French example of Robert Auzelle, we should not be misled. These exceptions, which run counter to a whole flood of pretentious tombs and which are a painful reflection of the suburban avalanche now covering the countryside with its pustules, are as rare as excellent architecture for the living.

18

Baron Haussmann

The architectural rationality that found expression under the Second Empire led Baron Haussmann to the grandiose project of replacing all the graveyards of Paris by a single 2,000-acre cemetery in the Oise. As he was destroying medieval—and lower-class—Paris (the Paris described by Eugène Sue in *Les Mystères de Paris* and by Victor Hugo in *Les Misérables*) and expelling the laboring class, which he identified as the "dangerous" class,[1] a population that was nevertheless to congregate around the city in new hovels, the beginnings of the uncontrolled urbanization of what was to be the suburbs, Haussmann was contemplating a second deportation: that of the dead.

We know that three cemeteries had already been set up outside the city boundaries, beyond the *boulevards extérieurs*, in the communes of Belleville, Montmartre, and Montrouge: Père-Lachaise, Montmartre, and Montparnasse. At first it was not Huassmann's intention to do anything

[1] Chevalier, *Classes laborieuses et Classes dangereuses*.

[261

about these three "external" cemeteries, but he considered it necessary to create new cemeteries, since those could not be extended, and the granting of freehold plots would eventually "freeze" the amount of land available.

In 1853, the population of Paris was 1,053,262. In 1859, it was to reach 1,174,346, and, after the absorption of the adjacent communes, it stood at 1,825,271 in 1866, and reached 2,000,000 just before the war of 1870. Since the average life expectancy was then forty-two, the prefect of Paris had to make provision for around 34,000 dead per year from 1853 to 1859, and for 44,000 to 47,000 dead between 1860 and 1869.

To the obstacle of freehold plots was added, after 1848, the obligation to preserve for five years in the common graves the dead who had been buried at public expense. Those coffins of the poor were piled up in sevens, in long, parallel contiguous lines. On September 14, 1850, Napoleon III forbade the placing of the coffins of the poor one on top of another, and decreed that henceforth they would be buried separately for five years. Haussmann writes:

> The thought that the bier containing the remains of some dear one would come into immediate contact with those of unknown persons whom one supposed to be victims of the most hideous diseases, the thought that one could not, at some later date, when one's fortunes had turned, go and seek out those precious remains, in order to take them elsewhere, clearly added, one can well believe, to the grief of those left behind . . .
>
> But the municipal administration was horrified at the consequences of the measure envisaged by the emperor. Instead of attributing to each gratuitous grave the surface area (2.5 meters) which it was customary to accord each paying burial, they merely refrained, in order to isolate them in a suitable fashion on every side, from placing the coffins of the poor one on top of another, while continuing to allow them to touch, head to head and side by side.[2]

The 17,000 free burials a year, allowing 1.7 meters (18.25 square feet) per corpse, required seven and one-half acres of land. If Napoleon III's wishes had been adopted (without distorting them), twenty-two acres would have been needed.

"The result of all these figures was that, within five years, our three Paris cemeteries would have to be closed for lack of space."[3]

[2] Baron Haussmann, *Mémoires*, vol. 3, chaps. 12, 13, *Grands Travaux de Paris* (1893). A reprint, *Mémoires d'Haussmann*, was published by Editions Guy Durier in 1979.
[3] Ibid.

The first steps were taken in 1853 with the founding of the cemetery at Ivry. But the extension of the boundaries of Paris to the fortifications, absorbing the communes of Belleville, Montmartre, Vaugirard, Ménilmontant, Auteuil, et cetera, brought the surface area of Paris to 19,500 acres, a Paris that could accommodate three million inhabitants, completely altered all the statistics for burial. Not only did deaths increase by half, but the three great cemeteries created at the beginning of the nineteenth century outside Paris (Père-Lachaise, Montmartre, and Montparnasse) were now within the city itself. The decree of 23 Prairial, Year XII, forbidding all burial within the boundaries of the city, implied, therefore, the immediate demolition of these three cemeteries and the removal of their dead.

An initial project was considered: the dead would be buried in ditches, or on the glacis of the counterscarps of the fortifications. But to surround Paris with cemeteries so close would be to arouse once again fears of polluting the city of the living with the miasmas of the dead carried in on the winds.

It seemed, therefore, that 58 acres a year would be needed for burials. But this figure would rise to 1,750 acres if thirty-year leases were granted, and to 2,875 if fifty-year leaseholds operated. Haussmann continues:

> Where, even in two sites, were such areas of land to be found, isolated on all sides, and suited in every respect to the use for which I intended them . . . I did not yet know how little Parisians care for new ideas . . . Nevertheless, for several years, I kept to myself, without daring to publish it, lest I compromise its success with over haste, the radical solution, conceived fairly rapidly in my mind, which is resistent to half-measures, compromises, and expedients, when the well-being of the future is at stake . . . To allow my administration to carry out the idea which haunted me, that is, to extend the duration of free burials to thirty years at least, fifty years, and even more if possible, in order to bring it much closer to the notion of perpetuity.[4]

It was only in 1864, though he had held the prefecture of Paris since 1853, that Haussmann published his great project,entrusting a commission with the task of finding sites around Paris suitable for the creation of new cemeteries. The three engineers who drew up the report—they included Belgrand, the creator of the Paris sewers—began by condemning the three cemeteries *intra muros* (Père-Lachaise, Montparnasse, Montmartre). These three urban cemeteries, said the commission, in-

[4]Ibid.

fected the water-bearing beds by the infiltration of decomposing organic matter. This water passed beneath highly populated districts. "The wells of these districts, situated downstream of the water courses coming from the cemeteries, receive nothing but completely polluted water, and this circumstance is all the more regrettable in that, among poor families, this water is used for various domestic uses, and, sometimes, even drunk."

In order to replace these three cemeteries, and to provide for all future burials, the commission proposed two sites, one to the south, on the plateau of the commune of Massy, the other to the north, on the outskirts of Pontoise. Haussmann accepted only the project for a cemetery in the 5,000-acre site proposed to the north of Paris. It was a huge deserted plateau, containing only a single ruined farmhouse, a sandy terrain, with a chalky subsoil. It was not an expensive site, and, in 1866, Haussmann was able to acquire 5,800 lots, that is 782 acres at 20 centimes per square yard.

The only inconvenience of this site was that it was nearly fourteen miles from Paris. But Haussmann commissioned Alphand, the marvelous creator of public parks under the Second Empire, to design a system of stations and railways exclusively for funerary use.

"I decided to concentrate at Méry all the burial services for Paris, by means of special railway which would bring the processions and visitors from the funerary stations, set up in our old cemeteries to the east, north and south, to which funeral processions would continue to proceed, as usual."[5] Haussmann also proposed to work out an agreement with the suburban railway companies for the movement of funeral trains on its lines, and for the connection of its track to the three departure stations. A mainline funerary station would also have to be built at the entrance to the northern cemetery (Montmartre).

The outcry that greeted this proposition may well have taken Haussmann by surprise, for it marked the appearance of a new attitude to burials. Haussmann was merely continuing the rationalization of space begun under Louis XVI and carried to its ultimate conclusion under the revolution and First Empire. Haussmann thought like Cabet, who, in his Icaria, pushed cemeteries and hospitals out to the edges of the city. In wishing to expropriate the three Paris cemeteries he was merely applying the law. But, after showing no interest in its burials for years, Parisians now regarded their cemeteries as museums. They refused to let anyone lay a finger on them. Death had become taboo.

[5] Ibid.

Haussmann is criticized for being "an Anglophile Protestant."[6] It is certainly true that this idea of linking cemeteries to the railways came from England. But the Second Empire was as Anglophile as Napoleon III, who had been so deeply affected by his exile in England. There already existed in England funerary stations, chapels, and warehouses, "machines intended to store coffins in special compartments, compartment-salons assignable to each family and guests," and special trains were envisaged for All Souls' Day and All Saints' Day.[7] The cult of the dead, which no longer exists in Great Britain, was already dying out. "In England, this service is almost nonexistent; there are no hangings, no visitors at the house of the deceased. The body is placed in a hearse and carried to the cemetery by horses at the trot."[8]

Since the law of 1850, burials were forbidden within London itself. Twenty cemeteries surround the English capital within a radius of between six and eight miles, most of them on the north bank of the Thames. Only two, the one specifically for the use of the City of London, and that known as London Necropolis, were at such long distances that they could be reached only by railway.

Léon Vafflard, funeral contractor for the city of Paris, criticized this connection between the railway and the cemetery, as he saw it practiced in London. Such a method, he declared, would not please the Parisian population. In England,

the body seems to be regarded as a parcel, which one is in a hurry to get rid of and which the entire population sees pass by without paying the slightest attention. We saw the arrival at Westminster Station of hearses bringing corpses from various parts of London; we watched the operations being carried out to place all these bodies in the carriages intended for them; we saw the relations, who, in very small numbers, accompanied these bodies, remaining in the waiting rooms, until it was time for the train to leave, and, without any apparent emotion, take their places in the first-, second-, or third-class compartments . . . After about a fifty-minute journey on this special train, we watched the unloading of the bodies, which were about thirty in number, saw them being taken to the chapel, where a single prayer for all was recited, and we attended their burial in common graves, prepared in advance.[9]

[6] Léon Pagès, *La Déportation et l'abandon des morts: Cimetière de Méry* (Paris, 1875).
[7] Ibid.
[8] Ibid.
[9] Léon Vafflard, *La Translation des cimetières de Paris* (Paris, 1864).

Curiously enough, in 1867 Léon Vafflard completely changed his opinion and became an enthusiastic supporter of Haussmann's project. The newspaper *Le Siècle* launched a campaign against the project for a cemetery at Méry-sur-Oise, and Vafflard replied with a pamphlet showing that the commune of Méry had given its unanimous approval and that this opinion was shared by all the communes of the arrondissement of Pontoise.[10] Vafflard wrote: "Insignificant commerce, and even more insignificant agricultural production, would be followed, in their district, by a great movement of affairs which should necessarily lead to the creation of a cemetery; the construction and maintenance of funerary monuments, which require the employment of monumental masons, bricklayers, stonecarvers, locksmiths, gardeners, and a large number of workmen in the various crafts and trades, could not fail to create a new era of prosperity and fortune for this humble village."[11]

One can see very well what converted Vafflard. Contrary to his earlier belief, the cemetery at Méry could be a source of considerable profit for the funeral business. And the campaign waged by *Le Siècle* was in fact supporting the Commission d'Assurances Générales, which owned the forest of Montmorency. This company wanted to obtain a railway concession that would serve the communes bordering on the forest of Montmorency; the forest could then be divided up into lots, and sold to the inhabitants attracted there by the new railway stations.

In fact, the real conflict between Haussmann and his adversaries was one involving economic interests. *La Curée*, which Zola was to turn into fiction and which dissected the tissue of Parisian urban life, might also be applied to the mortuary space which, for the first time, seems to have acquired commercial value. Haussmann has been criticized for his haste in acquiring land at Méry, even before the project for the cemetery had been accepted; but the researches of the commission had aroused suspicion, and Haussmann feared that if he did not act quickly the value of the land would rise so high that the cemetery would be impossible.

On April 5, 1867, Haussmann explained his project to the Senate: "I have no wish to burden the Senate with painful details; but I must add that the sites which have been used for so long for successive burials are becoming less and less suitable for that purpose. They absorb bodies with increasing difficulty; the ground is saturated and is even refusing its sad task, with the result that what can no longer be absorbed by the

[10] Léon Vafflard, *Plus de fosses communes!!! Le Cimetière de l'avenir, Méry-sur-Oise* (Paris, 1867).
[11] Ibid.

soil is given off into the air in the form of obviously very dangerous emanations." Then, answering the objection that the proposed cemetery was too far from Paris, he went on: "The transportation of the coffins would be carried out by special trains using the same equipment as the ordinary trains . . . Every day, trains, whose number, composition, and service would be fixed according to the recognized requirements of the population, would take visitors to the Great Necropolis. Departures could be doubled, trebled, or even more if necessary, every Sunday and feast-day. They could be increased tenfold for All Souls' Day and All Saints' Day. Free return tickets would be available to persons of slender means."[12]

Barbier, a councillor at the Cour de Cassation, supported the prefect's report with the following arguments:

> The use of the railways for the transportation of bodies is nothing new . . . Not to mention the examples which have been presented to us from foreign countries, it is a fact that our railway lines are frequently used to send bodies to family burial places far from Paris. It is this form of transport, hitherto reserved to the rich, that the city of Paris proposes to make generally available . . . One hardly needs to say that what is being proposed is not, as certain critics given to regrettable exaggeration have gratuitously supposed, to pile up bodies in the same compartment, as in a luggage van. On the contrary, each deceased person would have his own compartment.

In 1868 a number of objections to Haussmann's project were raised in the Chamber of Deputies. What was at stake was still the fear that the dead would not be shown proper respect. On January 28 Jules Simon, who was to be prime minister under the Third Republic, spoke on behalf of the 150 Parisians who died every day:

> I shall not speak, gentlemen, of the accidents which might occur, and of the exceptional gravity which they might assume; I shall not speak of those ten or twelve convoys of rich and poor, and of the difficulty of separating the funeral parties; I shall not speak of times of epidemic, or of the unexpected increase which would occur, or of that terrible thermometer of public health which everyone will have in his hand. Nor do I wish to speak of the danger to the living at times of plague, forced as they will be to pile in with the dead in the same train . . . Do you believe that the number of those who attend funerals will be in any way reduced by your new creation? Or the number of Sunday visitors, those working people, who, instead of going to places of

---

[12] Poverty under the ostentatious Second Empire must be measured by the number of free funeral processions in the Paris cemeteries (63%), and by the number of free religious services (75%).

pleasure, take their wives and children with them, buy a wreath of immor-
telles, and quietly go and place it on some dear grave . . . On All Souls' Day
and All Saints' Day nearly a million people visit cemeteries. Do you believe
that this number will diminish?

The cemetery as a guarantee of moral order was also a new idea.

On March 10, 1869, without consulting Haussmann, Rouher, the
minister of state, postponed the project for a cemetery at Méry. But
Haussmann was no longer what he had once been; neither was the Second Empire. A lot of shady dealings were going on around Napoleon
III. "Even the emperor," Haussmann writes, "constantly subjected to
the evil designs of personal enemies of mine around his person, and
among his ministers, no longer knew who to listen to."[13] The advent of
the Emile Ollivier ministry in 1870 was to send Haussmann off into
retirement.

But Alphand and Belgrand, who were to remain as civil servants
under the Third Republic, were nevertheless to get the new prefect of
the Seine, Léon Say, to adopt Haussmann's project. Say merely abandoned the idea of mortuary stations in the east and south; instead, all
funeral processions would leave from the northern cemetery. This was a
reasonable proposal for a prefect who, in addition to running Paris, was
a director of the Chemins de Fer du Nord.

Belgrand was constantly pointing to the danger that the cemeteries
of the inner suburbs might pollute well water. "In the cemetery of Père-
Lachaise," he declared, "the dead are buried in water . . . The soil reaches,
therefore, a permanent state of infection." He then offered this supreme
argument: "Today attacks are being levied at projects for great cemeteries; just as projects for a sewer system were once attacked; and just as
road-widening schemes were once attacked."

The creation of the single cemetery at Méry-sur-Oise was once more
discussed in 1874. On March 30 a letter from the cardinal-archbishop of
Paris, supported by 15,000 signatures, arrived at the municipal council:
"The idea of establishing a single cemetery at so great a distance is red-
olent of the spirit of a time when one wanted to turn Paris into a center
for every kind of human pleasure; it was then quite natural that one
should try to remove to a safe distance the sorrowful memories which
might have disturbed a perpetual round of pleasure."

This petition had the effect of postponing the project once again.

Like Haussmann, Léon Say was criticized for his Protestant back-

---

[13] Haussmann, *Mémoires*.

ground: "To say the least, he is indifferent to Catholic piety." The Municipal Council, on the other hand, were accused of being "for the most part strangers, born outside the city of Paris."[14] Their "revolutionary despotism" had led them "to remove the remains of the dead from the piety of the living, to transport coffins in overcrowded trains, where all the families would be mixed up together seventeen miles from the departure station, and twenty-five miles from the extremities of the city. These sacred remains, once buried in the huge necropolis, will be abandoned there forever."[15]

Hérold, the new prefect of the Seine in 1879, turned the cemetery at Méry into a project for optional burial. Abandoning the idea of the three mortuary stations at the three Paris cemeteries, he proposed a new site in the Rue du Faubourg-Saint-Denis, from which the funeral convoys would depart. But this proposal was not taken up. The creation of the cemetery at Méry was debated once more at the Municipal Council in 1881, seventeen years after Haussmann's initial proposal, but the Third Republic finally adopted the suburban cemeteries as a "temporary solution." And the three Paris cemeteries of the nineteenth century, contravening laws still in force, stayed where they were, becoming more and more like museums.

[14] Pagès, *La Déportation et l'abandon des morts*.
[15] Ibid.

19

The Radical Saving of
Space by Cremation

Thanks to cremation, the United Kingdom saved in 1967 an area
equivalent to 607 football fields.

President of the French Federation of Cremation, quoted
by Ruth Menahem, *La mort apprivoisée*, 1973

If in non-European civilizations cremation is often bound up with
fire worship, while in the ancient Greco-Roman world corpses were
burned both for reasons of hygiene and as a protection against the
desecration of graves, cremation in the modern world belongs rather
to our functionalism. It may even be regarded as the ultimate consequence of that functionalism. If the deceased is now merely a man who
has ceased to function, what is the point of "freezing" considerable areas
of ground in order to interpose corpses that one no longer believes will
rise again, or "come back," or be transformed into anything useful?

The saving of ground has always been the major concern of progressive town planners and architects from the beginning of industrial civilization—or at least the saving of ground reserved for dwellings, in contrast
to the space squandered on traffic, in response to the demands of the
new industrial and commercial civilization.

[271

In 1846 the Fouriérist polytechnician Considerant advocated the conversion of the individual dwelling into a collective dwelling with arguments that were to be exactly those of Le Corbusier, Gropius, and their successors a century later:

> Ask if it would be more economical and more sensible to house a population of some 1,800 or 2,000 persons in a single large building or to build 250 to 400 small separate houses . . . Add the boundary walls required, in this fragmented system, to enclose the houses, gardens, and courtyards . . . You would save 400 kitchens, 400 dining rooms, 400 lofts, 400 cellars, 400 stables, 400 barns . . . Quite apart from the saving in space and building, add that of two or three thousand doors, windows, bays, with their frames, their woodwork, and their ironwork; think of the ruinous maintenance that each of these houses requires each year.[1]

These irrefutable arguments concerning the use of space were to be taken up almost word for word by Le Corbusier to justify first his "vertical garden-city," then his "Unité d'habitation."

There are also arguments that were to be taken up by architects who, as we have seen, built "vertical" cemeteries, high-rise accommodation for the dead. But are these high-rise blocks for the accommodation of coffins "useful"? On a surface of 10 square meters (or 108 square feet) only four dead can be housed, whereas such an area would take two hundred funerary urns. A columbarium urn is, in fact, only 11 inches wide, 11 inches high, and 19 inches long. These containers hold between four and five liters (about a gallon) of ash, the amount produced by the average adult body, and more advanced cremation methods might considerably reduce this volume still further.

Just as the ideal vertical habitat has replaced the house by the cell, so, in funerary architecture based on cremation, tombs are being replaced by "compartments." Once again, the habitat of the living and the habitat of the dead show a parallel development.

"Thanks to cremation," writes the president of the French Federation of Cremation, with obvious satisfaction, "the United Kingdom saved in 1967 an area equivalent to 607 football fields."[2]

Indeed it is Great Britain that at present holds the record for cremations (60 percent of the deceased), against 46 percent in Denmark, 42 percent in Switzerland, and a mere 0.44 percent in France. But, apart

---

[1] Victor Considérant, *Exposition abrégée du système phalanstérien de Fourier, suivie de: Etudes sur quelques problèmes fondamentaux de la destinée sociale* (Paris, 1846).

[2] Menahem, *La mort apprivoisée.*

from the saving of land, the success of cremation in Great Britain stems no doubt from the almost total detachment felt by the British for their corpses. By destroying the deceased in a more radical way, "one is less attached to the remains and less tempted to visit them."[3]

In moving from the skeleton to the "remains," functionalism has had a great success. If the mere function of removing the dead were substituted for the funeral ceremonies, cremation would be better suited than any other technique to this removal.

In Greco-Roman antiquity, as in Asia today, cremation was very costly on account of the large quantity of wood required to burn a body. Two to three steres of wood were required to fuel a cremation that lasted for three to ten hours. In present-day Nepal, contrary both to the laws of the country and to religious custom, burial is spreading at the expense of cremation. This is on account of the scarcity of wood: the Nepalese are destroying their forests six times faster than the forests are growing.

But in the West, ovens fired by coke, oil, gas, or electricity can reduce incineration to fifty minutes in an oven heated up to 1,800 degrees centigrade. There is even the possibility of reducing the body to ashes more rapidly, and more completely still, with laser beams.

Crematorium ovens have the advantage over pyres of consuming the body without the human ashes mixing with those of wood. The ashes collected in the ovens are exclusively human and avoid "the inconvenience for which antiquity had no remedy, of confusing in a lamentable promiscuity the ashes of a hero with those of a log."[4]

The crematorium ovens are generally placed in the basement of a funerary building which also includes offices and a large hall to accommodate family and friends during the cremation. In order to conceal the noise of the oven, recorded music is transmitted. Then, in the presence of two witnesses, the ashes are placed in a sealed urn. The urn is handed back to the family, who generally place it in a compartment of the columbarium but who may also keep it in a family vault, and even, with official permission, on private property.

These various alternatives show the very great resistance of the French, and of Latins in general, to cremation. In France there are only nine crematoriums as opposed to 204 in Great Britain, 65 in West Germany, 63 in Sweden, 36 in Denmark, 32 in Norway, 29 in Switzerland. And the regulations concerning the transportation of a funerary urn are the

[3] Philippe Ariès, "La Vie et la Mort chez les Français d'aujourd'hui," *Ethnopsychologie,* 1 (1972).

[4] Augé, *Les Tombeaux.*

same as those governing a corpse. An entire railway carriage must be hired in France to transport a single urn.

Cremation has spread in modern Europe only in the northern, Protestant countries, largely because Catholicism forbade cremation until 1964. Jews, Orthodox Christians, and Muslims still prohibit it. Nevertheless, statistically, because of the immemorial custom of incineration in most Asian countries, cremation is at present the most widespread funerary practice in the world. Strangely enough, the United States shows the same repugnance for cremation as the Latin countries, since the number of incinerations does not exceed 3.6 percent; North Americans have returned to the ancient Egyptian custom of embalming.

Though rejected by the Hebrews, then by the two monotheistic religions deriving from Judaism—Christianity and Islam—incineration has been accepted by religions of highly developed civilizations: pre-Columbian Mexico, Hindus, Buddhists, Babylonians, Finno-Scandinavians, Southeast Asians. In Europe incineration seems to have appeared first among the Scythians, who gave it to the Thracians, who in turn handed it on to the Greeks.

Cremation was originally bound up with the cult of fire. Heraclitus, Sophocles, and Seneca believed that the end of the world would take the form of a great fire. The ancient Scandinavians, who saw the sky as a fire, thought that the pyre helped the soul to rejoin the celestial incandescence. Ancient philosophy also believed that fire, in purifying the body, helped it to release its spiritual part. The relation between the fire and the hearth and the cult of the dead among the ancients has always seemed an obvious one. Since fire was regarded as an emanation of the sun, the Vestal Virgins maintained a perpetual fire. The sepulchral lamps, placed in tombs, were supposed to give light to the manes, or shades. The early Christians continued this pagan tradition by also placing lamps in sepulchres. Our candles, our sanctuary lamp in front of the tabernacle, our eternal flame on the tomb of the unknown soldier, merely continue an immemorial cult of fire bound up with the cult of the dead— as does also our idea that paradise is a place of light and hell a place of darkness.

Burning offerings for the dead are a means of transmitting their quintessence to the invisible world. In China, Vietnam, and Korea, votive objects used to be made of paper stretched on a bamboo frame, intended to be destroyed by fire. A year after the death of an adult, paper gifts were once again burned, a letter containing an inventory of the objects being presented was burned with them, so that the deceased might check that all these gifts had reached him in the beyond.

Burning, then, was a way of reaching the spiritual through incandescence. Burning bodies also avoided rotting. Ashes, like embalming and cannibalism, make it possible to avoid a stinking corpse.

Last, the burning of bodies prevented their profanation by enemies and grave robbers.

The desecration of graves and the curses brought down on the profaners are as old as funerary cults themselves. If the peace of the grave seems to have always been regarded as indispensable to the correct functioning of the deceased in the beyond, if the defensive tactics to protect this peace against the desecrators of graves have given rise to splendid mausoleums, of which the Egyptian pyramids are the best known example, grave robbers have at the same time expended all their ingenuity in uncovering their secrets and do not seem to have been much affected by the curses. The best way of protecting one's posthumous peace was no doubt to have oneself buried very deeply in the earth, without any identifiable external sign—and, above all, not to take treasure with one into one's grave. For it is such treasure that has inevitably attracted grave robbers.[5]

At the beginning of the eighteenth Theban dynasty, all the tombs of the preceding Pharaohs had already been robbed. Under the twentieth dynasty the robbing of graves assumed unprecedented proportions. Cemetery guardians, priests, and functionaries acted as informants for the thieves. Breaking with a tradition 1,700 years old, Thotmes I decided to be buried a mile from the funerary temple, in a vault dug out of the ground. For greater safety, the workmen who had built the vault were put to death.[6] The mummy of Rameses III was transferred three times from burial-place to burial-place. Mummies were hidden in other places than the pyramids. The tomb of Amenhotep II provided shelter for no fewer than thirteen royal mummies.

Grave robbing was an occupation in Egypt as long ago as the thirteenth century B.C. Until very recently Gurna was a village inhabited

[5] It has seldom been noted that the Sythians and Normans, both great grave robbers, finally buried their loot in their own graves. Similarly, the Gauls, the Franks, and the Visigoths, despite their looting, were constantly poor, for their treasure was buried. So much rapine and murder ended in the city of the dead where it was, as it were, stored until some new grave robber appeared.

[6] It was the same for the workmen who built the tombs of Attila and Alaric. In 410 Alaric, king of the Goths, having died near Cosenza, his subjects, in order to make sure that his burial place would remain undiscovered and unviolated, diverted a stream. When the bed of the stream was dry, they dug a ditch in which they laid Alaric with his treasure. Then the water was allowed to resume its course. All the prisoners who carried out this task were slaughtered.

solely by grave robbers. It was one of these professional robbers from Gurna who, in 1881, guided Emile Brugsch-Bey toward the burial chamber in which he discovered the mummies of Seti I, Amenemhat I, Amenhotep I, Thotmes III, and Rameses II. In fact the Egyptian priests had removed these mummies from the pyramids of the Valley of the Kings in order to protect them from thieves. In their haste, they had merely leaned some of the sarcophagi upright against the walls. Forty mummies were thus found in this burial chamber.

But the tombs were not only robbed by professional (or amateur) thieves, or in the later "scientific" robberies of the archaeologists; they were also robbed by the kings themselves, who opened, out of curiosity or greed, the tombs of other monarchs. Alexander, master of Persia, had the tomb of Cyrus opened and, instead of the treasure which he expected, found only a sword, two bows, and a shield. One night Herod the Great went down to rob the common tomb of his nevertheless eminently sacred predecessors, David and Solomon, but a flame leapt out of the tomb and consumed the slaves entrusted with the task of removing the stone. Terrified, Herod ordered an expiatory monument to be built. In the eighth century A.D., the Lombard Giselpert, duke of Verona, had the grave of King Alboin, buried two centuries before, opened in order to rob him of his royal sword.

Curiosity and greed were opposed by anathema and vengeance. There was no worse punishment in antiquity than to be left a corpse without a tomb. On a tablet at Sippur is written: "Let his corpse fall and be given no tomb." Jeremiah speaks, as of a terrible vengeance, of the dead dragged out of their burial places. "He will drag from their burial places the bones of the kings of Judah, the bones of his chiefs, the bones of his priests, the bones of his prophets, and the bones of the inhabitants of Jerusalem . . . and will lay them out in the sun." At Susa, Assurbanipal says of the tombs of the kings of Elam: "The tombs of their kings, ancient and modern, who had not feared Assur and Isthar, my lords, I overthrew them, I demolished them, I exposed them to the light of the sun, and carried off their corpses to Assyria."

Victors regularly robbed the burial places of the kings of conquered countries, not only to take their treasure, but also to humiliate them. Cambyses had the body of Amasis, king of Egypt, exhumed, whipped, pricked with needles, its hair pulled out, then burned. A troop of Gauls opened the tombs of the kings of Macedonia, looted the treasure in the graves, and threw away the remains of the kings. Louis XIV acted no differently from Assurbanipal and Cambyses when, in 1711, he had the burial places of Port Royal destroyed, the nuns dragged out of their tombs, and the bodies piled up in the church before having them buried in a common grave. And the Revolutionaries acted no differently with Louis XIV when the royal graves of Saint-Denis were profaned.

The violation of stone sarcophagi was common in the Middle Ages, from the Roman sarcophagi to the Merovingian ones. And incineration did not necessarily protect from profanation. After being emptied of its ashes, the urn of Agrippina was used for a long time during the Middle Ages as a measure for wheat. Yet the Roman inscription had never been effaced: "Bones of Agrippina, daughter of Agrippa, niece of the divine Augustus, wife of Germanicus Caesar, mother of Caius." Such prestigious connections do not seem to have moved the already functionalist merchants of the Middle Ages.

The profanation of sarcophagi took an odd turn in the early Middle Ages, when the bodies of pagans were simply removed and replaced by bodies of Christians. Thus princes and prelates took over Roman sarcophagi. In the cloister of the cathedral of Salerno one can see Roman sarcophagi that contain the bodies of Norman paladins. A mitred bishop was buried in a sarcophagus on which bacchantes are carved. Sometimes several skeletons are found in a single stone sarcophagus.[7]

The salvage of tombs for other architectural purposes also has a long history behind it. Suetonius speaks of colonists who "demolished very ancient tombs to build country houses, and did so with even more enthusiasm when they discovered in the course of their exploration a quantity of vases of very ancient manufacture."[8]

Sometimes mausoleums have been put to some other purpose than their original functions. The monument erected to the memory of Augustus, in Rome, in which the ashes of Augustus, Tiberius, Caligula, and Claudius were laid, became a fortress in the Middle Ages and a theater in the nineteenth century. In 536, when the Ostrogoths attacked Rome, the Romans turned Hadrian's tomb into a citadel. As the Castel Sant' Angelo it has remained one, having also served as a prison.

The anathemas against profaners of tombs and the terrible punish-

[7] This squatting existed long before the Middle Ages. In antique Asia Minor people feared not only grave robbers but also kings, who reused particularly fine sarcophagi, or the parasitical dead who entered graves which were not their own. Tabnit, king of Sidon (fifth-sixth century B.C.), reused in this way the sarcophagus of an Egyptian general, without effacing the hieroglyphic epitaphs. And although he was a looter of tombs, he tried to dissuade future looters of tombs with the following inscription: "Whoever you may be, whatever man may find this chest; do not open my grave and do not disturb me; for there is no money with me; there is neither gold nor any kind of vase with me; stripped of everything, I lie alone in this chest" (Parrot, *Malédictions et Violations*).

[8] Suetonius, *The Twelve Caesars* (2d century A.D.).

ments reserved for them do not seem to have had much effect. On the gates of Syrian and Phoenician funerary galleries profaners were threatened with the annihilation of their posterity, the most terrible curse in the ancient East. In Egypt the curses were written on the tombs themselves. Anyone found guilty of profaning a tomb would be excluded from public functions, die before his time, be deprived of burial, attacked in water by a crocodile, stung by a serpent, and so on. The threats were the same for those who stole stelae or changed the names on them. Amenhotep III had engraved on his tomb, for the benefit of his future profaners, that God "will throw them into the brazier . . . They will perish in the sea, and their bodies remain engulfed . . . Their wives will be sullied under their eyes."

In Lycia, in the third century B.C., we see the beginning of funerary inscriptions laying down public fines for grave robbing. A lead tablet, found in a Cretan tomb, threatens: "May all evils strike him, fever, tertiary fever, quartan ague, leprosy, and fire." Henri Seyrig has deciphered at Salamina (Cyprus) an inscription dating from the early Christian centuries: "You, spirit, be full of resentment against that man [who profanes a dead man], and let him, being intact neither of feet, knees, nor eyes, see not the gentle light, let him enjoy no peaceful life, let him have absolutely no union, nor child . . . and let him at his death have no burial place in mother earth . . . Let him not be wept over."

There were a great many anathemas in the Roman and Gallo-Roman period. Fines of between 2,500 and 10,000 deniers were fixed, which had to be paid to the imperial treasury. But the profanation of tombs was also punished by deportation, forced labor, and sometimes death. The laws of the Franks, Burgundians, and Visigoths laid down punishments against those who unearthed the dead in order to rob them. The Visigoths punished the profaners with a hundred lashes, two hundred if the offender was a slave. In the codes of Theodicius and Justinian, profaners of tombs had their hands cut off. More clement, the Roman Church of the eighth century punished the profaner with no more than five years' penitence, three of which on a diet of bread and water.

A French author of the seventeenth century recounts how the Turks were so respectful of graves that they never touched the crusaders' tombs at Jerusalem, and they punished the profaners with the most terrible punishments: "They have so much veneration, not only for their own, but also for those of other Nations, that for them profaning a grave is one of the greatest crimes which may be committed. In fact, we read in the cosmography of Thevet, that Selim, one of the Ottomans, on leaving for a military expedition to Egypt, from which he returned triumphant, and master of all that country, had a number of his soldiers severely punished in Syria, simply for having opened the tombs of a Jewish doctor in which they hoped to find some treasure: fourteen were hanged, three impaled, and the others perished in various ways."[9]

The profanation of graves in the West may also have fetishistic motives. Goya was decapitated in his grave by an admirer, who carried off his head. The coffin of Marshal Pétain was secretely disinterred on the Île de Ré by followers who hoped to bury him at Douaumont. Chaplin's body was removed by thieves, who hoped to extract ransom from his family—a modern form of the hostage psychosis. I have said that the practice of incineration in Greek and Roman antiquity stemmed from a fear of profanation by the enemies of the city. Pliny confirms this when he says that the original purpose of burning a body "goes back to the wars which we have fought in distant lands; since the people of those countries disinterred our dead, we took to burning them." It should be noted here that warlike, migratory peoples, who cannot give permanent protection to cemeteries, burn their dead. This is so of the ancient Scandinavians, Saxons, and Armorican-Bretons. Before the Greeks undertook distant expeditions, they buried their dead. Burial was still common under Pericles. But, previously, Homer told of the cremation of warriors who fell in the Trojan War. The Athenians brought back in urns the ashes of the heroes who had died far from their country. But there can be no doubt that burial was the original method used by the Greeks. This is shown by the practice of throwing earth over the ashes, a custom that was to survive into the Roman civilization. "Throw earth three times on my ashes, and pass on," said Horace. And Cicero remarked: "Before the earth has been thrown on the dead, the place in which the dead has been burned has nothing religious about it." The memory of the body covered with earth became therefore a ritual simulacrum of the spadeful of earth thrown on the funerary urn.

To the fear of profanation was added a concern for hygiene. We know that the Greeks, like the Romans, first buried their dead in their own houses. From this practice was born the cult of the Manes, or shades. Since it had become illegal first to bury the dead in the houses, then in the city (legislation enacted under Solon), the only way of preserving one's dead in the house, without contravening the rules of hygiene, was to burn them. But it would seem that burial and cremation existed side by side in Ancient Greece and Rome, since bodies could only be buried outside the city, along the great highways that led to it. The Pythago-

[9]Jean Muret, *Cérémonies funèbres de toutes les nations* (Paris, 1675).

[279

reans, for example, buried their dead. From the time of Lycurgus, cremation did not exist in Sparta. Plutarch tells how the Spartans erected funerary monuments inside the city and placed their burial places around the tombs of the gods. No object was buried with the body, which was wrapped in a simple red sheet and surrounded by olive leaves. The different classes of citizens were not differentiated by any particular form of burial.

In Rome the custom in high society of having oneself cremated dates from the death of Sylla (78 B.C.). Having profaned the corpse of Marius and fearing a similar fate would be inflicted on his own corpse, Sylla had himself cremated in the Greek manner. Under the Roman monarchy kings and illustrious persons were buried in the Field of Mars, and the ordinary people cremated elsewhere. With the advent of the Republic burial for all appeared to be a democratic measure, but it was really an economic one, wood being scarce and expensive. The first Roman cemeteries appeared with the prohibition of burial in the city itself, and they reveal a social segregation that is hardly democratic: the emperors under the Capitol, the patricians along the roads leading into Rome, the people on the Esquiline (*extra muros*), corpses in disaffected wells (*puticoli*), executed criminals in special sites (*sesternium*).

The practice of cremation was never to lead to the complete abandonment in Rome of burial. Social segregation reappeared after Sylla, and under the Empire, between the rich, who could afford the expense of a funeral pyre, and the poor, who were buried in the ordinary way. The poor were burned only in times of epidemic, at the rate of one woman's body for every ten men's bodies—female bodies were thought to accelerate combustion. There were collective pyres for such occasions. Very high pyres were also erected from which a number of condemned criminals were hanged.

If poor Romans and slaves were not incinerated in normal times, it follows that the majority of the Roman population was buried. The funerals of the poor took place at night, by torchlight. The bodies were placed on a bier and covered by a toga. Juvenal remarked that, for most Romans, it was the first time that they had worn citizen's dress. The dead of the day were thrown pell-mell into a cistern, which was closed by a stone slab, and placed in a field some distance away from the town. When a cistern was full, the stone was sealed until such time as the corpses had rotted away, leaving room for the next batch. Cremations also took place at night (*funalia*, hence our word *funeral*). On the Appian Way, five miles from Rome, was a large burning place, surrounded on two sides by high walls, built of red sandstone, and paved with fire-resistant flagstones. All around were porticoes intended to shelter those attending the funerals. At one end were the apartments of the keepers and the sheds where the wood was kept.

The pyre was lighted by a relation of the deceased. Wood that caught fire easily—yew, larch, ash, juniper—was used: it was forbidden to use precious wood for cremation. A slow-burning cremation was regarded as a dishonor.

The funerals of the rich began with the lying in state in the atrium, the feet turned toward the street, the corpse exposed to the gaze of passersby. The procession consisted of professional mourners; the sacrificer, whose task it was to kill the deceased's favorite animals around the pyre; the archimime, dressed in the deceased's clothes, wearing a mask in his image, and imitating his walk and mannerisms; other individuals, masked according to the features of the deceased's ancestors; the family, the sons with covered heads, the daughters bareheaded, hair loose; the body of the deceased, borne on a litter, followed by a large number of funerary beds, rows of slaves and servants. An empty chariot brought up the rear. Often a wax body made in the image of the deceased was carried in the procession, a practice, as we have seen, that was to be taken up by the kings of France.

The corpse was laid on the pyre, with coins between his teeth to pay for the crossing of the Styx, and trumpets and flutes played funeral music. The sacrificer cut the throats of the deceased's favorite horses and dogs and spread libations of wine and milk over the earth.[10] Sometimes gladiators killed one another around their former master. Livy mentions a combat in which almost all the 120 gladiators perished. Sometimes, for the funerals of soldiers, prisoners were sacrificed. Finally, two bucks were immolated on the almost burnt out pyre, a priest sprinkling the mourners with a laurel branch dipped into pure water.

The ashes of the dead were placed in an urn, usually of terracotta, sometimes of glass, marble, bronze, or gold. These Roman urns, round or ovoid, smooth, fluted, or scored, were inscribed with the name and age of the deceased. The funerary vases were placed in the niches of subterranean chambers, each niche containing two urns, "like pigeons in their nest," said the Roman poets—hence, no doubt, the term *columbarium*, the comparison being even closer in the case of multi-story cell-

---

[10] Numa Pompilius forbade libations of wine at his death, lest he arrive in the otherworld drunk. Meat dishes were also cooked on the human funeral pyres; these were intended for the gods, but the poor ate them with great relish. There is a more moving custom: before burning the corpse, the eyes were opened so that he might see his soul fly off.

ular monuments. There were both family and common columbariums, belonging to private persons who sold or let niches to families. There, again, the comparison may be made with the *insulae*, those multi-storied buildings, sometimes fifty-six feet high, in which the people lived very uncomfortably in tiny rooms. Octavia, Nero's wife, had a columbarium erected for the funeral urns of her emancipated slaves. A symbol of the loneliness of power, Trajan's funerary urn was placed at the top of Trajan's column.

Though unknown in Egypt, Phoenicia, and Persia, cremation was used at one time, according to Justinian, by the Cathaginians, who copied the practice from the Greeks (Virgil had Dido dying on a pyre). Darius sent them an ambassador requesting them to give up eating dog meat and burning their dead.

The Gauls buried their dead at the time of the Fall of Rome, but cremated them at the time of Vercingetorix. At the beginning of La Tène III incineration appeared in Provence under the Roman influence and in Belgian Gaul under the Germanic influence. By the end of the La Tène period, all the tombs found in the Vosges had contained cremated remains. Under the Roman occupation, although incineration was the more widely practiced, the two forms remained side by side until, under the influence of Christianity, burial became, from the fourth century on, once more preponderant.

The Gallo-Roman poor got the funerals they could afford. Sometimes their ashes were put in a broken urn or a small wooden box, nails from which have been found. On occasion the ashes were even placed directly on the ground, with only a piece of broken jar as a lid. The funerary container became rarer and more expensive as the Roman world declined. This accounts for the robbery of sarcophagi by princes who, themselves, could not afford the luxury of paying a stonecutter.

At the end of the bronze age cremation supplanted burial throughout Europe. The Teutons incinerated their dead. "The weapons of the deceased," writes Tacitus, "and sometimes even his horse, were thrown into the flames before him." From the time of Odin the Scandinavians also burned their dead with whatever was dearest to them in life: weapons, horses, servants, dependents, friends, wife.

In the early Christian period each converted people continued at first to practice its own funerary customs. Thus the first Egyptian Christians, to the great scandal of Saint Anthony, and of later bishops, continued to embalm their dead and to preserve the mummies. Similarly, the first Greek and Roman Christians practiced cremation. Saint Peter and

Saint James said that it was not necessary to inconvenience the Gentiles by imposing Jewish customs upon them, and cremation continued therefore in Christian Europe until the fourth century. In the fifth century incineration was abandoned in Rome by the pagans themselves. But at the end of the eighth century cremation still remained in force among the Saxon Christians.

Christianity did not lead, then, to an immediate substitution of cremation by burial, as has often been thought. This did not occur until an edict of Charlemagne in 785 forbade cremation under pain of death for those practicing it.

The burial of Christians, like that of Muslims, shows a direct link with Jewish custom. Indeed, cremation was regarded with horror by the Jews. Even during the Egyptian and Babylonian captivity, the Jews persisted in burying their dead. Tobias incurred great danger in order to ensure that the bodies of the Hebrews executed by Sennacherib were buried.

No doubt Christianity, too, wished to mark itself off from the Roman pagan world. Cremation was to be practiced in the Christian world only as a punishment reserved for sorcerers, criminals, and heretics. Fire no longer signified the sun, but hell.

From the beginning of the Reformation, the Protestants advocated cremation, after eight centuries of eclipse in Europe, in order to devalue the body at the expense of the soul. But the custom of burial was to prevail, even for Protestants. Similarly, the attempt to revive the Roman custom of incineration, in a period which saw a return to the antique, under the French Revolution, was short lived.

In Year V of the Republic, Legrand d'Aussy submitted to the Conseil des Cinq-Cents a bill on the right to cremation: "Each individual is free to have burned or buried in whatever place he considers suitable the body of his relations or dear ones, in compliance with the laws of public order and health."

Louis-Sébastien Mercier, than a deputy, spoke vehemently against this project, as against any revival of funerary practices:

No, I do not want those hateful pyres; I do not want those domestic cemeteries, those gardens paved with dead, those cupboards in which one can show one's grandfather on this side and one's great uncle on the other. Private sepultures are an affront to the calm and repose of society . . . Those private sepultures, demanded by the most false sensibilities, those hateful pyres, those cadaverous flames, that subtraction of the dead from the earth, our common mother, all these innovations against long-established practice, are an affront to my mind, my reason, my feelings; and what is being suggested today? To bring back the household gods, the domestic altars, the funerary urns, the phials, the lacrymatories of the Ancients, or to revive the mummies of Egypt, to wrap us in bands and thus throw us back into the errors and extravagances of paganism.[11]

But, in his vehement attack, Mercier adds a quite "modern" argument, that of the "profitability" of the dead, their posthumous functionalism. He says in fact that the corpses of our dear ones do not belong to us and should be returned to the earth, "which gave them its elements." So the incineration demanded by the proposer of the bill seems to him to be "a gross error, if not actually a physical attack, a sacrilege, perpetrated on nature." Fire "would rob the earth of what it had a right to expect for the reproduction of vegetable life and for the building up of chalky soil. Fire would give everything to the air, which would be an utter loss. Moreover, the funeral pyre would require fuel, and our forests would go up in useless smoke, instead of heating our hearths and forges."

That was an argument that must have carried weight!

In 1814, when the Germans burned on great pyres, over two weeks, the 4,000 soldiers who had died before Paris, cremation on the field of battle appeared as a hygienic measure intended to avoid the epidemics that almost always followed on wars. But in 1867, at the International Congress of Aid to the War Wounded, in Paris, Piero Castiglioni and Agostino Bertani again proposed, but without success, the cremation of the war dead. We saw above how, after Sedan, the corpses of the dead soldiers had been piled up in ditches, covered with tar, and burned with straw soaked in oil.

Curiously enough, in the late nineteenth century, propaganda in favor of cremation was centered in the Latin countries. This movement was organized as a political party of anticlerical and freemasonic inspiration. The first congresses of cremationists took place at Padua in 1869 and in Rome in 1871. The first cremation since the fall of the Roman Empire took place in Italy in 1822, when, in an act of romantic homage, Byron set fire to Shelley's drowned body. But the cremation of the poet Shelley, performed in a spirit of identification with the ancient Greek poets, was a gesture that found no imitators. On the other hand, when

[11] L. S. Mercier, *Corps Législatif*. Conseil des Cinq-Cents. *Sur les sépultures privées* (Paris: 18 Frimaire, Year V—1796).

the Chevalier Keller asked in his will to be cremated in Milan, in 1874, in the crematorium temple which he had had built at his own expense, there was a problem. Official permission was refused, and Keller had to be embalmed until permission for the cremation was granted in 1876. From that date, a royal decree made the preservation or destruction of corpses legal.

In 1872, a society for cremation got permission to carry out cremations in New York. In 1884 Great Britain followed suit.

Between 1874 and 1886 twelve years of polemic finally forced the authorities to allow cremation. On August 14, 1874, the prefect of the Seine was invited to open a competition to find the best method of incineration. In 1880, despite the opposition of the prefect of the Seine, the Society for the Propagation of Cremation, which had just been founded, renewed the demand for a competition. Among the committee members of this new society were two architects, Normand and Emile Trelat. Most of the others were doctors. In 1882 the Municipal Council of Paris was won over to the principle of incineration but refused to make it obligatory as one of its members, Cadet, proposed. On July 11, 1883, the Municipal Council of Paris asked the prefect of the Seine to install crematorium ovens in the Paris cemeteries. Once again the request was refused. In spite of everything, on July 25, 1885, the Municipal Council voted funds for the erection at Père-Lachaise of "a monument capable of disposing of entire corpses as soon as the law authorizing optional cremation is passed."

On March 31, 1886, cremation was discussed in the Chamber of Deputies. The opponents argued that cremation placed an obstacle to legal investigations in cases of suspected poisoning. But the proposition of M. Blatin, the deputy for Puys-de-Dôme, that everybody might freely decide "the mode of his sepulture, to opt for burial or incineration," was finally adopted by 321 votes to 174. On November 15, 1887, the law on the freedom of sepulture was passed, and Formigé's crematorium was opened at Père-Lachaise the same year—opened, but not used, for Parisians showed so little enthusiasm at being cremated that the first "customer" did not arrive until two years later.

At the beginning of modern cremation, a number of disputes concerning the efficiency of the ovens split the pro-cremation movement into a number of different societies. Wood having been excluded on grounds of cost, the gas-burning model designed by an Italian, Professor Polli, enjoyed the greatest support.

Although Italy and France had become the champions of cremation after 1875, this funerary technique enjoyed practically no success in those two countries, whereas it spread rapidly in all the Protestant countries, with the exception of the United States.[12] In 1885 the Italian G. Pini, secretary of the Milanese Cremation Society, wrote this sentence which, in the light of the events of World War II, had a particularly sinister irony: "We must, chronologically speaking, assign the first place to learned Germany for the research and work which have been carried out there in favor of cremation."[13]

From the crematorium ovens of the concentration camps to the incineration of Hitler and his familiars after their suicides in the Berlin bunker, and of the bodies of the survivors of the Third Reich, after their hanging at Nuremberg, their ashes being thrown to the wind, as were once those of heretics, modern Germany has felt the effects of the sinister invention of Professor Polli. But, as with Dr. Guillotin's guillotine, its use went well beyond his wildest expectations.

Certain late nineteenth-century economists, who were advocates of cremation, proposed clearing the sites lost by cemeteries and turning them over to agriculture. Others proposed quite simply to manufacture fertilizers with the remains of the dead. "Could one not make a better use of those storehouses of putrefaction we call cemeteries, which render sterile huge areas of valuable land."

Louis-Sébastien Mercier feared that cremation would prevent the return of useful material to the earth. He was unaware that ash is an excellent fertilizer. His defense of burial belonged rather to the pantheistic ideology of a return to nature. What would he have thought of the English surgeon Henry Thompson, founder, in 1874, of the first British cremation society, who calculated the damage done to British agriculture by the nonuse of the ashes from the 80,000 who died in 1871: "Of the 3,254,260 inhabitants who, in 1871, formed the population of London, 80,430 died in that year. The quantity of remains in bones and ashes, which a perfect combustion of all those corpses would have produced, in weight, is about 206,820 pounds. This residue represents a very large sum of money, for it corresponds to six or seven times its weight in dried bones."

Dr. Thompson regretted the enormous cost of importing bones, al-

---

[12] In 1963 the World Incineration Congress declared that it had 400 million supporters. In June 1964 the pope accepted incineration for Catholics. But the Christian belief in the resurrection of the body in an identical form had long ago fallen into disuse. Furthermore, so many Catholic martyrs had been burned, in particular Joan of Arc, that it could no longer be sustained that those whose bodies had been burned would be unable to rise at the Last Day.

[13] G. Pini, *Cremation in Italy and Abroad, from 1774 to the Present* (Milan, 1885).

most all of which were used as fertilizer, "while we bury our own, not near the surface, where they might be useful, but deep down where they infect the water we drink."[14]

The dispersal of the ashes from cremation, which is forbidden in France, is common in Great Britain, where the family often scatters the remains of its "loved ones" in the countryside or out at sea. Henry de Montherlant asked for his ashes to be thrown to the wind. One of his disciples took the funerary urn to Italy and dispersed Montherlant among the ruins of the Forum.

But here we come to the negation of funerary architecture. The space of death is no longer enclosed by a structured space. It is Space, all Space. And the volatile body becomes as immaterial as the soul.

[14] L'Echo du Grand Orient, *Etudes sur la crémation des morts* (Nîmes, 1884).

20

The American Way of Death

The Thanatos Centers will be responsible for death, as the Eros Centers are responsible for sex.

Jean Baudrillard
L'Echange symbolique et la mort, 1976

The space of dying is tending to become more and more a specialized space, that of the hospital. From being a space of refuge for the old, the mentally sick, the poor, in the nineteenth century, and in the first half of the twentieth a place of sickness and cure, the hospital is gradually being transformed, on the analogy of the "dormitory," into a "moritory."

"Apart from operative cases or extremely serious cases, [the hospital] no longer houses the sick . . . . The hospital is becoming the place where death, in cases of chronic disease, is decided on, decreed, according to automatic protocols, and it is the job of a section of the medical personnel to prepare the patients."[1]

But although in the United States the "thanatos centers" are perfectly designed for a precise use, which is, in a sense, to give the dying person a gentle death, the status of the European hosptial still remains ambiguous. It is the place of death, but it is also the place of cure. More-

[1] Attali, *L'Ordre cannibale*.

[289

over, the hospital personnel are not at all prepared for playing the role of "undertaker." Doctors, interns, and nurses all show embarrassment when confronting the dying: they all fob them off in their own way. They change the room of the "condemned" person so that the other patients will not notice anything. Or they surround the dying person with screens, a crude way of masking an event that fools no one, least of all the dying person, who knows that the screen is part of the ritual of death in the ward.

But the patient is never told the truth in the hospital. The worse he gets, the more one tries to reassure him, gradually leading him to an infantilization that makes him more docile, which is in any case one of the aims of the medical personnel. Nevertheless, 80 percent of the sick in hospital know instinctively when they are going to die and refuse medication and treatment. Though the old are generally resigned to the fact, seldom revolted by it, but anxious, though some die refusing food, those who die in the prime of life, on the other hand, often prove to be aggressive in the solitude in which they are held.[2] Faced with this attitude, the nurses become exaggeratedly maternal, and the doctors, who are ashamed of lying, overcome their sense of guilt by an offhandedness, even an insensitivity, which creates around the dying person an atmosphere of aggressiveness: aggressiveness on the part of the patient against the medical personnel, on the part of the doctor against the dying person, who is a testimony of his failure, and on the part of the family against both patient and doctor. We are a long way from the "beautiful death" of the eighteenth century, with its deathbed scenes, death surrounded by relations and friends, with no other specialist but the priest, who brings extreme unction, the final sacrament, the required ritual. We are far, too, from that "journey" of the dying, of which Alexandra David-Neel speaks: the Tibetan lamas guiding the dying person, preventing him from falling asleep, from sinking into a coma, indicating to him the successive departures of consciousness. It is a technique of departure which has much in common with the technique of arrival, that is to say, giving birth. The lamas assist the dying person to die rather as the midwife helps a woman to give birth.

In our mechanized, functionalist society, are we to expect, as Jacques Attali claims that we are, ever greater shortages of equipment, increased

---

[2] There appears to be little difference in the degree of anxiety experienced by the religious invalid and the atheist one: 20% of the first category experienced anxiety, 24% of the second. On the other hand, the dying who have a lukewarm faith or a perfunctory religious observance are the most anxious: 56% (Maurice Berger and Françoise Hortala, *Mourir à l'hôpital* [Paris: Le Centurion, 1974]).

deficits in the social security system, and a consequent decline in the services provided by many hospitals?[3] "The next phase of economic crisis," he writes, "is a crisis in health equipment and in its financing . . . We shall see the setting up of parallel circuits of decision, long waiting lists for operations, a black market in treatment, and, the ultimate sign of penury, pre- or post-operative euthanasia."

A foretaste of this policy was provided by a consultative committee, made up of doctors and ordinary citizens, which, in Seattle in 1968, defined the norms governing the use of the kidney machine, thus exercising a right of life or death. "The center has worked out a series of criteria which must be strictly adhered to: deterioration of the renal functions, an absence of lasting hypertension, the responsibility and emotional maturity of the patient, his desire to cooperate, age to be between seventeen and fifty, six months' residence in the Seattle region; a minimum level of financial resources, a certain value for the community, a potential for recovery, psychological and psychiatric balance."[4]

According to these criteria the following were excluded from the selection, and therefore condemned to death: a beatnik between the age of twenty and thirty, a lady of substantial means but dubious reputation, and a lumberjack, who fulfilled all the criteria except that he had no money.

Another modern space of death is the morgue. Not that the morgue did not exist in the past. Zola describes in *Thérèse Raquin* the morgue of the Quai de l'Archevêché, with its well-furnished slabs and curious passersby peering in through the windows at the rotting remains. There is nothing like that today and we do not regret it. But, as a sign of the times, the dead are hidden from view. Modern morgues are underground parking lots, strongrooms, refrigerated safes.[5] There, with the help of cotton wool or sawdust, and, for the benefit of the families, with as much verisimilitude as they can muster, the specialists reconstitute bodies that have undergone autopsy.

The American "funeral homes" reproach us with our own inadequacy. In the United States, funerals, far from having disappeared, have on the contrary been taken over by commerce and industry. They have even become the third industrial power in the country. In a society of rational production and consumption, there was obviously no reason why death should not become as profitable as anything else.

[3] Attali, *L'Ordre cannibale*.
[4] Ibid.
[5] Jean-Luc Henning, *Morgue* (Paris: Ed. Libres-Hallier, 1979).

"Die, we'll do the rest" was one slogan produced by an efficient advertising agency.

American funerals have specific spaces at their disposal: "funeral parlors," in which the families are received; "funeral homes," where the dead are embalmed and presented in their familiar attitudes; "thanatos centers," mortuary complexes, just as there are "shopping centers." To these specific spaces corresponds a whole specialized vocabulary, a language intended to remove the image of the deceased and to make the tools of death "harmless." The coffin is called a casket, the hearse a professional car, the wreaths floral homages, the ashes of the cremated or the corpse, the "loved one." The undertaker is given the more technical-sounding title of "mortician," while the practitioners of the "thanatos centers" are known as "thanatopractors."

Americans long felt as great a repulsion for the funeral vault as for cremation. The country graveyard, so dear to eighteenth-century England, long resisted the assaults of the morticians. In the end the professionals managed to reconcile the American love of nature with the requirements of the market. Private companies have converted into cemetery-parks vast green spaces that they have divided up into funerary lots. In 1915 only 5 percent of Americans opted for the funeral vault, but the morticians have managed to raise that figure to 60 percent. All that was needed was to persuade their customers that the vault was more chic than bare earth, that the embalmed body resisted the deterioration of time much better in a vault than in a mere coffin. Funerary marketing has stressed "the same desirable qualities that we have all been schooled to look for in our daily search for excellence: comfort, durability, beauty, craftsmanship."[6] Coffins in solid bronze offer the customer who wants "long-term protection" a product of "magnificent quality."[7] Some are equipped with foam-rubber mattresses, others with "innerspring mattresses," all lined with satin rayon with a choice of some sixty colors. The catalogues of the thanatopractors also offer a wide choice of brassieres, for "Post Mortem Form Restoration," and "Practical Burial Footwear" (for the dead, of course), and a wide range of makeup for embalming.[8]

For men, this makeup is divided into three main categories: rural, athletic, and scholarly—that is to say, red, brown or white.

Embalming is so universally practiced in the United States and Can-

[6] Jessica Mitford, *The American Way of Death* (London: Hutchinson, 1963).
[7] Ibid.
[8] Ibid.

ada that the "mortician" applies it automatically, without consulting the deceased's relations. In fact, almost all Americans are embalmed, even those who ask to be cremated afterwards. In Great Britain embalming has gone beyond 50 percent. In France embalming is rare, but may nevertheless be carried out with the authority of the mayor or prefect of police. A police inspector or a country policeman must attend the embalming and take away a phial of the liquid used, to make sure that no prohibited substances—lead, arsenic, mercury—have been used.[9] Jean Cocteau, Edith Piaf, and Maurice Chevalier, for example, all insisted on being embalmed.

Since the eighteenth century the inalterability of the body has been guaranteed by a preservative injected into the circulation system according to a method developed by the English physician Hunter. The blood is pumped out of the veins and replaced in the arteries by formaldehyde, glycerine, borax, phenol, alcohol, and water. But, in the United States, embalming is intended above all to present to those left behind, called in the jargon of the morticians the "waiting ones" (as opposed to the "loved ones") a dead body that does not look dead. Smeared with cream, made up, wearing new clothes, the deceased has nothing of the corpse about him. Half-exposure is recommended for gentlemen, "because the legs never look so well."[10] But usually the deceased is sitting in an armchair, in some familiar attitude, reading the paper, smoking a pipe, or knitting. Evelyn Waugh describes visiting one such "loved one": "He found a little room, brightly furnished and papered. It might have been part of a luxurious modern country club in all its features save one. Bowls of flowers stood disposed about the chintz sofa and on the sofa lay what seemed to be the wax effigy of an elderly woman dressed as though for an evening party. Her white gloved hands held a bouquet and on her nose glittered a pair of rimless pince-nez."[11]

Evelyn Waugh also takes us to a funeral park inspired no doubt by Forest Lawn Memorial, near Los Angeles, a California cemetery decorated with flowerbeds, lakes, swans, fountains, statues, lawns, and where one can also be baptized or married in one of the three churches: "The Park is zoned. Each zone has its own name and appropriate Work of Art. Zones of course vary in price and within the zones the prices vary according to their proximity to the Work of Art. We have single sites as low as fifty dollars. That is in Pilgrims' Rest, a zone we are just devel-

---

[9] Emile Martin, *Funérailles et sépultures: Traité pratique de police et d'administration* (Paris: 1935).

[10] Evelyn Waugh, *The Loved One* (London: Chapman and Hall, 1949).

[11] Ibid.

oping behind the Crematory fuel dump. The most costly are those on Lake Isle. They range about 1,000 dollars. Then there is Lovers' Nest, zoned about a very, very beautiful marble replica of Rodin's famous statue, the Kiss. We have doubled plots there at 750 dollars the pair."[12]

If these cemeteries resemble recreation parks, the "funeral homes" in no way resemble the sinister premises of French undertakers. Lighted by neon, they look for all the world like nightclubs. They have smoking rooms and restrooms, and their lobbies are filled with plants. The other rooms sport tapestries, statues, and knickknacks of all kinds. Everything is designed so that sorrow is overcome by astonishment, well-being, and an impression of comfort and wealth. A Buffalo company distributes publicity matchboxes with this slogan: "Recourse to one of our branches guarantees the maximum comfort and pleasantness in a family atmosphere."

After a reception given in honor of a "loved one," the corpse is laid in the coffin decorated with tulle bows and muslin streamers and taken to the cemetery in a car. Of the "waiting ones," only the relations and close friends accompany the deceased, and they retire without attending the burial.

Roger Caillois has studied this suppression of death in a study of the American cinema. "A society describes itself very well," he writes, "in the way it represents the passage from this world to the next, and that other world itself." When the American cinema represents the other-world, there is nothing terrifying about it. In their Christian, or antique, mythology, there is no skeleton, no scythe, no devil, no boiling cauldron, no heaven, and no hell. The survival which it invents is a "negation of the sacredness of death" to the advantage of "an administrative beyond."[13]

The deceased, who does not know that he is dead, arrives in a grassy terrain, which is rather like an airfield. The mist lifts as he moves forward. The vague outlines of hangers appear. Employees wearing caps take charge of the newcomer, lead him to an officeblock for the administrative formalities. He has to fill out forms and wait patiently in line before being attended to. Finally, a courteous functionary explains to him that he is dead (*A Matter of Life and Death*, 1941). In Ernst Lubitsch's *Heaven Can Wait* (1943), Satan is more like a corporation president sitting in his office, surrounded by files and secretaries. The dead are brought

[12] Ibid.
[13] Roger Caillois, *Quatre essais de sociologie contemporaine*, chap. 1, "La Représentation de la mort dans le cinéma americain" (Paris: Olivier Perrin, 1951).

up to him in luxurious elevators. In most of these films the traditional ladder or steps are replaced by elevators or vertiginous escalators. Nothing could be more normal. This bureaucratic aspect, which is an extension of the bureaucratic environment on earth, means that we pass only from one administration to another, just as the ancient Egyptian found his beloved Nile in the underworld. But the bureaucratic world of the beyond is more precise, more implacable, smoother-running. One communicates only with underlings. There is, however, one noteworthy difference with earthly bureaucracies: the functionaries are not ill-tempered. And that, no doubt, is the only way one can recognize that one is in the otherworld.

This representation of the beyond in American movies is not far removed from what we also see in the French theater and cinema when they dabble in metaphysics. Sartre's *Huis Clos* is set in an ordinary-looking hotel lounge, and the devil who appears is like some obsequious waiter. In Cocteau's *Orphée*, there are the same bureaucratic personnel, with the brilliantly original touch that the angels of death are motorcyclists, the same motorcyclists who, in France, escort senior members of the government and bureaucracy, thus according them a kind of deification.

But no doubt this bureaucratic vision of death also stems from the fact that, in the United States, death is (and before long will be in France) "insured as a social service," possibly with reimbursement. This is the case with natural death, but Jean Baudrillard envisages a situation in which suicide may be performed in specialized motels where "for a substantial sum, one can procure death in the most pleasant conditions (like any other kind of consumer good, with perfect service, everything necessary laid on, even hostesses, who try to revive your wish to go on living, then, with professional conscientiousness, let the gas enter your room)."[14]

[14]Baudrillard, *L'Echange symbolique.*

21

The Space of Death
The Situation Today and
in Prospect: Futurology

And the world of the dead, like a continent adrift, will move farther
and farther away from the world of the living.

Edgar Morin
L'Homme et la Mort dans l'Histoire, 1951

A lthough in industrial societies death is becoming ever more discreet, although the dying are gradually taking the place of plague
victims, even of criminals, although a sort of indifference to
death links us to the stoicism of the ancients, although fewer
and fewer people visit cemeteries, especially in our cities,
an apparent cult of the dead is nevertheless maintained—even if this cult
is carried out by proxy, by maintenance workers paid as such, who make
sure that our cemeteries and graves are kept in a good state of repair.
Indeed, our industrial society is constantly extending this system of proxy.
Children are being entrusted from a very early age to crèches and the
old put into retirement homes. Coming into life and leaving it are matters for specialists—as, too, are death and the beyond.

[297

Recent statistics show that 55 percent of the French population between the ages of eighteen and forty-five regard the problem of the upkeep of graves as unimportant.[1] But eight French persons out of ten are
nevertheless given a religious burial.[2] Hence the abundance of crosses in
the cemeteries, far more numerous in fact than the number of practicing
Christians. However, no other norm exists for the aesthetics and ideology of graves. The mayor may oppose neither the erection of a monument of a religious character, of whatever religion, nor the erection of a
monument of a political character. The mayor may only refuse permission for the erection in cemeteries of monuments "contrary to safety,
good order, health, and decency."[3] This reservation makes possible a
number of exclusions. The inscriptions on graves, theoretically free, may
also be rejected by the municipal authorities: "As long as these inscriptions contain nothing injurious or aggressive which might compromise
public order or the decency appropriate to burial places, the mayor cannot forbid them without exceeding his powers."[4]

It should be added that no regulation forbids the digging of a grave
as deep as one likes. The height of the monument is not limited either.
A municipal regulation forbidding the erection in a cemetery of a monument more than nine feet high was annulled by the Conseil d'Etat on
July 30, 1915. There is nothing to prevent one decorating a grave just
with grass or planting a tree over it. In spite of everything, most graves
are covered with a gravestone, which used to be of marble and which is
nowadays more generally of granite, which is less fragile than marble,
or of concrete, or plastic imitating granite. A plastic gravestone costs half
as much as a granite one, and a concrete one a quarter as much.[5]

Although burials are still forbidden in churches, places of worship,
and public buildings, we have seen how this rule is circumvented, since
burials are still taking place in the Panthéon and in the Invalides. The
founders and benefactors of hospitals may still be buried in the grounds
of a hospital, as Pasteur was in his Institut. What is more, anybody is
allowed to have himself buried in a piece of land or garden which belongs to him on condition that this site is situated thirty-five meters from
the boundaries of a built-up area and that he obtain the permission of
the local mayor. In cases where ownership of the ground changes hands,

[1] Thomas, *Anthropologie.*
[2] Heuse, *Guide de la mort.*
[3] Martin, *Funérailles et sépultures.*
[4] Ibid.
[5] Heuse, *Guide de la mort.*

the grave may not be interfered with or moved, and the former owners retain the right of perpetual access.

The increase of the urban population, the longer preservation of corpses by the use of plastic coverings for coffins, which slows down the rate of putrefaction, and the rise in the standard of living, which makes it possible for more and more families to buy freehold or long-lease plots, mean that the dead are becoming once more a nightmare for town planners. The difficulty of finding a site for a new cemetery is increased by the fact that, contrary to the situation in the United States, the space of death is, in Europe, unproductive.[6] In West Berlin, despite 116 cemeteries, there is a six-week wait for burial. In Japan only members of the Imperial family may be buried in Tokyo. Although cremation is obligatory in Japan, the room taken up by urns is still too great, since the keepers of cemeteries have to organize a lottery twice a year to choose those families whose ashes are buried, the others being kept in underground cellars.[7]

At a time of housing developments and high-rise apartment buildings, it is natural enough that cemeteries should also be expected to inter a maximum number of bodies in the minimum amount of space, and as cheaply as possible. The standardization of death will reflect more and more the normalization of life.

But, at present, just as functionalism in housing is contradicted by the individualism of the detached suburban house, mortuary standardization is held back in Latin Europe by a sort of expressionism of the tomb and a taste (which goes back to prehistory) for property that is taken with one into the beyond. Although it is uncommon today to be buried with one's wealth, one insists nevertheless on marking the site through which one enters the world of the dead. The grave is no longer a mausoleum, but it is still a door, or rather a trapdoor, bearing the name of the "departed." It seems that a certain awareness persists that, behind

---

[6]American cemeteries no doubt show us the way of the future, the problem of space being resolved by highly profitable financial operations, based on property investment. The selling of plots is a highly planned affair, with advertisements in the papers, door-to-door salesmen, highly trained in the techniques of persuasion, and easy terms. Nothing is forgotten in the death trade. Paths are eliminated to make room for more sites, mausoleums are replaced by mere standardized identity plaques, "conjugal spaces" are sold where the bodies are placed one on top of another, tombs with six or seven stories are sold under co-ownership. The space of death here follows strictly the contemporary space of the living (Marie-Claude Volfin, "Lieux et objects de la mort," *Traverses*, I [August 1975]).

[7]*Newsweek*, September 16, 1968.

this trapdoor, there may be a subterranean path. The trapdoor-grave is the ultimate door closed behind one, after leaving a word, a mark, on the door.

Although the minimum space granted to the dead in French cemeteries is two square meters, the area of a cemetery is calculated at a rate of between four and five square meters per inhabitant living in the community.

A curious reversal of funerary ecology is observable at present. Although in the eighteenth century demands were made that the cemetery should be removed from the town to protect the living from being polluted by the dead, and although in the twentieth century cemeteries are still placed at a distance from the towns (though most of the towns overtake their cemeteries and surround them), this is now done to protect the dead from being polluted by the living.

The few contemporary architects and town planners who are concerned with the space of death want to integrate this space into the environment. This concern to adapt the funerary composition to the site is obviously new. In the past it was the cemetery which itself created the site.

We are far removed from the cemetery as urban spectacle that existed before the late eighteenth century, when the authorities of Marseilles were inundated with complaints against the Jewish cemetery on the hill of the Trois Lucs, on the grounds that the prayer for the dead disturbed the bowls players.[8] One no longer wants cemeteries under one's window.

So the architects and town planners now conceive of cemeteries in a natural setting and integrated with that setting. This represents a revival of the naturalism of the funerary garden, so dear to the preRomantics of the eighteenth century. Thus, according to Robert Auzelle, the cemeteries of the future will be divided into four categories, all of them a form of landscape:

1. The Park Cemetery, a composition of English-style gardens, with luxurious vegetation;

2. The Forest Cemetery, of a Germanic type, the first example of which is the Waldfriedhof in Munich, designed by Hans Grässel in the late nineteenth century, the forest used as a cemetery with a counterpoint of sculpture and architecture;

3. The Architectural Cemetery, a composition based on groups of graves, separated from one another by hedges, clipped trees, and small

[8] Thomas, *Anthropologie.*

terraces. One of the oldest examples of this type of cemetery is the Cimetière du Nord, in Strasbourg.

4. The Landscape Cemetery, a Swiss formula that consists of designing groups of landscapes with the help of trees and shrubs. A good example is provided by Robert Auzelle, who designed the cemetery at Clamart. This type of cemetery subscribes to the present architectural myth of the green space. Indeed, it is generally accepted as such by the visitors, who tend to regard it more as a park for walking in than as a cemetery. In Holland the Protestant cemetery at Haarlem is of a similar type, with its vistas of majestic trees.

In 1937, at the Journées Internationales de la Santé Publique, Dr. Clavel presented a project for "Sacred Woods," huge parks in which 25 square meters (270 square feet) would be reserved for each grave.

Robert Auzelle also went so far (and much further than Haussmann, who wanted to open a cemetery for Paris in the adjacent department of the Oise) as to propose the creation of a single cemetery for the whole of France, in a very underpopulated region, such as the Lozère or the Creuse. Free freehold plots could be granted in this department given up almost entirely to the dead.

A single radical method which would make it possible to solve this appalling problem of cemeteries would be to eliminate death. The *Conventionels*, practitioners of the Age of Reason, functionalists before the term had been invented, dreamed of annihilating, at one and the same time, poverty, sickness, and death. "Man is made neither for the hospital nor for the poorhouse," said Saint-Just. In 1790 some *Conventionels* suggested that disease might be eliminated by abolishing hospitals and doctors. The medical faculties were closed. "No more alms, no more hospitals," cried Barère. Hounded by the Terror, the *Conventionel* and scientist Condorcet wrote his final pages: "Thanks to the progress of the sciences, men will reach a stage in the future when he can eliminate death . . . Science will have conquered death. And then one will no longer die."[9]

The wonderful utopianism of the Enlightenment! And it was one which the scientism of the nineteenth century was to take up. But because of the new diseases born of industrialization and urban overcrowding, life expectancy regressed in the nineteenth century, though, later, child medicine managed to overcome the terrible infant mortality rate. Thus an illusion was created that life was being extended, whereas only

[9]Michelet, *Histoire de la Révolution Française.*

[301

the average life expectancy was extended, by considerably reducing infant mortality, mature mortality being very little altered. Between 1850
and 1935 the mortality rate of adults between 55 and 65 remained constant. Similarly, between 1950 and 1960 the life expectancy of men over
35 did not alter, despite the deployment of a formidable arsenal of medication and machinery intended to prolong life. The all-out efforts of the
medical profession extended life in the United States only by 15 percent
between 1940 and 1975, whereas the expenditure on health in the same
country, for the same period of time, showed an increase of 314 percent.
This is what Jacques Attali meant when he remarked that life expectancy in certain countries exceeds the norm of profitability.[10]

Everything leads one to believe that life expectancy will not be increased, even in the rich countries, before the end of this century, and
the statistics tell us that wealth cannot necessarily deliver a longer life.
Although geographic situation counts a great deal in life expectancy at
birth (to be born in Bangladesh is a much greater handicap than being
born in the Île de France), although the physiological poverty of the
parents remains a not inconsiderable factor, occupation also comes into
play. In France the life expectancy of an unskilled worker, for example,
is seven years below that of a teacher. Or, to put it another way, although
three-quarters of the teachers aged thirty-five have every chance of reaching
seventy, an unskilled laborer has only one chance out of two of reaching
that age. Right at the top of the statistical column of longevity are, in
decreasing order, teachers, the liberal professions, senior managers, the
Catholic clergy, middle managers. At the bottom are agricultural laborers and unskilled industrial workers. So life in the open air is not necessarily favorable to health (agricultural workers die young), and wealth
does not necessarily make any difference, since teachers and the clergy,
professions which provide large numbers of healthy old people, are poorly
paid. In the nineteenth century, owing to the complete lack of hygiene
in poor districts and the harassment of interminable hours of work, the
mortality gap between middle-class and working-class districts was 42
percent. In 1946 it was no more than 1 percent. After sixty-five there is
even greater mortality among the rich than among the poor, no doubt
because of overeating.[11] Similarly, in a poor country like Cuba, the extension of life is greater than in a rich country like the United States.

The richest country in the world is not the one with the largest pro-

[10] Attali, *L'Ordre cannibale*.

[11] Fabre-Luce, *La mort a changé*. Contrary to the seventeenth century, when the life
expectancy of the rich was double that of the poor.

portion of old people. The proportion of people over the age of 65 is, in fact, only 10.7 percent in the United States, 9.3 percent in the U.S.S.R., 8 percent in Japan, as opposed to 13.6 percent in France, 14.9 percent in West Germany, and 14.4 percent in Great Britain. The average in the nine countries of the European Community taken together is 13.7 percent.[12]

We can expect not immortality, then, but extension of life: life expectancy at birth. One calculates, one makes suppositions. Disease and death are regarded today no longer as deviant, as a sign of marginality, but as sin, as a breakdown in the human machine. To limit the machine's breakdowns and to slow down as far as possible the wearing-out process are imperatives of good productive functioning in industrial societies. The body is "economically useful to protect." That is why, since 1965, health has become "the most important market in the American economy, outstripping the automobile and steel sectors."[13]

But a defense of absolute life would involve unbearable constraints: prohibition of alcohol, tobacco, speeding in cars,[14] guns, even passion; a very restrictive diet; the prevention of all harmful effects caused by industry, and, by that very fact, an end to certain industries, and increased unemployment.

Rather than forbid the accident, one commercializes the prosthesis. The artificial limb, even the artificial organ, is an adumbration of that artificial, immortal being, the robot. Since they are unable to make the man of flesh and blood immortal, are industrial societies eventually going to create a man of steel, or synthetic materials, less fragile, unaffected by microbes, and perfectly conditioned?

For the moment, fear of breakdown leads to increased stocking of artificial limbs and graft organs. The cardiac pacemaker, which was invented in 1935 and which, in twenty years, has reduced its weight a hundredfold, now extends the life of a million people in the world. Similarly, the kidney machine has been reduced to the size of a suitcase, and now weighs only nine pounds. But these artificial organs seem to belong to an artisanal age when compared to the electric heart now being developed, or to the electronic prosthesis of the pancreas, or to the prostheses of the nervous system, such as supplementary memories. "Pharmaceut-

---

[12] After heart disease and cancer, alcoholism, with 30,000 deaths a year, is the third cause of death in France. Road accidents account for between 13,000 and 16,000 deaths a year.

[13] Attali, *L'Ordre cannibale.*

[14] Fabre-Luce, *La mort a changé.*

ical, oil, chemical, even car corporations manufacture surgical implants, finger joints in silicone rubber, artificial crystaline lenses for the eye, artificial knees, ears, bones, valves, intraaortic balloons, limbs."[15]

When death meant the flight of the soul, the mark of death seemed to be the cessation of breathing (the last breath). Then a mechanistic society imagined that death was linked to the stopping of the heart. Our electronic society believes (is certain, but other societies were also certain) that absolute death is the death of the brain. All that would be required would be to develop an artificial brain for the robot to live and last forever.

A method of embalming known as the "cryonic" method now makes it possible to preserve a corpse in perfect condition until such time as a complete medical cure has been found for the disease from which it died. There are at present only thirty-two cryogenized corpses, all in the United States. On top of our organ banks, are we now going to see banks of ressuscitatable corpses?

This insatiable activity of medical science is curiously linked to euthanasia. In the mail received by a weekly paper, an eighty-year-old lady demands "a pill to put an end to it all": "After the pill to avoid giving life involuntarily, let us demand the pill to leave life voluntarily."

Since 1978 several American states have included this right to death in their legislation (Natural Death Act). They are California, Oregon, Idaho, New Mexico, Nevada, Texas, North Carolina, and Arkansas. Euthanasia, then, is becoming legal in the United States. However, since its adoption by the first state quoted above, few patients have demanded the disconnection of the machines that give them artificial survival.

The rationalism and functionalism of industrial society go even farther when one sees that certain theoreticians are proposing that each individual should receive from the state, at birth, a specific sum of money which he would use during his life both for his leisure and for his health. It would be up to him to shorten his life by wasting his capital (the phrase "burning the candle at both ends" is here given its full sense), or to keep a sum in reserve for expensive medical treatment that may be able to extend his life. In other words, instead of the state administering "social security," each individual would have an overall sum for health, which might perfectly well be spent for anything else, except that, at the point at which there is nothing left, one would have to demand euthanasia prematurely.

[15] Attali, *L'Ordre cannibale*.

The space of death? Again that obsessive question we have found throughout this book: What is to be done with the corpse? Eat it, bury it in the earth, cast it on the river, embalm it, preserve it in sealed vaults? Ecologists have recently proposed placing the corpse directly in the soil, without a coffin, without any visible tomb. It is an old, pantheistic notion, dear to the preromantics. Louis-Sébastien Mercier describes the "futuristic" burial of a peasant who used the same "return to nature": "His children carried him on three loose sheaves of wheat, buried him, as he had wished, and placed on his grave his bushhook, his spade, and a plowshare."[16]

But then a new space of death, a new postmortem space appears from scientific research. Some believe in an extension of life in Einsteinian space-time; others in the interplanetary travel. Did not Norbert Wiener say that one day man would travel by telegraph and cable himself to a star?

Although all that remains of man is a small pile of calcium, although "the system of man, like every system, returns to physical systems," "a certain consciousness of the consciousness of man's central nervous system" tells him that something must survive, cannot totally disappear, something which is not physical, which does not see, "which one guessed or postulated beyond immediate experience, and which has been called the soul, a sort of immaterial, that is to say, transphysical reality."[17]

The philosophy of science has led Stéphane Lupasco, a rationalist thinker, to wonder about the "soul," as it is more convenient to go on calling it. That is interesting.

It is all the more interesting in that a physicist, Jean E. Charon, published in the same year (1979) a work which tends to prove that, although man is mortal in his physical appearance, he is immortal in his mind, which is contained in electrons. Everything returns to dust, of course, "but our person is still enclosed in that dust, whereas everything which made up our physical appearance has completely disintegrated."[18] And not only my person is enclosed during my own life in that dust, but it was already enclosed before my birth, and will be again after my death. The physical laws described by Charon guarantee me not only immortality in a process of change, but also an immortality in the past. Not so long ago we were told that only God had always existed and

---

[16] Louis-Sébastien Mercier, *L'An 2440* (Paris, 1792).
[17] Stéphane Lupasco, *L'Univers psychique* (Paris: Denoël-Gonthier, 1979).
[18] Jean E. Charon, *Mort voici ta défaite* (Paris: Albin Michel, 1979).

would exist forever. The response of modern physics is: we, too, have always existed and will exist forever. But in that case would not we ourselves be God or, rather, gods. Thales, six hundred years before Christ, said as much: "All things are full of gods."

Although protons and neutrons are matter, only electrons, objects without volume and definable geometric form which can only be located by the trace of their point of contact, only electrons are spirit. And, among those electrons, only those which form part of the constitution of our DNA are immortal. Our spirit, therefore, is made up of the spirit of the electrons of our bodies, whose "life is measured in billions of years, and is therefore comparable to the age of the universe itself . . . This also means that our minds possess spiritual elements whose roots lie billions of years in the past."[19]

There is nothing surprising, then, in the fact that our culture retains with such sharpness the terrified memory of the precarious life of the first men. There is nothing surprising in the fact that our modern culture is impregnated with myths and thoughts inscribed in our collective unconscious for millennia.

"Every phenomenon that ceases to exist in its present form, *cannot have not existed*. It is preserved somewhere. We say in the past. But where? In an area, certainly, of potentialities."[20]

To Lupasco's question, Charon responds that in the course of billions of years the electrons that make up our minds have amassed information. "It is those electrons of our DNA that preserve and extend. The electrons entering our DNA will pursue their existence *after* our physical death, whereas our nature will be returned to dust . . . My Self continues its spiritual adventure in the universe for all eternity."[21]

This is an odd reappearance of the soul, at the moment when everything seemed to prove that it would be effaced forever. It is an odd reappearance, too, of the ghost, those electrons traveling from the depths of time, passing from body to body, from matter to matter, and escaping to the stars. It is an unexpected alliance of physics and metaphysics.

An immense people appears "disseminated in the totality of the space of our universe, a people possessing the enormous advantage of immortality; this people is that of the thinking electrons."[22] My Self grows up with them, with the dimensions of the universe. The space of death is no longer reduced to an antiquated coffin or to a ridiculous grave. The

[19] Ibid.
[20] Lupasco, *L'Univers psychique.*
[21] Charon, *Mort voire ta défaite.*
[22] Ibid.

space of death goes beyond the cemeteries, which no longer have any purpose. Indeed, what is the point of a tomb-house, what is the point of cities and villages of the dead, what is the point of all the funerary furniture, those monuments to the dead, those mausoleums, those funeral decorations, those "thanatos centers," intended only to commemorate the space of the remains? If our spirit lives in the electrons, the space of death goes beyond the space of the corpse and all the rites surrounding its ephemeral preservation. And only in the spaces of passage, with its very moving symbols, the space of the journey remains: a journey in time and space, a journey into the cosmos and immateriality. Is not the soul wandering without a house the electron (which may be identified with the aeon of the Gnostics) in search of a new body, that is to say, a new house? The architecture of the beyond is not the childish image of paradise, purgatory, and hell but the urbanism of the cosmos.

The space of death, seen from this point of view, would be ALL space, since it would be one with the space of life.

BIBLIOGRAPHY

Architecture and Town Planning

Bertholon, Pierre Abbé. *De la salubrité de l'air des villes et en particulier des moyens de la procurer.* Montpellier, 1786.

Considérant, Victor. *Exposition abrégée du système phalanstérien de Fourier, suivie des Etudes sur quelques problèmes fondamentaux de la destinée sociale.* 1846.

Viollet-le-Duc. *Dictionnaire raisonné de l'architecture française du XIe au XVIe siècle.* Paris, 1854–1864.

Horeau, Hector. *Assainissement, Embellissement de Paris ou Edilité urbaine mise à la portée de tout le monde.* Gazette des Architectes et du Bâtiment. Paris, 1868.

Guadet. *Eléments et théorie de l'architecture.* Paris, 1901–1904.

Magne, Emile. *L'Esthétique des villes.* Mercure de France, 1908.

Lavedan. *Histoire de l'urbanisme.*

Aalto, Alvar. *Œuvres.* Zurich: Girsberger, 1963.

Guiomar, Michel. *Principes d'une esthétique de la mort.* Ph.D. diss. José Corti, 1967.

Pérouse de Montclos, J.-M. *E. L. Boullée.* Paris, 1969.

Rykwert, Joseph. *On Adam's House in Paradise.* New York: Museum of Modern Art, 1972.

Kaufmann, Emil. *Trois architectes révolutionnaires.* Paris: SADG, 1978.

Le Temps des Gares. *Catalogue du C.C.I.* Centre G. Pompidou, 1978.

Descamps, Olivier. *Les Monuments aux morts de la guerre 14–18, chefs-d'œuvre d'art public.* Paris-Lyon: Francis Deswartes, 1978.

Horeau, Hector. *Catalogue Musée des Arts Décoratifs.* Paris, 1979.

Rudofsky, Bernard. *L'Architecture insolite.* Tallandier, 1979.

Girardin, René-Louis de. *De la composition des paysages.* Afterword by Michel H. Conan. Ed. du Champ Urbain. 1979.

Cemeteries

Borsbeek, Robiano de. *De la violation des cimetières.* 1824.

Cochet, Abbé. *La Normandie souterraine ou Notices sur les cimetières romains et les cimetières francs explorés en Normandie.* 1854. Reprint. Portulan, 1970.

Vafflard. *De la translation des cimetière de Paris*. 1864.

Vafflard. *Plus de fosses communes! Le cimetière de l'avenir Méry-sur-Oise*. 1867.

Gossi, Max. *Le Catholicisme et ses cimetières*. Paris-Brussels, 1874.

Pagès, Léon. *La Déportation et l'Abandon des morts, cimetière de Méry*. Paris, 1875.

Schaeck-Jaquet, C. *La Sépulture, particulièrement les cimetières et les nécropoles*. Geneva, 1876.

Courtois-Suffit, J. *Projet de cimetière perpétuel par la crémation lente des gaz*. Le Moniteur des Architectes, no. 3, Paris, 1881.

Nicaise, Auguste. *Les cimetières gaulois dans la Marne*. 1884.

Dufour, Abbé Valentin. *Les Charniers des églises de Paris*. 1884.

Coupry, Paul, fils. *Les Cimetières barbares du XIXe siècle remplacés par les cimetières de l'avenir*. Brochure rose publiée à Nantes en 1887.

Haussmann, Baron. *Mémoires*. Vol. 3, chaps. 12 and 13. *Grands travaux de Paris*. 1893. Reprint. Guy Durier, 1979.

Delattre, A.-L. *Les Cimetières romains superposés de Carthage*. 1899.

Baudouin, Marcel. *Découverte d'une nécropole gallo-romaine à puits funéraire à Apremont, Vendée*. La Roche-sur-Yon, 1907.

Puaux, René. *Le pèlerinage du roi d'Angleterre aux cimetières du front et le poème de Kipling*. Association France-Grande-Bretagne, 1922.

Bourde la Rougerie. *Le Parlement de Bretagne, l'évêque de Rennes et les ifs plantés dans les cimetières 1636–1637*. Rennes, 1931.

Morin, Alfred. *Un cimetière gallo-romain*. 1934.

Dauvergne, Robert. *Le Cimetière mérovingine de Chevigny*. 1936.

Paul-Albert, N. *Histoire du cimetière du Père-Lachaise*. Paris: Gallimard, 1937.

Auzelle, Robert. *Les Problèmes de sépulture en urbanisme*. Thesis, l'Institut d'Urbanisme. Paris, 1942.

Ebersolt, J.-C. *Les Cimetières burgondes du Doubs et du Jura à l'époque barbare*. 1950.

Julian, Philippe. *Le Cirque du Père-Lachaise*. Fasquelle, 1957.

Hillairet, Jacques. *Les 200 cimetières du vieux Paris*. Ed. de Minuit. 1958.

Auzelle, Robert. *Dernières demeures*. Paris, 1965.

Dansel, M. *Au Père-Lachaise: Son histoire, ses secrets, ses promenades*. Fayard, 1973.

Cimetières de Martinique. "Crér," no. 29, June 1974.

Chabot, André. *Le Petit monde d'Outre-Tombe*. Ed. Cheval d'Attaque. 1978.

Le Clère, Marcel. *Cimetières et sépultures de Paris*. Les Guides Bleus. Hachette, 1978.

Tombs

Diderot. *Salon de 1761*.

Druon, Dom. *Journal historique de l'extraction des cercueils royaux dans l'eglise de Saint-Denis, fait par le citoyen Druon, ci-devant bénédictin*. Cahier 16 × 20 de dix feuillets. Archives Nationales.

Girard, Joseph-François-Henri. *Des tombeaux et de l'influence des institutions funèbres sur les mœurs*. Paris, 1801.

Daly, César. *Architecture funéraire contemporaine.* Paris, 1871.

Le Blant, Edmond. *Etude sur les sarcophages chrétiens antiques de la ville d'Arles.* Paris, 1878.

Augé, Lucien. *Les Tombeaux.* Hachette, 1879.

Michel, Albin. *Nîmes et ses tombeaux chrétiens.* 1881.

Hornstein, Edouard de. *La Liberté des tombeaux ou les cimetières neutralisés en violation du Concordat.* 1882.

Le Blant, Edmond. *Les Sarcophages chrétiens de la Gaule.* Paris, 1886.

Delattre, A.-L. *Les Tombeaux puniques de Carthage.* Lyon, 1890.

Chabat, Pierre. *Les Tombeaux modernes.* Paris, 1890.

Delattre, A.-L. *Les Tombeaux puniques de Carthage:La nécropole de Saint Louis.* Paris, 1891.

Giraud, Pierre. *Les Tombeaux: Essai sur les sépultures.* Paris, 1901.

Billard, Max. *Les Tombeaux des rois sous la terreur.* Lib. Acad. Perrin, 1907.

Baye, baron de. *Les Tombeaux des Goths en Crimée.* Nogent-le-Rotrou, 1908.

Ingersoll-Smouse, Florence. *La Sculpture funéraire en France au XVIIIᵉ siècle.* Ph.d. diss. Université de Paris, 1912.

Van Tieghem, Paul. *Le Préromantisme.* Vol. 2, 1930. Previously published as *La Poésie de la Nuit et des Tombeaux en Europe au XVIIIᵉ siècle.* Alcan, 1921.

Colas, Louis. *La Tombe basque.* Paris: Champion, 1923.

Segalen, Victor, Gilbert de Voisins, Jean Lartigue. *Mission archéologique en Chine, 1914–1917: La Sculpture et les monuments funéraires. Atlas, vol. 1.* Paris: Lib. Orientaliste Geuthner, 1923.

Levaillant, Maurice. *Les tombes célèbres.* Paris, 1926.

Barbedette, L. *Le Symbolisme des tombeaux gallo-romains.* Revue Archéologique, ed. E. Leroux. Paris, 1926.

Parrot, André. *Malédictions et violations de tombes.* Paris: Lib. Orientaliste Geuthner, 1939.

Ceram, C.-W. *Des dieux, des tombeaux, des savants.* Plon, 1952.

Bihalgi-Merin, Oto. *L'Art des bogomiles.* Arthaud, 1963.

Broëns, Maurice. *Ces souterrains: refuges pour les vivants ou pour les esprits? La clef d'une énigme archéologique.* Paris: Picard, 1976.

Burial Places

Mercier, Louis-Sébastien. *Corps législatif sur les sépultures privées.* 18 frimaire, an V, 1796.

Legouvé. *Sépulture.* Poème lu le 5 octobre 1793 à l'Institut de France. 1801.

Legrand d'Aussy, Pierre J.-B. *Des sépultures nationales, An VII, 1798.*

Murcier, Arthur. *La Sépulture chrétienne en France d'après les monuments du XIᵉ au XVIᵉ siècle.* Paris, 1855.

Hornstein, Edouard de. *Les Sépultures devant l'histoire, l'archéologie, la liturgie, le droit ecclésiastique, la législation civile.* Paris, 1868.

Barrière-Flavy, C. *Etude sur les sépultures barbares de l'époque wisigothique dans le midi de la France.* Moscow: Congrès International d'archéologie, August 1892.

Van Gennep, Arnold. *Essai d'un classement des modes de sépulture.* Actes et mémoires de congrès d'histoire religieuse, October 1923.

Linckenheld, Emile. *Les Stèles funéraires en forme de maison chez les Médiomatriques et en Gaule.* Université de Strasbourg, 1927.

Martin, Emile. *Funérailles et sépultures, traité pratique de police et d'administration.* Paris, 1935.

Salin, Edouard. *La Civilisation mérovingienne.* Les sépultures, 1952.

Joffroy, René. *La Sépulture à char de Vix.* Bulletin archéologique et historique du Châtillonnais, no. 5, 1953.

Joffroy, René. *Les Sépultures à char du premier âge du fer en France.* Picard, 1958.

Niel, Fernand. *Dolmens et menhirs.* Paris: PUF, Que Sais-Je, 1961.

L'Helgouach, Jean. *Les Sépultures mégalithiques en Armorique,* Ph.d. diss. Rennes, 1966.

Boisse, Claude. *Fouilles de sépulture.* N.d.

Mulot, Abbé François-Valentin. *Vue d'un citoyen sur les sépultures.* Paris, N.d.

Egypt

Graves, John. *Pyramidography.* London, 1646.

Volney. *Voyage en Syrie et en Egypte.* 1787.

Montet, Pierre. *Les Scènes de la vie privée dans les tombeaux égyptiens de l'Ancienne Egypte.* Fac. Lettres, université de Strasbourg, 1925.

Kopp, René. *Variétés sur la vérité, I, La Science de la mort dans l'Ancienne Egypte.* Paris, 1932.

Lauer, Jean-Philippe. *Le Problème des pyramides d'Egypte.* Payot, 1948.

Lacouture, Simone. *Egypte.* Petite Planète, Seuil, 1962.

Livre des Morts des Anciens Egyptiens, Livre des morts des Tibétains. Edit. du Cerf. 1967.

Funerals

Muret, Jean. *Cérémonies funèbres de toutes les nations.* Paris, 1675.

Sévigné, Madame de. *Lettre à Mme de Grignan,* 6 May 1672.

Bossuet. *Oraisons funèbres.*

Ménestrier, Père Claude-François. *Des décorations funèbres.* Paris, 1683.

Ménestrier, Père C.-F. *Description de la décoration funèbre de Saint-Denis pour les obsèques de la Reine.* Paris, 1683.

Hérault de Séchelles. *Discours à la Fête du 10 août 1793.*

Mulot, Abbé François-Valentin. *Discours sur les funérailles etet le respect dû aux morts,* N.d.

The Space of the Beyond
(PURGATORY, HEAVEN, HELL)

Virgil. *Aeneid*, Book VI.

Dante. *The Divine Comedy.*

Milton, John. *Paradise Lost.*

Swedenborg, Emmanuel. *Heaven and Its Wonders and Hell from Things Heard and Seen.* 1758. Reprint. London: Swedenborg Society, 1958.

Collin de Plancy. *Démoniama.* 1820.

Collin de Plancy. *Dictionnaire infernal.* 1863.

Delepierre, Octave. *Le Livre des visions ou l'enfer et le ciel décrits par ceux qui les ont vus.* London, 1870.

Louvet, Abbé. *Le Purgatoire d'après les révélations des saints.* Paris, 1883.

Brémond, Abbé Louis. *La Conception catholique de l'enfer.* Paris: Bloud et Barral, 1900.

Hauvette, Henri. *La Forme du purgatoire dantesque.* Bordeaux, 1902.

Monnier, Jean. *La Descente aux enfers.* D.Theol. diss. La faculté protestante de Théologie de Paris, 1904.

Amélineau, E. *L'Enfer égyptien et l'enfer virgilien.* Etude de mythologie comparée. Ecole Pratique des Hautes Etudes, Annuaire 1914–1915.

Bar, Francis. *Les Routes de l'Autre Monde, descente aux enfers et voyages dans l'au-delà.* Paris: PUF, 1946.

Goubert, J., and Christiani, L. *Les plus beaux textes sur l'au-delà.* La Colombe, 1950.

Carrouges, Michel. *Images de l'enfer dans la littérature*, in "L'Enfer," Ed. Revue des Jeunes, 1950.

Ghisoni, Paul. *Eschatologie infernale.* La Colombe, 1962.

Lalouette, Abbé Philippe. *L'Enfer, le ciel, le purgatoire.* 1969.

Vovelle, Gaby and Michel. *Vision de la mort et de l'au-delà en Provence d'après les autels des âmes du purgatoire, XVᵉ-XXᵉ siècles.* Cahier des Annales. A. Colin, 1970.

El Saleh, Soubhi. *La Vie future selon le Coran.* Vrin, 1971.

Brunel, Pierre. *L'Evocation des morts et la descente aux enfers; Homère, Virgile, Dante.* Paris: Société d'édition d'enseignement supérieur, 1974.

Votive Offerings

Berger, Philippe. *Notes sur trois cents nouveaux ex-voto de Carthage.* Paris, 1887.

Müller, Sophus. *Trouvailles danoises d'ex-voto des âges de pierre et de bronze.* Copenhagen, 1888.

Decouflé, Pierre. *La Notion d'ex-voto anatomique chez les étrusco-romains.* 1964.

Catalogue du Musée Carnavalet. 1966.

BIBLIOGRAPHY

Ex-voto. Exposition Goethe Institut. Catalogue 1967.

Public Torture and Execution

Peltier, Gabriel. *Le Martyrologue ou l'histoire des martyrs de la Révolution.* 1792.
Peltier, Gabriel. *Tableau du massacre des ministres catholiques et des martyrs de l'honneur exécutés dans le couvent des Carmes et à l'abbaye Saint-Germain, les 2, 3, 4 septembre 1792 à Paris.* Paris, 1797.
Anchel, Robert. *Crimes et châtiments au XVIIIᵉ siècle.* Lib. Acad. Perrin, 1933.
Mandrou, R. *Introduction à la France Moderne, 1500–1640.* Albin Michel, 1961.
Soubiran, André. *Le Bon Docteur Guillotin et sa simple mécanique d'après les documents de Pierre Mariel.* Lib. Acad. Perrin, 1962.

Cremation

Vanderpol, A. *La Crémation et les funérailles à Rome.* Lyon, 1882.
La L*⁎⁎*. *L'Echo du Grand Orient: Etude sur la crémation des morts.* Nîmes, 1884.
Clarens, J.-P. *Terre ou feu.* Paris, 1885.
Pini, G. *Cremation in Italy and Abroad from 1774 to Our Day.* Milan, 1885.
Hornstein, Edouard de. *La Crémation devant l'histoire, la science et le christianisme.* Paris, 1886.
Salomon, Georges. *La Crémation en France, 1797–1889.* Paris, 1890.
Leclère, Adhémard. *Cambodge: la crémation et les rites funéraires.* Hanoi, 1906.
Marsille, Louis. *La Crémation chez les bretons chrétiens,* Vannes, 1912.

It is significant that the catalogue of the Bibliothèque National, in Paris, cites a great many works on cremation published between 1882 and 1894; that no such works are mentioned for the period from 1936 to 1959 (the idea has gained acceptance and the time for polemics has ended); and that since 1960 only German works on the subject are referred to.

Hospital

Berger, M., and Hortola F. *Mourir à l'hôpital.* Le Centurion, 1974.
Hennig, Jean-Luc. *Morgue.* Ed. Libres-Hallier. 1979.

The Vegetal Setting of Death

Girardin, Stanislas de. *Promenade ou itinéraire des jardins d'Ermenonville.* Paris, 1811.

Gibault, Georges. *Les Fleurs et les tombeaux*. Paris, 1902.

Gibault, Georges. *Les Fleurs et les couronnes de fleurs naturelles aux funérailles*. Revue Horticole, 16 Nov. 1902.

Death in History

Procopius. *The Gothic Wars*. c. 550 A.D.

Chastenet de Puységur, Jacques. *Mémoires*. 1632.

Voltaire. *Le Siècle de Louis XIV*. 1751.

Michelet, Jules. *Histoire de la Révolution française*. 1847.

Heilley, Edmond G. d'. *Morts royales*. 1866.

Heilley, Edmond G. d'. *L'Extraction des cercueils royaux à Saint-Denis en 1793*. Hachette, 1868.

Marais, Mathieu. *Journal et Mémoire sur la Régence et le siècle de Louis XV, 1715–1737*. 4 vols. 1868.

Guibert, Louis. *Livres de raison, registres de famille et journaux individuels limousins et marchois*. Limoges, 1888.

Aulard, Fr.-Alph. *Le Culte de la raison et le culte de l'Etre Suprême, 1793–1794*. Alcan, 1892.

Ridder, André de. *De l'idée de la mort en Grèce à l'époque classique*. 1897.

Enlart, Camille. *Manuel d'archéologie française*. Picard, 1929.

Cumont, Franz. *Recherches sur le symbolisme funéraire des Romains*. Paris, 1942.

Carlier, Alfred. *Histoire des coutumes funéraires*. Brochure de la bibliothèque du Travail, no. 41, Nov. 1946.

Gorce, Denys. *Le Grand siècle-devant la mort*. Ed. du Cèdre. 1950.

Guerry, Liliane. *Le thème du Triomphe de la mort dans la peinture italienne*. Maisonneuve, 1950.

Morin, Edgar. *L'Homme et la mort dans l'histoire*. Corréa, 1951.

Tenenti, Alberto. *La Vie et la mort à travers l'art du XVᵉ siècle*. Cahier des Annales, no. 8. A. Colin, 1952.

Chastel, André. *L'Art et le sentiment de la mort au XVIIᵉ siècle*. Bulletin de la Société d'Etudes du XVIIᵉ siècle, nos. 35–36, July-Oct. 1957.

Heurgon, Jacques. *La Vie quotidienne chez les Etrusques*. Paris: Hachette, 1961.

Eger, J.-C. *Le Sommeil et la mort dans la Grèce antique*. Ed. Sicard. 1966.

Huizinga, J. *Le Déclin du Moyen Age*, chap. 11. Payot, 1967.

Carrière, 'Ch., Courdurié, M., Rebufat, F. *Marseille ville morte; la peste de 1720*. 1968.

Lebrun, Fr. *Les Hommes et la mort en Anjou*. 1971.

Les Pleurants dans l'art du Moyen Age. Catalogue. Exposition à Dijon 1971.

Ariès, Philippe. *La Vie et la mort chez les Français d'aujourd'hui*. Ethnopsychologie I, 1972.

Vovelle, Michel. *Piété baroque et déchristianisation en Provence au 18ᵉ siècle: Les attitudes devant la mort d'après les clauses des testaments*. Plon, 1973.

Vovelle, Michel. *Mourir autrefois: Attitudes collectives devant la mort au XVIIe et au XVIIIe siècle*. Collection Archives Gallimard-Julliard, 1974.

Ariès, Philippe. *Essais sur l'histoire de la mort en Occident, du Moyen Age à nos jours*. Ed. du Seuil. 1975.

Le Roy Ladurie, Emmanuel. *Montaillou, village occitan*. Gallimard, 1975. *Montaillou*, tr. Barbara Bray. London: Scolar Press, 1978.

Ariès, Philippe. *L'Homme devant la mort*. Ed. du Seuil. 1977.

Chaunu, Pierre. *La Mort à Paris*. Fayard, 1978.

Chevalier, Louis. *Classes laborieuses et classes dangereuses*. Plon, 1958; paperback ed., 1978.

Favre, Robert. *La Mort au siècle des lumières*. Presses Universitaires de Lyon, 1978.

Gascar, Pierre. *L'Ombre de Robespierre*. Gallimard, 1979.

Ethnology—Ethnography

Le Braz, Anatole. *La Légende de la mort chez les Bretons Armoricains*. 1874. Alpina, 1958.

Granet, Marcel. *La Vie et la Mort: Croyances et doctrines de l'antiquité chinoise*. Ecole Pratique des Hautes Etudes, Annuaire 1920–1921.

Frazer, James. *The Golden Bough*, esp. chap. 3, "Killing the God." London: Macmillan, 1900.

Frazer, James. *The Fear of the Dead*. London: Macmillan, 1933.

Van Gennep, Arnold. *Manuel de folklore français contemporain*. Vol. 2. *Du berceau à la tombe: Funérailles*. Picard, 1946.

Leenhardt. Do Kamo: la personne et le mythe dans le monde mélanésien. Gallimard, 1947.

Lévi-Strauss, C. *Les Vivants et les Morts*. In *Tristes Tropiques*. Plon, 1955; trans. John and Doreen Weightman, Athenaeum, 1964.

Villasenor, Eduardo. *La Farce et la mort au Mexique*. Mexico, 1957.

Roux, Jean-Paul. *La Mort chez les peuples altaïques anciens et médiévaux d'après les documents écrits*. Paris: Maisonneuve, 1961.

Decary, Raymond. *La mort et les coutumes funéraires à Madagascar*. Maisonneuve, 1962.

Henry, Françoise. *L'Art irlandais*. Zodiaque, 1963–1964.

Marcireau, Jacques. *Rites étranges dans le monde*. Laffont, 1974.

Rites de la Mort. Catalogue de l'Exposition du laboratoire d'ethnologie du Muséum d'Histoire Naturelle, dirigé par Jean Guiart, Musée de l'Homme. Paris, 1979.

Crooke, William. *Death and Disposal of the Dead*. Encyclopedia of Hastings, N.d.

Religion—Spiritualism

Salvianus. *Of the Government of Providence*. Fifth cent. A.D.

Theresa of Avila. *The Life of St Teresa of Avila*. Trans. David Lewis. London: Burns and Oates, 1962.

Nicole, Pierre. *Essais de morale*. 1678.

Bossuet. *Discours sur l'Histoire Universelle*. 1681.

Blanchard, Antoine. *Nouvel Essay d'Exhortation*. 1718.

Kardec, Allan. *Qu'est-ce que le spiritisme?* 1854.

Chevreul, L. *On ne meurt pas: preuves scientifiques de la survie*. Paris: Jouve, 1916.

Bernard, A. *Les Vies successives*. 1921.

Flammarion, Camille. *La Mort et son mystère*. Vol. 3. *Après la mort*. Flammarion, 1922.

Flammarion, Camille. *Les Maisons hantées: En marge de la mort et de son mystère*. Paris, 1923.

Michel, A. *Les Fins dernières*. Paris, 1929. Reprinted as *Les Mystères de l'au-delà*. 1953.

David-Neel, Alexandra. *Mystiques et magiciens du Tibet*. Plon, 1929.

Menoud, Ph. *Le Sort des trépassés d'après le Nouveau Testament*. Cahiers Théologiques de l'Actualité Protestante. Delachaux et Niestlé, 1945.

Dimier, Marie-Anselme. *La Sombre Trappe: Les légendes et la vérité*. Ed. de Fontenelle. 1946.

Bernard, A. *Notre destinée: Ce que nous apprennent les révélations spirites*. Psychic Collection, N.d.

Philosophy

Morelly. *Code de la Nature ou le Véritable esprit de ses lois de tout temps négligé ou méconnu*. 1755.

Voltaire. *Dictionnaire philosophique*. 1764.

Denis, Léon. *Après la mort*. 1923.

Natavel, L. *La Peur de la mort et sa guérison infaillible*. Paris, 1934.

Chauchard, Paul. *La Mort*. PUF, 1947.

Larcher, Hubert. *Le Sang peut-il vaincre la mort?* Gallimard, 1957.

Sertillanges. *De la mort*. Robert Morel, 1963.

Jankelevitch, V. *La Mort*. Flammarion, 1966.

Cioran, E.-M. *Précis de décomposition*. Idées-Gallimard, 1966.

Oraison, Marc. *La Mort et puis après?* 1967.

Choron, Jacques. *La Mort et la pensée occidentale*. Payot, 1969.

Lupasco, Stéphane. *Du rêve, de la mathématique et de la mort*. Ch. Bourgeois, 1971.

Lupasco, Stéphane. *L'Univers psychique*. Denoël-Gonthier, 1979.

Charon, Jean-E. *Mort, voici ta défaite*. Albin Michel, 1979.

BIBLIOGRAPHY

Sociology

Caillois, Roger. *Quatre essais de sociologie contemporaine.* Chap. 1, *La représentation de la mort dans le cinéma américain.* Paris: Olivier Perrin, 1951.

Fourastié, Jean. *Machinisme et bien-être.* Paris: PUF, 1951.

Fargue, Marie. *L'Enfant devant le mystère de la mort.* 1963.

Fabre-Luce, Alfred. *La Mort a changé.* Gallimard, 1966.

Menahem, Ruth. *La Mort apprivoisée.* Ed. Universitaire. Paris, 1973.

Thomas, Louis-Vincent. *Anthropologie de la mort.* Payot, 1975.

Ziegler, J. *Les Vivants et la mort.* Seuil, 1975.

Heuse, Georges. *Guide de la mort.* Masson, 1975.

Jaulin, R. *Morbidité et économie occidentale.* "Traverses," I, Ed. de Minuit, Aug. 1975.

Volfin, M.-C. *Lieux et objets de la mort.* "Traverses," I, Ed. de Minuit, Aug. 1975.

Baudrillard, Jean. *L'Echange symbolique et la mort.* Gallimard, 1976.

Urbain, J.-D. *La Société de Conservation.* Payot, 1978.

Sansot, P., Strohl, H., Verdillon, C. *L'Espace et son double: De la résidence secondaire aux autres formes secondaires de la vie sociale.* Ed. Champ Urbain. 1978.

Attali, Jacques. *L'Ordre Cannibale: Vie et mort de la médecine.* Grasset, 1979.

Literature

Suetonius. *Lives of the Twelve Caesars.* Second cent. A.D.

More, Thomas. *Utopia,* Book II. 1516. Trans. Ralph Robinson. London: Burns and Oates, 1937.

Young, Edward. *The Complaint, or Night Thoughts.* London, 1744.

Harvey, James. *Meditations among the Tombs.* London, 1745.

Gray, Thomas. "Elegy Written in a Country Churchyard." 1751.

Diderot. *Lettre à Sophie Volland,* 6 Oct. 1759.

Mercier, Louis-Sébastien. *Tableau de Paris.* 1781.

Rétif de la Bretonne. *Les Nuits de Paris.* 1788–1794.

Saint-Simon, duc de. *Mémoires.* Abr. ed. 1788, complete ed. 1829–1831.

Mercier, Louis-Sébastien. *L'An 2440.* Paris, 1792.

Chateaubriand. *Le Génie du christianisme.* 1802.

Mérimée Prosper. *Notes d'un voyage dans l'Ouest de la France.* Paris, 1836.

Chateaubriand. *Mémoires d'Outre-Tombe.* 1849; tr. London, 1902.

Tolstoy, Leo. *Three Deaths.* 1859.

Tolstoy, Leo. *The Death of Ivan Illich.* 1886.

Valéry, Paul. *Le Cimetière marin.* 1920.

Hamel, Maurice, *Un vivant chez les morts.* Figuière, 1936.

Bachelard, Gaston. *L'Eau et les rêves.* J. Corti, 1942.

Cohen, Gustave. *Essai d'explication du cimetière Marin.* 1946.

Waugh, Evelyn. *The Loved One.* London: Chapman and Hall, 1949.

Berl, Emmanuel. *Présence des morts*. Gallimard, 1956.

Huxley, Aldous. *Brave New World*. 1932. Reprint. London, 1959.

Huxley, Aldous. *Brave New World Revisited*. London, 1958.

Mitford, Jessica. *The American Way of Death*. London: Hutchinson, 1963.

Lély, Gilbert. *Sade*. Gallimard, 1966.

Steiner, Jean-François. *Treblinka*. Paris: Fayard, 1966; trans. Helen Weaver. New York: Simon and Schuster, 1967.

Sabatier, Robert. *Dictionnaire de la mort*. Albin Michel, 1967.

Cayrol, Jean. *De l'espace humain*. Seuil, 1968.

Malraux, André. *Oraisons funèbres*. Gallimard, 1971.

Charpentier, F. *La Mort*. Classiques Hachette, 1973.

Malraux, André. *Lazare*. Gallimard, 1974.

Calvino, Italo. *Invisible Cities*. Trans. William Weaver. New York: Harcourt Brace Jovanovich; London: Secker and Warburg, 1974.

Index

Index

Index